Christian Origins
and the Ancient Economy

Christian Origins and the Ancient Economy

DAVID A. FIENSY

CASCADE *Books* · Eugene, Oregon

CHRISTIAN ORIGINS AND THE ANCIENT ECONOMY

Cascade Books
An Imprint of Wipf and Stock Publishers
199 W. 8th Ave., Suite 3
Eugene, OR 97401

www.wipfandstock.com

ISBN 13: 978-1-62564-181-6

Cataloging-in-Publication data:

Fiensy, David A.

 Christian origins and the ancient economy / David A. Fiensy.

 xvi + 226 p. ; 23 cm. Includes bibliographical references and index.

 ISBN 13: 978-1-62564-181-6

 1. Galilee (Israel)—Antiquities. 2. Galilee (Israel)—Economic conditions. 3. Palestine—Social life and customs—To 70 A.D. 4. Sociology, Biblical. 5. Jesus Christ—History and criticism. I. Title.

BS2417 E3 F54 2014

Manufactured in the U.S.A.

Dedicated to
Addison Phoebe and Alexa Rae

עטרת זקנים בנות בנות

(Prov 17:6, adapted)

Contents

Contents

Part Three: The Early Church

Acknowledgments

Chapter 8 has not previously been published. It was presented to the Society of Biblical Literature in Chicago in 2012. The following chapters are previously published articles and are reprinted with permission of the publishers. The author and publisher gratefully acknowledge the cooperation of these publishers.

Chapter 1, "Jesus' Socio-Economic Background," first appeared in *Hillel and Jesus*, edited by James H. Charlesworth and Loren Johns, 225–55. Minneapolis: Fortress, 1997.

Chapter 2, "Leaders of Mass Movements and the Leader of the Jesus-Movement," first appeared in *JSNT* 74 (1999) 2–27.

Chapter 3, "Jesus and Debts: Did He Pray about Them?" first appeared in *Restoration Quarterly* 44 (2002) 233–39.

Chapter 4, "The Ancient Galilean Economy: A Model," first appeared as "Ancient Economy and the New Testament." In *Understanding the Social World of the New Testament,* edited by Dietmar Neufeld and Richard E. DeMaris. 194–206. London: Routledge, 2009.

Chapter 5, "The Nature of the Galilean Economy: The Debate between the Archaeologists and the Sociologists," first appeared in *A City Set on a Hill: Festschrift for James F. Strange,* edited by Daniel Warner and Donald Binder. Mountain Home, AZ: BorderStone, 2014.

Chapter 6, "Did Large Estates Exist in Lower Galilee in the First Half of the First Century CE?" first appeared in *JSHJ* 10 (2012) 1–22.

Chapter 7, "Assessing the Economy of Galilee in the Late Second Temple Period," first appeared in *The Galilean Economy in the Time of Jesus,* edited by David A. Fiensy and Ralph Hawkins, 165–86. Atlanta: Society of Biblical Literature, 2013.

Chapter 9, "Poverty and Wealth in the Jerusalem Church," first appeared in *Faith in Practice: Studies in the Book of Acts*, edited by David A. Fiensy and William Howden, 300–323. Atlanta: EES, 1995.

Chapter 10, "The Composition of the Jerusalem Church," first appeared in *The Book of Acts in Its Palestinian Setting*, edited by Richard Bauckham, 213–36. Grand Rapids: Eerdmans, 1995.

Chapter 11, "What Would You Do for a Living?" first appeared in *Handbook of Early Christianity*, edited by Anthony J. Blasi, Jean Duhaime, and Paul-André Turcotte, 555–74. Walnut Creek, CA: Altamira, 2002.

Abbreviations

SECONDARY WORKS

AB	Anchor Bible
ABD	*Anchor Bible Dictionary.* Edited by David Noel Freeman. 6 vols. New York: Doubleday 1992
ABRL	Anchor Bible Reference Library
AGJU	Arbeiten zur Geschichte des antiken Judentums und des Urchistentums
ALGHJ	Arbeiten zur Literatur und Geschichte des hellenistischen Judentums
ANRW	*Aufstieg und Niedergang der römischen Welt: Geschichte und Kultur Roms im Spiegel der neueren Forschung.* Edited by H. Temporini and W. Haase, Berlin: de Gruyter, 1972
ASP	American Studies in Papyrology
BA	*Biblical Archaeologist*
BAR	*Biblical Archaeology Review*
BASOR	*Bulletin of the American Schools of Oriental Research*
BFCT	Beiträge zur Förderung christlicher Theologie
BJPES	*Bulletin of the Jewish Palestine Exploration Society*
BJS	Brown Judaic Studies
BTB	*Biblical Theological Bulletin*
CGTC	Cambridge Greek Testament Commentary
CIJ	*Corpus Inscriptionum Iudaicarum*
CQ	*Classical Quarterly*
CRINT	Compendia Rerum Iudaicarum ad Novum Testamentum
DJS	Duke Judaic Studies
EncJud	*Encyclopaedia Judaica.* 16 vols. Jerusalem: 1972.
ExpTim	*Expository Times*
EKKNT	Evangelisch-katholischer Kommentar zum Neuen Testament
HTKNT	Herders theologischer Kommentar zum Neuen Testament
HTR	*Harvard Theological Review*
HUCA	*Hebrew Union College Annual*
IDB	*The Interpreter's Dictionary of the Bible.* Edited by George Arthur Buttrick. 4 vols. Nashville: Abingon, 1962
IEJ	*Israel Exploration Journal*
Int	*Interpretation*
JAC	*Jahrbuch für Antike und Christentum*

Abbreviations

JBL	*Journal of Biblical Literature*
JESHO	*Journal of the Economic and Social History of the Orient*
JJS	*Journal of Jewish Studies*
JQR	*Jewish Quarterly Review*
JRA	*Journal of Roman Archaeology*
JRS	*Journal of Roman Studies*
JSHJ	*Journal for the Study of the Historical Jesus*
JSJ	*Journal for the Study of Judaism in Persian, Hellenistic, and Roman Periods*
JSNT	*Journal of the Study of the New Testament*
JTS	*Journal of Theological Studies*
LSJ	H. G. Liddell, R. Scott, and H. S. Jones, *A Greek-English Lexicon.* 9th ed. with revised supplement. Oxford: Oxford University Press, 1996
NEAEHL	*The New Encyclopedia of Archaeological Excavations in the Holy Land.* Edited by Ephraim Stern. 4 vols. Jerusalem: 1993
NICNT	New International Commentary on the New Testament
NovT	*Novum Testamentum*
NovTSup	Novum Testamentum Supplements
NTL	New Testament Library
NTS	*New Testament Studies*
NTTS	New Testament Tools and Studies
OBT	Overtures to Biblical Theology
OtSt	*Oudtestamentische Studien*
PEQ	*Palestine Exploration Quarterly*
ResQ	*Restoration Quarterly*
RevExp	*Review and Expositor*
RevQ	*Revue de Qumran*
RIDA	*Revue internationale droits de l'antiquité*
RQ	*Römische Quartalschrift für christliche Altertumskunde und Kirchengeschichte*
SBL	Society of Biblical Literature
SBLSP	*Society of Biblical Literature Seminar Papers*
SJ	Studia judaica
SJLA	Studies in Judaism in Late Antiquity
SUNT	Studien zur Umwelt des Neuen Testaments
YCS	*Yale Classical Studies*
TDNT	*Theological Dictionary of the New Testament.* Edited by Gerhard Kittel and Gerhard Friedrich. Translated by Geoffrey W. Bromiley. 10 vols. Grand Rapids: Eerdmans 1964–1976
THKNT	Theologischer Handkommentar zum Neuen Testament
TNTC	Tyndale New Testament Commentaries
ZAW	*Zeitschrift für die alttestamentliche Wissenschaft*
ZDPV	*Zeitschrift des deutschen Palästina-Vereins*
ZNW	*Zeitschrift für die neutestamentliche Wissenschaft*

PRIMARY WORKS

Jewish Sources

1QS	Qumran Community Rule
11QT	Qumran Temple Scroll
'Abot R. Nat.	*Abot de Rabbi Nathan*
Ant.	Josephus, *Antiquities of the Jews*
b.	Babylonian Talmud
Abod. Zar.	*Abodah Zarah*
'Arak	*'Arakhin*
BB	*Baba Bathra*
Ber.	*Berakhoth*
Bik.	*Bikkurim*
BM	*Baba Metzia*
BQ	*Baba Qama*
C. Ap.	Josephus, *Contra Apionem*
Deut. Rab.	*Deuteronomy Rabbah*
Eccl. Rab.	*Ecclesiastes Rabbah*
'Ed.	*Eduyoth*
'Erub.	*'Erubin*
Gen. Rab.	*Genesis Rabbah*
Git.	*Gittin*
Hag.	*Hagigah*
Hor.	*Horayoth*
Hull.	*Hullin*
Hypoth.	Philo, *Hypothetica*
L.A.B.	*Liber Antiquitatum Biblicarum* (also called Pseudo-Philo)
Lam. Rab.	*Lamentations Rabbah*
Lev. Rab.	*Leviticus Rabbah*
Life	Josephus, *Life*
m.	Mishnah
Ketub.	*Ketuboth*
Ma'as.	*Ma'aseroth*
Mak.	*Makkoth*
Meg.	*Megillah*
Menah.	*Menahoth*
Mo'ed Kat. (or Qat.)	*Mo'ed Qatan*
Mur	Document from Wadi Muraba'at
Ned.	*Nedarim*
Pesah.	*Pesahim*
Pesiq. Rab.	*Pesiqta Rabbati*
Pirqe R. El.	*Pirqe Rabbi Eliezer*
Qidd.	*Qiddushin*
Sanh.	*Sanhedrin*
Shabb.	*Shabbath*
Sheb.	*Shebiith*
Shebu.	*Shebuoth*

Abbreviations

Sot.	Sotah
Spec. Laws	Philo, The Special Laws
Sus	The Book of Susanna
t.	The Tosephta
Ta'an.	Ta'anith
War	Josephus, Jewish War
y.	Talmud Yerushalmi (Palestinian Talmud)
Yebam.	Yebamoth
Zebah.	Zebahim

Non Christian Greco-Roman Sources

Aristotle, Pol.	Aristotle, Politics
Cicero, Brut.	Cicero, Brutus
Cicero, Off.	Cicero, de Officiis
Cicero, Rep.	Cicero, de Republica
Dio Chrysostom, Or.	Dio Chrysostom, Orationes
Diod.	Diodorus Siculus
Herodotus	Herodotus, Histories
Livy	Livy, From the Founding of Rome
Lucian of Samosa, Fug.	Lucian, Fugitivi
Plato, Resp.	Plato, The Republic
Pliny, HN	Pliny the Elder, Natural History
Polybius	Polybius, Histories
Strabo	Strabo, Geography
Tacitus, Ann.	Tacitus, Annales
Xenophon, Oec.	Xenophon, Oeconomicus

Christian Primary Texts

Acts Thom.	Acts of Thomas
Athenagoras, Leg.	Athenagoras, Legatio pro Christianis
Augustine of Hippo, Civ. Dei	Augustine, Civitas Dei
Christ. Mart.	Acts of the Christian Martyrs
Clement of Alexandria, Paed.	Clement, Paedagogos
Cyprian, Ep.	Cyprian, Epistles
Eusebius, H.E.	Eusebius, Ecclesiastical History
Gos. Naz.	Gospel of the Nazoreans
Gos. Thom.	Gospel of Thomas
Hippolytus, Trad. Ap.	Hippolytus, Apostolic Traditions
Inf. Gos. Thom.	Infancy Gospel of Thomas
Irenaeus, Haer.	Irenaeus, Adversus Haereseis
Justin Martyr, Dial.	Justin Martyr, Dialogue with Trypho
Lactantius, Inst.	Lactantius, Institutes
Minucius Felix, Oct.	Minucius Felix, Octavius
Origen, Cels.	Origen, Contra Celsum

Prot. Jas.	*Protevangelium Jacobi*
Tertullian, *Apol.*	Tertullian, *Apology*
Tertullian, *Cor.*	Tertullian, *de Corona*
Tertullian, *Idol.*	Tertullian, *de Idololatria*
Tertullian, *Spect.*	Tertullian, *de Spectaculis*
Theophilus of Antioch, *Auto.*	Theophilus, *ad Autolycum*

SCRIPTURE REFERENCES

Hebrew Bible

Gen	Genesis
Exod	Exodus
Lev	Leviticus
Num	Numbers
Deut	Deuteronomy
Josh	Joshua
1 Sam	1 Samuel
2 Sam	2 Samuel
1 Kgs	1 Kings
1 Chr	1 Chronicles
Neh	Nehemiah
Isa	Isaiah
Jer	Jeremiah
Mal	Malachi
Zech	Zechariah

New Testament

Matt	Matthew
Rom	Romans
1 Cor	1 Corinthians
2 Cor	2 Corinthians
Gal	Galatians
Eph	Ephesians
Col	Colossians
1 Thess	1 Thessalonians
2 Thess	2 Thessalonians
2 Tim	2 Timothy
Jas	James
1 Pet	1 Peter

MISCELLANEOUS ABBREVIATIONS

Aram	Aramaic language
Byz	Byzantine period (363–640 CE)
ER	Early Roman period (37 BCE-70 CE)
Gr	Greek language
Heb	Hebrew language
Hell	Hellenistic period (333–37 BCE)
LR	Late Roman period (250–363 CE)
LXX	The Septuagint Greek Translation of the Old Testament
MR	Middle Roman period (70–250 CE)

Introduction

IN THE CONTEMPORARY QUEST for the historical Jesus, the socioeconomic background of Jesus and its impact on his message and ministry is the subject of intense debate. Among many, it is accepted that the Galilee in which Jesus was born and raised was plagued by grinding poverty, that his followers were primarily poor people, and that his audience was made up of the masses of the poor.[1] Others, however, have argued that Galilee was an egalitarian and economically prosperous society.[2] These contradictory viewpoints have made it cliché that the quest for the historical Jesus is at the same time a quest for the historical Galilee.[3] The geographical and cultural location of Jesus's youth, it is surmised, may help us understand his later message or his pattern of ministry. Certainly scholars of the past have thought as much; the current group seems to have the same opinion.[4]

But we might amend slightly the common currency: it is not so much a quest for the historical Galilee but more precisely a quest for the economy of Galilee. Therefore the quest is a study in contrasts: 1) Some look at Galilee through the lenses of cultural anthropology and macrosociology; others look at Galilee through the lenses of archaeology and reject the use of social theories. 2) Some maintain that the relations between rural villages and the cities were hostile; others propose that the relationship was one of economic reciprocity and goodwill. 3) Some suggest that Galilee was typical of other agrarian societies—with poor peasants who lived in the rural areas, and exploitative wealthy people

1. Crossan, *Historical Jesus*; Crossan, *Birth of Christianity*; and Horsley, *Galilee*.

2. Overman, "Jesus of Galilee"; Edwards, "Socio-Economic and Cultural Ethos," 53–91; and Groh, "Clash," 29–37.

3. Freyne, "Geography, Politics, and Economics," 76; and Moxnes, "Construction of Galilee—Part I" and "Part II."

4. See the surveys in Moxnes, "The Construction of Galilee"; and Rapinchuk, "Galilee and Jesus in Recent Research."

who lived mostly in the cities; others respond that life was pretty good for everyone in Galilee and that it was an egalitarian society.

How does one sort through the arguments, the data, and even the rhetoric? The following essays will attempt to take a fresh look and propose this author's answers. Throughout the volume a common theme runs: I have sought to avoid the polar opposites. I do not think Jesus was a desperately poor man, nor do I think that most Galileans were landless and half-starving. Yet neither do I think that Galilee was an economic boom center. I do not think that the majority of early Christians were from the poorest rung of society. On the other hand, there were a few elites in the group but not many. The church did, however, take its ministry to the poor very seriously.

The eleven chapters that follow fall into three parts: Part One (chapters 1 and 2) focuses on the historical Jesus and his socioeconomic background. I will argue that Jesus came from a middling class of artisans, was not poor (though his family possessed modest means), and was experienced in urban culture enough to serve as a leader of a mass movement.

Part Two (chapters 3–8) investigates the economic conditions of first-century-CE Galilee. These chapters will find no evidence for widespread indebtedness, landlessness, abject poverty, or starvation. Nor will they argue that the economy was humming along splendidly. There was some prosperity in Galilee at this time, but to speak of an economic boom seems an exaggeration.

Part Three (chapters 9–11) will handle the early church and the economic standing of its members. These chapters will conclude that most early Christians were from about the same middling artisan class that Jesus came from. There certainly were some desperately poor persons in the church and a significant number of slaves, but most were not from those levels. One would even have seen some wealthy persons of high social standing in the ancient church but not many.

PART ONE

The Historical Jesus

1

Jesus's Socioeconomic Background

THE RISING INTEREST IN the past twenty years in the sociological investigation of the Bible results from the insight that the history presented in
its pages was not only religiously but also socioeconomically influenced.
To fail to appreciate those factors in the study of biblical history is to miss
the richness of interpretive possibilities. One of the earlier advocates of
the new methodology, H. Kreissig, lamented works that fail to distinguish Jews of the Second Temple period both religiously and socially "as
if they had been a homogenous mass who lived only from religion."[1]

Scholars who have studied the socioeconomic conditions of Herodian Palestine have concurred with Kreissig's complaint. S. Freyne has
produced a description of Galilee from Alexander to Hadrian that seeks
to understand it as a peasant society. R. A. Horsley and J. S. Hanson have
attempted to understand the Jewish rebellion as a class conflict between
the rural peasants and the urban elite. S. Applebaum, A. Ben-David, and
D. E. Oakman emphasize the economic plight of the agricultural worker.
B. J. Malina has described peasant categories and values in New Testament period Palestine to make us aware of the otherness of this society.[2]

Jesus lived under conditions typical of ancient agrarian societies.
To understand him in this background is to add new contours to the
investigation. He not only dialoged with numerous religious groups, but

1. Kreissig, *Die sozialen Zusammenhänge*, 89. Cf. more recently Charlesworth, *Old
Testament Pseudepigrapha and the New Testament*, 19–23.

2. Freyne, *Galilee*; Horsley and Hanson, *Bandits*; Applebaum, "Economic Life in
Palestine"; Oakman, *Economic Questions*; Ben-David, *Talmudische Ökonomie*; Malina,
New Testament World.

he interacted with certain socioeconomic classes. His parables were not only imbued with theological insights but with economic content as well. His lifestyle did not simply reflect the necessities of itinerant preaching; it also resulted from conscious socioeconomic choices.

This essay seeks to place Jesus in his Galilean, socioeconomic environment by asking two questions: What was the socioeconomic environment structure of Galilee during the tetrarchy of Antipas? From which socioeconomic rung did Jesus come? First we will sketch the structure of Galilean society. Then we will review what evidence exists for Jesus's own socioeconomic origins.

The Economic Structure of Galilean Society

Greco-Roman Society

The economic structure of Galilean society was essentially similar to the economics in the rest of the Mediterranean world. The agrarian economies of the ancient empires followed remarkably familiar patterns. Therefore we can benefit from insights gained from studies of Greek and Roman societies. The works of eminent classical scholars can be especially valuable in putting the Galilee of Herod Antipas in its historical and economic setting.[3]

The same holds true for using sociological models. Although one must be cautious in applying sociological theories to the study of ancient society, some interesting insights can nevertheless result from such attempts. If the sociological model has been informed by ancient sources and is judiciously eclectic in its selection of modern sociological theory, we can be reasonably assured that we are not guilty of merely molding the past to fit the present. On the other hand, to ignore sociology or anthropology is surely to invite ethnocentrism. The work of G. E. Lenski[4] meets these criteria as well.

3. E.g., Rostovtzeff, *Roman Empire*; de Ste. Croix, *Class Struggle*. Jones, *Greek City*; Jones, *Cities of the Eastern Roman Provinces*; MacMullen, *Roman Social Relations*; Brunt, *Italian Manpower*; Frayne, *Subsistence Farming*; Garnsey, *Non-Slave Labour*; White, *Roman Farming*; Grant, *Social History*; Alföldy, *Die römische Gesellschaft*.

4. Lenski, *Power and Privilege*. Cf. Crossan, *The Historical Jesus*, 44–45, who also has used Lenski's work as a check against viewing Jesus's world through uninformed, ethnocentric spectacles. Crossan writes: "One can obviously debate Lenski's master model in whole or in part, but I accept it as a basic discipline to eliminate the danger of

Our structuring of Galilean society is heavily dependent on economic standing, as was Lenski's in his work on agrarian societies in general. Some of the categories important to theologians may not even be mentioned.

Galilee had Gentiles from various geographical and ethnic backgrounds in addition to the majority of Jews (Strabo 16.2.34). But for the purposes of this socioeconomic classification, these variations are often irrelevant. A well-to-do merchant is about on the same level regardless of his or her ethnic origins. Likewise, a poor day laborer suffered the same plight whether he or she was a Jew, a Phoenician, an Arabian, or a Greek.

Society in the ancient empires was divided into urban and rural. G. Alföldy and many other historians have noted this condition.[5] The rural population in the eastern Roman empire generally maintained its native language and customs[6] whether Coptic in Egypt,[7] Lycanonian or Celtic in Asia Minor,[8] or Aramaic in Syria and Palestine.[9]

On the other hand, in the cities, people spoke Greek. Many were literate and most were in touch with the great institutions and ideas of Greco-Roman society. This was especially true of the aristocrats, but to some extent even of the urban poor, according to de Ste. Croix, since the urban poor may have been "mixed with the educated" in some way.[10] Such mixing could take place in Galilean cities, not only in synagogues but in theaters, amphitheaters, and hippodromes, as well as in the courts of justice.[11] Thus even the urban poor had different cultural experiences

---

imposing presuppositions from advanced industrial experience on the world of an ancient agrarian empire." The descriptions of Roman social structure by Gager (*Kingdom and Community*, 93–113) and Alföldy (*Die römische Gesellschaft*, 10), based on legal standing, are also helpful. But Lenski's analysis is more socioeconomically nuanced.

5. Alföldy, *Die römische Gesellschaft*, 10.

6. De Ste. Croix, *Class Struggle*, 10, 13; Rostovtzeff, *Roman Empire*, 193, 343; MacMullen, *Roman Social Relations*, 46.

7. MacMullen, *Roman Social Relations*, 46; Jones, *Greek City*, 293.

8. Jones, *Greek City*, 290; Acts 14:11.

9. Schürer, *History of the Jewish People*, 2:26: "The prominence of Aramaic at every level as the main language of Palestinian Jewry is now solidly backed by evidence." The same was true for the native languages of North Africa, Britain, Gaul, Spain, and others. See Rostovtzeff, *Roman Empire*, 193–94; Jones, *Greek City*, 290–91; Brunt, *Social Conflicts*, 170–72. For Aramaic as the nearly exclusive language of Upper Galilee, see Meyers, "Galilean Regionalism" 93–101.

10. De Ste. Croix, *Class Struggle*, 13.

11. See Schürer, *History of the Jewish People*, 2:46, 48, 54–55. As the authors say

from those of the rural peasants. As L. White has observed, for medieval agrarian societies, "cities were atolls of civilization . . . on an ocean of primitivism."[12]

This description of ancient society, while typical for classical historians, should be modified somewhat for Lower Galilee. In the first place, E. Meyers has shown that Greek made strong inroads into that region.[13] Thus the linguistic differences between urban and rural areas, so marked in other parts of the empire, were less striking—though still existent—in Lower Galilee. Second, D. R. Edwards has argued persuasively for economic reciprocity and cultural continuity between urban and rural areas of Lower Galilee.[14] Yet Edwards also indicates that even in this region there were cultural differences between urban and rural.[15] We do not need to posit a radical cultural gulf between city and country to appreciate that living in the one was not the same culturally as living in the other.

The natural result of different cultural experiences was a sense of superiority on the part of the urbanite over the country peasant. Lenski shows that in agrarian societies in general, the urban elite viewed peasants as subhuman.[16] M. Rostovtzeff observed that city residents in the Roman Empire regarded the farmer as an inferior, uncivilized being.[17] R. MacMullen writes that the urbanite regarded the peasant as an "unmannerly, ignorant being."[18]

---

(55), even though Josephus (*Ant.* 15.268) declared that theaters and amphitheaters were alien to Jewish custom, "it should not be assumed that the mass of the Jewish population did not frequent them." On the benefits for the urban proletariat of living in the city, see Jones, *Greek City*, 285. See Overman, "Who Were the First Urban Christians?," 160–68, for a description of the cities of Galilee and their public institutions.

12. White quoted in de Ste. Croix, *Class Struggle*, 10

13. Meyers, "Galilean Regionalism" 97.

14. Edwards, "First-Century Urban/Rural Relations," 169–82.

15. Ibid., 176: "While ideological tensions may have existed between rural and urban inhabitants . . ."; and on 179 Edwards allows that there were in Lower Galilee: "rural areas that were largely conservative, Aramaic speaking enclaves."

16. Lenski, *Power and Privilege*, 271.

17. Rostovtzeff, *Roman Empire*, 192

18. MacMullen, *Roman Social Relations*, 32; see also Jones, *Greek City*, 295–96.

Palestine

Did this attitude prevail in Palestine? L. Finkelstein maintained that all the residents of Jerusalem, both wealthy and poor, agreed in their contempt for the provincials (country peasants).[19] One detects such contempt in Josephus, a Jerusalemite. He has the high priest refer to the Zealots—many of whom came from the rural districts of Palestine[20]—as "slaughtered victims" and "offscourings" (*War* 4.239–241). G. Cornfield's translation captures the tone of these words: "the dregs and scum of the whole country."[21] Whether these words are the high priest's or Josephus's own words, they represent words of someone from the elite, urban class describing the lower, rural classes. Josephus himself calls the Zealots "slaves, rabble, and bastards," which Cornfield renders, "slaves, the dregs of humanity and bastard scum."[22]

Although Josephus is somewhat later than the time of Jesus and Antipas, these same attitudes likely prevailed in the early first century CE. Such attitudes were common in antiquity. Further, although Josephus likely had an apologetic purpose in blaming the Jewish War on rural riffraff, the way he discredited his scapegoats is instructive. He attacked them in these passages as much on socioeconomic grounds as on any other.

We have no direct evidence that such an attitude prevailed in Galilee itself. Perhaps the urban snobbery was less pronounced in Lower Galilee because of the greater economic reciprocity between city and village. But we should probably not conclude that it did not exist at all in that region.[23]

19. Finkelstein, *Pharisees*, 1:24. For Palestine, see also Applebaum, "Judea as a Roman Province," 370–71; and Theissen, *Sociology of Early Palestinian Christianity*, 47–58.

20. This conclusion is convincingly argued by Horsley and Hanson, *Bandits*, 220–23. See, e.g., *War* 4.135, 419–39, 451.

21. Cornfield, *Josephus*, 227.

22. *War* 5.433; Cornfield, *Josephus*, 388.

23. Second-century-CE rabbinic statements about the Galilean ʿ*am haʾ-arets* (people of the land) should caution us against such a conclusion. Disparaging comments about the עם הארץ may reflect not only religious but also social differences. The עם הארץ are called בור in Hebrew, which means "uncultured" or "mannerless" (cf. Jastrow, *Dictionary*, 1:148). They are consistently represented as ignorant and unteachable. Their wives are "like reptiles." See Moore, *Judaism* 1:60; 2:72–73, 157; and Vermes, *Jesus the Jew*, 54–55. Cf. also Urbach, "Class Status and Leadership," 71, where Rabbi would open his storehouses during the famine but not for the עם הארץ and Heinemann, "Status of the Laborer," 267. Although the עם הארץ was a religious designation

It is unlikely that Lower Galilee escaped the kind of urban prejudice that was common in the Greco-Roman world.

Ancient agrarian societies tended to be structured around two groups: the takers (i.e., the elites) and the givers (i.e., the large class of rural peasants). The total makeup of these societies was complex. The society included several socioeconomic classes and subgroups (as we will attempt to establish below), but these classes and subgroups were oriented toward one of the two main groupings—the takers or the givers—listed below.

The socioeconomic distance between these two classes was typically enormous. As Lenski notes, "One fact impresses itself on almost any observer of agrarian societies, especially on one who views them in a broadly comparative perspective. This is the fact of the *marked social inequality*."[24] The extent to which Galilee fits or deviates from a typical agrarian society must now be demonstrated.

The Elites of Galilee

The elites of Galilee consisted of Herod Antipas and his family, as well as certain other wealthy families. They almost always lived in urban centers as absentee landlords and government officials. Their wealth derived from the surpluses of the peasants in the form of taxes or rents on land.

At the top of Galilean society stood Antipas, the tetrarch, and his family. Antipas evidently received an annual income of 200 talents (*Ant* 17.318) both from taxes and from his large estates in Perea, on the Great Plain, and in Galilee.[25] His family exceeded all other members of the elite class not only in political power but also in wealth. Because these political overlords enriched their top government officers and other friends with

and not a social class, as Oppenheimer (*Am Ha-aretz*, 18–21) argued, most of them were rural residents. See Finkelstein, *Pharisees*, 1:24–25, 2:754–61; and Zeitlin, "The Am Haaretz," 45–61.

24. Lenski, *Power and Privilege*, 210 (emphasis is Lenski's).

25. For Perea, see *Life* 33 where the estate at that time belonged to Crispus, one of Agrippa I's former prefects. For the Great Plain, see *Life* 119 where there is reference to an estate there of Bernice, Agrippa II's sister. These lands then were passed down to members of the Herod family. For Galilee, see *Ant*. 18.252 and Hoehner, *Herod Antipas*, 70. See additionally, Fiensy, *Social History*, 21–73; and Charlesworth, *Jesus within Judaism*, 139–48.

large land grants,[26] commanded the army, and levied taxes, their power over even other aristocrats was enormous.

Another social group within the elite class was the group of non-noble aristocrats. They were called elders (Mark 15:1; Acts 4:5), leaders (*Life* 194), first men (*Life* 9, 185; Mark 6:21), notables (*War* 2.318, 410), powerful ones (*War* 2.316, 411), those first in rank and birth (*Ant* 20.123), and honored men (m.Yoma 6:4). These men and their families were the nonpriestly and nonroyal members of the elite class who, because of their wealth, influence, and achievements, were leaders of their communities. Some were local magistrates (*War* 2.237=*Ant*. 20.123; *Life* 134; cf. *Life* 246, 278),[27] and some apparently had to assist the tax farmers in collecting the taxes (*Ant*. 20.194; *War* 2.405).[28]

We clearly find nonnoble aristocrats in Tiberias. Josephus says (*Life* 32–39) there were three groups in Tiberias at the outbreak of the war: a group of the most insignificant persons, a group led by Justus, and the respectable citizens. In the latter group were Julius Capellus; Herod, son of Miaris; Herod, son of Gamalus; and Compsus, the son of Compsus. T. Rajak[29] surmises that, judging by his name, the first man listed by Josephus was a Roman citizen, and that the next two are from the Herodian family. She also notes that Compsus's brother Crispus was the former prefect of Agrippa I (*Life* 33). These men are clearly from the upper class of Tiberias.[30]

Apparently this social group also existed at Sepphoris. We do not possess information about the leaders of Sepphoris from the Herodian period, but the later rabbinic material about Sepphoris indicates a class of aristocrats. A. Büchler[31] affirmed that these leading citizens were called "the great ones," "the great of the generation," and "Parnasim" (i.e., leaders or managers). These great ones were large landowners. In a Talmud passage quoted by Büchler, a sage from the third century CE distin-

---

26. As did Herod the Great to Ptolemy of Rhodes (*War* 1.473, 667; 2.14–16, 24, 64) and Agrippa I to Crispus (*Life* 33).

27. Jeremias, *Jerusalem*, 224.

28. Ibid., 228; Baron, *A Social and Religious History*, 1:274; McLaren, *Power and Politics in Palestine*, 204–6.

29. Rajak, "Justus of Tiberias" 345–68. Cf. Kippenberg, *Religion und Klassenbildung*, 129–30.

30. Goodman, *State and Society*, 33, seems correct that Mark 6:21 refers to the aristocrats of Galilee. This reference probably pertains more specifically to Tiberias.

31. Büchler, *Political and Social Leaders*, 7–10.

guishes three social classes based on wealth: the landowners, the peasants עַמ הָאָרֶץ and the "empty ones" (i.e., the poor).[32] Probably every town of good size had its wealthy and influential citizens, such as John of Gischala (*Life* 43–45)[33] or Simon of Gabara (*Life* 123–25).

It is important to emphasize that ancient agrarian societies, with poor agricultural technology, could support only a small group of elites. The surplus was simply too meager. J. H. Kautsky's statement accurately assesses what was typical:

> The Aristocracy can be initially defined simply as consisting of those in an agrarian economy who, without themselves engaging in agricultural labor, live off the land by controlling the peasants so as to be able to take from them a part of their product. Of course, only a small percentage of the population can be aristocrats, because each peasant produces only a relatively small surplus and the average aristocrat consumes far more than a peasant.[34]

Thus the elite groups, although highly significant in wealth and power, were only a very small percentage of the population.

R. MacMullen, G. Alföldy, and R. Rilinger estimate that the upper classes of the Roman Empire (the senators, knights, and decurions) composed no more than 1 percent of the total population.[35] One would expect this percentage roughly to hold true in Galilee, for the nature of agrarian societies, as Kautsky observed, prevented a large elite class.

The Retainers

The class termed by Lenski[36] "the retainers" stood between the elite and the peasants. Lenski maintains that most agrarian societies have employed retainers to mediate between the common people and the ruling class. Lenski suggests that retainers deflected some of the hostility of the

32. *b. Hull.* 92a; Büchler, *Political and Social Leaders*, 35. The comments of Stuart Miller, "Studies," 141–71, are also interesting in this connection.

33. See Rappaport, "John of Gischala," 479–93.

34. Kautsky, *Politics of Aristocratic Empires*, 79–80.

35. MacMullen, *Roman Social Relations*, 89; Rilinger, "Moderne und zeitgenössische Vorstellungen," 302; Alföldy, *Römische Sozialgeschichte*, 130. Cf. Lenski, *Power and Privilege*, 228, who gives a similar figure for other agrarian societies.

36. Lenski, *Power and Privilege*, 243–48. Lenski estimates the average number of retainers for agrarian societies at 5 percent of the population (245).

lower classes toward the elite, since the peasants and small craftsmen could never be sure whether their trouble came mainly from the retainers or higher up.

The retainers administered the financial and political affairs of the upper class and enforced their goals. For this service, says Lenski, they "shared in the economic surplus." That is to say, they were elevated economically above the ordinary mass of people. As with nearly all social distinctions, however, the line between the lower aristocrats and upper retainers was fuzzy, as was the line between the lower retainers and upper peasantry.

Tax collectors were obvious examples of retainers, whether one speaks of the small tax farmers—who, F. Herrenbrück[37] maintains, were mainly responsible for collecting the revenue—or of toll collectors. John, the tax collector who resided at Caesarea (*War* 2.287); Zaccheus, the chief tax collector who lived at Jericho (Luke 19:1–10); and Levi of Galilee (Luke 5:29) belonged to this class. The first two examples indicate that the retainers could become quite wealthy.

We should also expect the estate overseers or bailiffs to have played a significant role in Galilean society. The office of bailiff was known all over the empire.[38] These important officials are mentioned twice in Luke (12:42–48; 16:1–8). The example in Luke 16:1–8 of the dishonest bailiff is especially revealing. Here we see the far-reaching authority the bailiff exercised over his master's economic affairs. Since bailiffs could be either slaves or freedmen,[39] the slaves referred to in Mark 12:2 and Matt 24:45 are probably also bailiffs.[40]

In spite of the lowly origins of many of the bailiffs, their skills at administration must have made them invaluable to absentee landlords. Columella (*de Re Rustica* in the first century CE) described at length the characteristics that both the bailiff and his wife should possess (11.1.3–29, 12.1.1–6). They must be of sober and nonindulgent dispositions and

---

37. Herrenbrück, "Wer warren die 'Zöllner?,'"178–94. Cf. Stern, "The Province of Judea," 308–76.

38. For the Latin term *vilicus*, see Jones "Colonus." For the Greek term οἰκονομος, see LSJ; and Michel, "οἰκονομος," 149–51. For the Hebrew terms איקונומוס and סנטר see Jastrow, *Dictionary*. For the wide distribution of the Greek term, see Ziebarth, "Oikonomos" XVII. 2: 2118–19. For the terms in the rabbinic literature, see *Lev. Rab.* 12; *Pesiq. Rab.* 10; *b. Shabb.* 153a; *t. BM* 9:14; *t. BM* 4:9; *t. BB* 3:5; *m. BB* 4:7.

39. Jones, "Colonus."

40. Michel, "οἰκονομος," 149–51.

must work hard. They must by example and by use of authority ensure that everyone does a full day's work.[41]

In addition to tax collectors and bailiffs, a third type of retainer is the judicial magistrate, whom S. Freyne finds in *War* 21.571 and Luke 12:58 (=Matt 5:25).[42] Luke 18:2 may also refer to this official. They evidently judged legal disputes and served in nearly every town of any size. To these officials we should also add soldiers, both Roman and Herodian.[43] The lower officials of the royal court would also be retainers.[44]

The governing class and their retainers stood over the lower classes both in the urban centers and in the country. They extracted rents and taxes, the surplus, from the peasantry and others, and they lived mostly in the cities, usually in wealth and luxury.

Rural Peasantry

Most of the population in ancient agrarian societies belonged, as Rostovtzeff affirmed, to the rural peasantry.[45] MacMullen suggests, for example, that 75 percent of the people of ancient Italy were peasants.[46] De Ste. Croix accepts the figure of L. White, the medievalist, who estimated that ten people were needed in the country to produce enough food to enable one person to live away from the land. This figure agrees with those offered by sociologists of agrarian societies.[47] In light of the works of J. A. Overman and D. R. Edwards[48] on the urbanization of Galilee, we may wish to incline somewhat toward MacMullen's lower figure, but we should still conclude that the rural, agricultural workers composed by far the majority of the population in first-century Galilee.

---

41. Cf. Cato, *Agricultura* CXLII–CXLIII.

42. See Freyne, *Galilee*, 198. These local judges appear also in the rabbinic literature. See *b. Shabb.* 139a and Urbach, "Class Status and Leadership," 67.

43. For Roman soldiers, see Matt 8:5–13. For Herodian soldiers, see *Ant.* 18.113–14.

44. See Jeremias, *Jerusalem*, 88–90, for a description of these officials.

45. Rostovtzeff, *Roman Empire*, 346.

46. MacMullen, *Roman Social Relations*, 253.

47. De Ste. Croix, *Class Struggle*, 10; White, "Ausbreitung der Technik," 1:92. See also Sjoberg, *The Preindustrial City*, 83. Sjoberg affirms that no more than 10 percent of agrarian populations usually lived in cities. Sometimes it was less than 5 percent. Lenski's figure is similar (*Power and Privilege*, 199).

48. Overman, "Who Were the First Urban Christians?" 160–68; Edwards, "Urban/Rural Relations," 169–82.

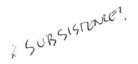

The agricultural workers included small freeholders, tenant farmers, day laborers, and slaves. The small freeholders (see t. Pe'ah 2:2) were generally subsistence farmers, though some may have been somewhat more prosperous. A survey of farm plots from ancient Galilee indicates that they ranged from 1 to 15 acres, with most of them being around 4 acres.[49] These farm sizes are in line with the survey of Samaria done by S. Dar.[50] As A. Ben-David has concluded, that size farm is only large enough for a subsistence at best[51] if the peasant had a large family of six to nine people. Still, Freyne is probably correct that the small freeholders of Galilee do not appear, in Josephus's references to them, to have been starving, but earned their living with little or no margin for error.[52]

There is ample evidence—literary,[53] inscriptional,[54] and archaeological[55]—that many large estates existed in Herodian Palestine, just as they certainly existed in other parts of the Roman Empire.[56] Large estates needed a pool of cheap labor. Hence, they were worked by varying combinations of tenant farmers, day laborers, and slaves.

If Jesus's parables are descriptions of ordinary life in Galilee, then Galilee too had its share of workers on large estates. As J. Herz, M. Hengel, and J. H. Charlesworth have demonstrated,[57] the parables of the Wicked Tenants (Mark 12:1–12), the Rich Fool (Luke 12:16–21), the Laborers in the Vineyard (Matt 20:1–15), the Tares (Matt 13:24–30), the Prodigal Son (Luke 15:1–32), and others[58] describe conditions on large estates with tenants, day laborers, and slaves. Furthermore, there were

49. Golomb and Kedar, "Ancient Agriculture," 136–40.

50. Dar, *Landscape and Pattern*, 46, 60–76; cf. esp. 262.

51. Ben-David, *Talmudische Ökonomie*, 44.

52. Freyne, *Galilee*, 193–194, 208.

53. See the collected evidence in Fiensy, *Social History*, 21–73.

54. Cf. the Hefzibah inscription. See Landau, "Greek Inscription," 54–70.

55. See especially Dar, *Landscape and Pattern*, 230–45.

56. See MacMullen, *Roman Social Relations*, 6; Brunt, *Social Conflicts*, 34; Finley, *Ancient Economy*, 99.

57. Herz, "Grossgrundbesitz," 98–113; Hengel, "Das Gleichnis von der Weingärtnern," 1–39; Charlesworth, *Jesus Within Judaism*, 139–48.

58. See also the large sums of money and produce mentioned. These indicate large estates (cf. Luke 16:1–12; Matt 25:14–30; Luke 7:41–43; Matt 18:21–31; and Mark 10:17–22). Freyne is correct, however, to caution against placing too much emphasis on the parables alone in determining socioeconomic conditions. See Freyne, *Galilee*, 165–66.

quite likely imperial estates in Galilee (*Life* 71–73), as well as Antipas's own large holdings.[59]

Thus we may conclude that estates large enough to support an absentee urban landlord and his family[60] did exist in Galilee in the first century CE. The corollary of this conclusion is that there were people working these estates who often lived in extreme poverty.

The tenant farmer[61] (אריס) farmed a small section of the landlord's estate and paid him a percentage of the harvest, anywhere from 25 percent to 50 percent (*m. Pe'ah* 5:5; *t. BM* 9:11). Day laborers and hirelings were very poor workers who found work especially at harvest time (*t. Ma'as.* 2:13, 2:15; *t. BM* 7:5–6; *m. BM* 7:4–7:7; *m. Pe'ah* 5:5). Agricultural slaves, though probably less numerous than in other parts of the empire, did exist in Galilee (Matt 13:27; Luke 17:7).

Although agriculture was clearly the most important form of rural livelihood, it was not the only form. There were also shepherds. Some of the shepherds undoubtedly owned their own flocks. Others were day laborers or slaves (Luke 17:7; John 10:11–12) who tended the flocks of large-estate owners or the collected village flocks.

The socioeconomic standing of the rural people of Galilee probably ranged from the comfortable (those with more than sufficient land) to the subsistence level (those with little or no margin for error in the year's crops) to the destitute (poor day laborers and beggars).

Village and Urban Trades

Others lived in the cities and towns besides the absentee landlords: merchants, artisans, and urban day laborers. Wealthy merchants eventually entered the aristocratic class. The smaller merchants include what J. Jeremias called the "retail traders" and those who engaged in either foreign or local trade on a small scale.[62]

One of the major Galilean export items was fish. The Sea of Galilee contained many varieties of fish edible for both Jews and Gentiles (*War*

---

59. See Alt, *Kleine Schriften*, 395; Rostovtzeff, *Roman Empire*, 664 n. 32; and Hoehner, *Herod Antipas*, 70.

60. One usually required at least fifty acres to live as an absentee landlord. See White, *Roman Farming*, 385–87.

61. Other forms of tenancy were probably land entrepreneurs, according to Ben-David, *Talmudische Ökonomie*, 63. Cf. Krauss, *Talmudische Archäologie*, 109–10.

62. Jeremias, *Jerusalem*, 35–51, 100.

3.508, 520; *m. 'Abod. Zar.* 2:6). These fish were pickled or salted (Strabo 16.2.45; *m. 'Abod. Zar.* 2:6; *m. Ned.* 6:4) and then sold all over Palestine. Many were involved in this trade, from the fishermen—who could be day laborers (Mark 1:19-20)—to the owners of the fishing boats and the merchants who marketed the fish. Josephus could allegedly round up 230 boats on the Sea of Galilee (*War* 2.635). The Gospels also attest to a thriving fishing trade (Matt 4:17-22; Mark 1:16-17; Luke 5:11).[63]

There were also cloth industries in Galilee. Linen, grain, and olive oil were exported.[64] Pottery was also an important item of trade. The pottery of Kefar Hananya and Kefar Shikhin were especially famous (*m. Kelim* 2:2; *b. BM* 74a; *b. Shabb.* 120b) and were sold all over Galilee and the Golan.[65] The distribution for such trade would have required an active mercantile class.

Just below the merchants in socioeconomic status were the artisans or craftsmen. These workers were able, because of their skills, to demand a higher wage than the ordinary, unskilled day laborer, yet they were usually not as comfortable as the merchants. The crafts in the ancient world included making leather products, cloth products, and pottery. Carpentry, masonry, and metal working were also prominent.[66] All of these trades are attested in the sources for Palestine as well.[67]

Historians agree that most artisans worked hard but were able to earn just enough to live simply.[68] They were not usually wealthy, but neither were they starving. However, craftsmen could attain a level of

---

63. See Hoehner, *Herod Antipas,* 67; Wuellner, *Fishers of Men,* 45-63; Clark, "Sea of Galilee," 349.

64. See Hoehner, *Herod Antipas,* 68; and Edwards, "Urban/Rural Relations," 175.

65. See Adan-Bayewitz, "Kefar Hananya, 1986" 178-79; and Adan-Bayewitz and I. Perlman, "Local Trade," 153-72.

66. See Michel, *The Economics of Ancient Greece,* 170-209.

67. Klausner, *Jesus of Nazareth,* 177, lists over forty trades.

68. Burford, *Craftsmen,* 138-43; Mossé, *Ancient World at Work,* 79; Hock, *Social Context,* 35. Dio Chrysostom, *Or.* 7.112-113, says that those who know a trade will never worry about a living. Lucian, *Dialogi Meretricii* 6.293, says that as long as Philenus the smith was alive, his family had plenty of everything. In *b. Sanh.* 29a the Talmud says that as long as one knows a trade he need have no fear of famine. *T. Qidd.* 1:11 compares knowledge of a trade to a vineyard with a wall around it. *Didache* 12:3-4 assumes that a person without a craft may need financial assistance. Cf. also Glotz, *Ancient Greece at Work* , 359, who notes that craftsmen at Delos earned twice as much per day as unskilled laborers in the fourth and third centuries BCE.

affluence if their skills were especially in demand,[69] or if they could afford slaves to mass-produce their goods.[70] Archaeology has discovered a family of well-to-do artisans in Palestine as well: the family of Simon the temple builder, buried in Tomb I on Givat ha-Mivtar, north of Jerusalem.[71] This was a family of craftsmen which did hard manual labor but attained enough financial success to afford both a tomb in a rather high-priced area[72] and ossuaries.[73]

Artisans did not enjoy a high social standing among the Greeks or the Romans. Herodotus (*Histories*, in the fifth century BCE) writes that the Egyptians and other foreigners regarded craftsmen as low on the social scale, and that the Greeks also accepted this attitude (2.167). Aristotle (fourth century BCE) allows that some of the crafts are necessary for a society (*Pol.* 4.3.11–12; cf. Plato, *Resp.* 2.396b–371e). Nevertheless, he regards the artisans as inferior beings. Artisans are much like slaves (*Pol.* 1.5.10) and they, the day laborers, and the market people are clearly inferior to other classes, even farmers (*Pol.* 6.2.7; 7.8.2).

Xenophon (fourth century BCE) has Socrates denigrate the artisans. In some cities, says Socrates, they cannot be citizens (*Oec.* 4.1–4). The same attitude can be found in later Greek authors, such as Dio Chrysostom (first century CE; see *Or.* 7.110), Lucian of Samosata (second century CE; see *Fug.* 12–13), and Celsus (second century CE; see Origen, *Cels.* 6:36). Important Roman authors, such as Cicero (first century BCE; see *Off.* 1.42 and *Brut.* 73) and Livy (first century BCE; see 20.2.25)[74] also reflect this attitude, although Cicero also admits that artisans are useful to the city (*Rep.* 2.22).

This attitude stemmed from the effect that some of these trades had on the body, disfiguring it or making it soft because of a sedentary life

---

69. Burford, *Craftsmen*, 141; Hock, *Social Context*, 34, cites the case of Tryphon the weaver (Papyrus Oxyrhynchus 2.264), who earned enough to buy his own half of a three-story house.

70. Mossé, *Ancient World at Work*, 90–91, refers to three famous affluent tanners in classical Athens.

71. This tomb and its contents are described by Tzaferis, "Jewish Tombs," 18–22; Haas, "Anthropological Observations," 33–37.

72. See Smith and Zias, "Skeletal Remains, 115. They note that this was an expensive area in which to purchase a tomb.

73. Tzaferis, "Jewish Tombs," 30, indicates that only the well-to-do could afford ossuaries.

74. See especially Hock, *Social Context,* 35–36; Burford, *Craftsmen,* 29, 34, 39–40; and MacMullen, *Roman Social Relations,* 115–16.

(Socrates in Xenophon, *Oec.* 4.1–4; Dio Chrysostom, *Or.* 7.110). In addition, an artisan was not considered an adequate defender of his city, in contrast to a peasant farmer (Socrates in Xenophon, *Oec.* 4.1–4). We must bear in mind, however, that this was the attitude of the elite toward artisans, not the attitude of the artisans themselves or of other classes.

The same attitude seems not to have prevailed among Palestinian Jews. The rabbinic sources extol both manual labor (*m. 'Abot* 1:10; *'Abot R. Nat.* B XXI, 23a) and teaching one's son a craft (*m. Qidd.* 4:14; *t. Qidd.* 1:11; *b. Qidd.* 29a). Artisans often receive special recognition (*m. Bik.* 3:3; *b. Qidd.* 33a), and many of the sages were artisans. Josephus also seems to have regarded artisans highly. He praises their skills in building the temples (*Ant.* 3.200, 8.76), sacred vessels (*Ant.* 12.58–84), and towers (*War* 5.175). He never refers to artisans using the pejorative term "mechanical workers."[75]

It is also interesting that Origen (third century CE), the Christian scholar of Alexandria, tried to deny that Jesus was a carpenter (*Cels.* 6.36). Justin (second century CE) on the other hand, although he was also a Christian philosopher-apologist, was quite willing to admit that Jesus had been a carpenter and maintained that he had made yokes and plows *(Dial.* 88.8). Justin grew up in Samaria, the semi-Jewish region between Judea and Galilee, and evidently did not have the Greek elitist view regarding artisans.

In addition to the craftsmen, who were associated both with the urban centers and small villages, there were also in the cities the unskilled day laborers. Some were burden bearers, others messengers, and others working assistants to artisans. Some were paid to be watchmen over children, over the sick, even over the dead. One can even find reference to manure gatherers and thorn gatherers.[76] Their lack of skills made these persons less capable of earning a living.[77]

75. For rabbinic sages as artisans, see Büchler, *Economic Conditions,* 50; Klausner, *Jesus of Nazareth,* 177; Strack and Billerbeck, *Kommentar,* 2:745–46. For further citations on the rabbinic view of craftsmen, see Krauss, *Talmudische Archäologie,* 2:249–51. For the pejorative connotation of the term βαναυσος see LSJ and MacMullen, *Roman Social Relations,* 138, and the citations given by each.

76. See Krauss, *Talmudische Archäologie,* 2:105–6, and the copious references cited there.

77. See Sperber, "Costs of Living in Roman Palestine," 248–71. Sperber shows that skilled labor usually received greater wages than unskilled (see 250–51). Cf. also Glotz, *Ancient Greece at Work,* 359, who notes that craftsmen at Delos in the fourth and third centuries BCE earned twice as much per day as unskilled workers.

✝ Unclean and Degraded Classes

Below all the classes already discussed existed, according to Lenski, the unclean and degraded classes. They were found both in the city and the countryside and consisted of people "inferior to that of the masses of common people" due to occupation, heredity, or disease.[78]

The occupations that were scorned were, among others, prostitutes, dung collectors, ass drivers, gamblers, sailors, tanners, peddlers, herdsmen, and usurers.[79] Those groups inferior to the common people due to heredity included mainly those born illegitimately. *M. Qidd.* 4:1 lists a hierarchy of births ranging from priests to the lowly four: bastards, Gibeonites, those that must be silent when reproached about their origins, and foundlings. The Hebrew word usually translated "bastard" (ממזר) does not refer to any illegitimate child. This person is the child of an adulterous or incestuous union (as defined by Leviticus 18 and 20). Bastards could not "enter the congregation of the LORD" (Deut 23:3, my translation).[80] That is, they could not intermarry with Israelites.

The second of this lowly four was a descendent of the Gibeonites, whom Joshua (Josh 9:27) made temple slaves. According to later rabbinic law (*b. Yebam.* 78b), they were also excluded from the Israelite community.[81] The third of the four must be silent when reproached about his descent because he does not know who his father was (*m. Qidd.* 4:2).[82] The foundling is a child taken up from the street, whose father and mother are unknown (*m. Qidd.* 4:2).[83]

Mishnah Yebam. 4:13 indicates that records were kept of one's ancestry. Rabbi Simeon ben Azzai (second century CE) reports that he found a family's register in Jerusalem that indicated that a certain person was a bastard. The precise definitions of these terms were debated by the sages, but the stigma attached to them was not. It "marked every male descendant . . . forever and indelibly."[84] One Mishnaic passage, for

---

78. Lenski, *Power and Privilege*, 280–81.

79. Luke 7:37–39; Matt 21:31. See the rabbinic lists of unacceptable occupations: *m. Qidd.* 4:14; *m. Ketub.* 7:10; *m. Sanh.* 3:3; *b. Qidd.* 82a; *b. Sanh.* 25b. See also Jeremias, *Jerusalem*, 303–12.

80. Dembitz, "Bastard."

81. See Jastrow, *Dictionary*, 943, נתין

82. Jastrow, *Dictionary*, 1637, שחוקי

83. Ibid., 89, אסופי B. BM 87a says a man should not marry a foundling.

84. Jeremias, *Jerusalem*, 342. For his definition of these terms, see 337–44.

example, demands that an Israelite who marries a bastard or a Gibeonite be scourged (*m. Mak.* 3:1).

Another category of those scorned are those included in the unclean and degraded class due to disease. We should think here especially of the lepers, who seem to have abounded in Palestine.[85] Such people were declared unclean by a priest (Lev 13:11, 25) and had to remain apart from everyone else, crying out from a distance, "Unclean!" (Lev 13:45–46). Lepers lived a life of social ostracism.

✗ The Expendables

At the very bottom of the social structure, according to Lenski, were the "expendables." This group consisted of "criminals, beggars, and underemployed itinerant workers." Lenski remarks concerning this class: "Agrarian societies usually produced more people than the dominant classes found it profitable to employ." Lenski estimates, based on statistics from Europe from the sixteenth to the eighteenth century, that in most agrarian societies, about 5 to 10 percet of the population were in this class.[86]

First in the list of expendables were the bandits. Hengel was one of the first scholars to describe bandits in Palestine in sociological terms. Banditry was a problem throughout the Greco-Roman world in the time period we are considering. The ranks of bandits were swollen by runaway slaves, deserting soldiers, and impoverished peasants.[87] One sociologist, E. J. Hobsbawn, has described the phenomenon of banditry in agrarian societies generally as "a primitive form of organized social protest."[88] This thesis has been taken up most recently by R. Horsley and J. S. Hanson in their work on Palestine in the first century C.E.[89]

That banditry in the ancient world was rooted in social and economic factors is hardly deniable.[90] We also find examples in Palestine of

85. See Mark 1:40; 14:3; Luke 17:2; *m. Meg.* 1:7; *m. Mo'ed Kat.* 3:1; *m. Sotah* 1:5; *m. Zebah.* 14:3; *L.A.B.* 13:3; Apocryphal Syriac Psalm 155 (see Charlesworth, *Pseudepigrapha,* 2:629). The word seems to have been used for infectious skin diseases in general. See Zias, "Death and Disease," 147–69.

86. Lenski, *Power and Privilege,* 281–83.

87. Hengel, *Zealots,* 33–34.

88. Hobsbawm, *Primitive Rebels,* 13.

89. Horsley and Hanson, *Bandits.*

90. See MacMullen, *Enemies of the Roman Order,* 255–68; Shaw, "Bandits in the Roman Empire," 3–52.

banditry originating in poverty and hardship. But we must be cautious about attributing to bandits the Robin Hood heroic stature that Horsley and Hanson describe.[91] They attempt to show that bandits often enjoyed the support and protection of the peasant villagers and were even their heroes. Their two examples are Hezekiah and his men, who were executed by Herod the Great (*Ant.* 20.118–36; *War* 2.228–31), and Eleazar ben dinai, to whom the Galileans turned to get justice on a group of Samaritans for murdering some Jewish pilgrims (*Ant.* 20.118–36; *War* 2.228–31).

Horsley and Hanson point out that the execution of Hezekiah and his men brought a storm of protest. But those protesting in the case of Hezekiah were the relatives of those slain, and their protest was primarily against Herod's summary execution of these men without trial. Even the Sanhedrin, certainly no lover of bandits, was appalled by Herod's handling of the matter (*Ant.* 14.165–67). Furthermore, Josephus writes that they sang Herod's praises in the villages and cities because in getting rid of Hezekiah, he had granted security and peace to the region (*Ant.* 14.160). Josephus may be stretching the truth here in presenting the viewpoint of the urban elite rather than of the peasant villager, but it is also possible that many peasants honored bandits as much from fear as from hero worship, and that there was a general relief when Hezekiah was executed.

In the case of Eleazar ben Dinai, the peasants turned to him as a last resort only after Cumanus dallied about giving them justice. The Mishnah, on the other hand (*m. Sot.* 9:9), remembers ben Dinai as a murderer. Perhaps he was a local hero or even a "freedom fighter" or Zealot,[92] but this is hardly provable.

Even if one could produce a few examples of bandits as social protesters representing the will of the common people, it would not change the verdict on banditry in general. Bandits were generally considered objects of dread and animosity in the Jewish sources. They were dangerous, ruthless criminals who preyed on innocent people. The rabbinic sources, Josephus, and the New Testament all reflect this attitude.[93]

91. Horsley and Hanson refer to the bandits of Palestine as "Jewish Robin Hoods" (*Bandits*, 74).

92. Bientenhard, *Tosefta-Traktat Sota*, 153–55, regarded Eleazar ben Dinai as a Zealot freedom fighter.

93. See, e.g., Mark 14:48, Luke 10:30, John 10:1, 2 Cor 11:26; *m. Shabb.* 2:5; *t. Ta'an.* 2:12; *m. BM* 7:9; *War* 2.253; 4.135, 406; *Ant.* 14.159; 17.285, 256. Some authors in antiquity romanticized the brigand and pirate leaders as heroic figures. However,

Beggars also appear frequently in Palestine. They are lame (Matt 21:14; Mark 10:46; Luke 16:20; John 5:3; Acts 3:2; *m. Shabb.* 6:8) or blind (John 9:1) and sit along the roadside in the country (Mark 10:46) or along the streets and alleys in the city (Luke 14:21). A favorite place for beggars was the temple (Acts 3:2), since almsgiving was considered especially meritorious when done there.[94]

To conclude the first part of this essay we can say that the size difference between the rich and poor populations was enormous. Perhaps only about 1 percent of the population belonged to the elite class. What percentage of the population lived in extreme poverty? We can only estimate based on statistics from other societies. MacMullen notes that in Europe in the fourteenth and fifteenth centuries, one-third of the population lived in "habitual want." According to MacMullen, the person living in "habitual want" "devoted the vast bulk of each day's earnings to his immediate needs and accumulated no property or possessions to speak of."[95]

MacMullen estimates that the poor consisted of about one-third of the Roman Empire. This figure may be somewhat out of line for Antipas's Galilee, but probably not by much. The figure includes not only many of the expendables but most of the day laborers among the urban and rural workers—and probably many of the tenant farmers. Most of the rest lived more or less also in poverty, but at least had their physical needs met. The average peasant or artisan was very poor compared to the elite classes but was not destitute and did not live in habitual want.

Where Did Jesus Fit?

Where did Jesus fit into the socioeconomic structure of Galilee? Many scholars in the past have pictured Jesus as coming from the poorest rung of Galilean society.[96] Others have added to Jesus's supposed poverty the

---

the bandits also caused untold hardship on the general population. See Hengel, *Zealots*, 5–34.

94. Jeremias, *Jerusalem*, 116–17.

95. MacMullen, *Roman Social Relations*, 93.

96. See Plummer, *Gospel according to Luke*, 32, 65. But Plummer adds astutely: "Neither here (Luke 2:24) nor elsewhere in the New Testament have we any evidence that our Lord or His parents were among the abjectly poor." See Manson, *Gospel of Luke*, 20–21; Branscomb, *Teachings of Jesus*, 213–14; Bowman, *Jesus' Teaching*, 27; Batey, *Jesus and the Poor*, 5. Furfey, "Christ as τεκτων," 215, also concludes that Jesus was poor, but like most people of his day.

dimension of social or political activism.[97] Still others maintain that Jesus came from a middle-class background.[98] At least one scholar has claimed for Jesus membership in the wealthy class.[99] Many scholars either assume that Jesus was poor or place too much emphasis on a few verses in the Lucan birth narrative that are capable of various interpretations.[100] Others unwisely use economic terms (*middle-class*) appropriate only for industrial society.

To understand Jesus's socioeconomic origins, we must explore what it meant for Jesus to be an artisan in ancient Galilee. Next we should look for any hints in the Gospels themselves about Jesus's background.

We should consider it probable that Jesus was a τεκτων, or carpenter. This assertion is found only in Mark 6:3, while in the parallel passage in Matt 13:55 he is called "the son of the carpenter." Nevertheless, the historical probability that Jesus was a carpenter remains high. All the major Greek manuscripts—except one[101]—and many of the early versions have the reading "Is not this the carpenter?"[102] Furthermore, these words are found in a text describing Jesus's rejection at his hometown, a narrative unlikely to have been invented by the early church. Third, the passage in Matthew ("Is not this the son of the carpenter?")—even if one were to argue that it is more accurate or authentic—actually supports the meaning of Mark, since fathers usually taught their craft to their sons.[103] Thus, we should conclude that Jesus came from the artisan class.[104]

97. Von Pöhlmann, *Geschichte der sozialen Frage*, 2:467–73; Mayer, *Der zensierte Jesus*, 21–45. There are other recent studies of Jesus from this perspective, but one cannot discern how the authors view Jesus's socioeconomic background. See, e.g., Trocmé, *Jésus et la Révolution*; Yoder, *Politics of Jesus*; Hollenbach, "Liberating Jesus," 151–57; Oakman, *Economic Questions*; Horsley, *Jesus and the Spiral of Violence*.

98. Hengel, *Property and Riches*, 27; and Meier, *Marginal Jew*, 282.

99. Buchanan, "Jesus and the Upper Class," 195–209.

100. Scholars point especially to the offering paid by Mary (Luke 2:24), which seems to be that of a poor person. But we must be cautious about the meaning of *poor*. What might seem poor (i.e., destitute or nearly so) to moderns could have been quite average to ancients. At most, this offering indicates only that Jesus's family was not wealthy at that time.

101. Papyrus 45 from the third century CE has the text of Mark 6:3 read like that of Matt 13:55.

102. See Metzger, *Textual Commentary*, 88–89; and Cranfield, *Mark*, 194–95. But for an opposing view, see Taylor, *Mark*, 299–301.

103. Buford, *Craftsmen*, 82; Klausner, *Jesus of Nazareth*, 178.

104. The Aramaic term for "carpenter" sometimes is used in the Talmud metaphorically of a scholar (see Vermes, *Jesus the Jew*, 21–22) even as the Greek word for

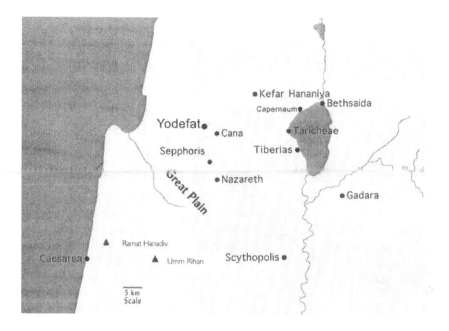

Figure 1.1: Galilee in the first century CE

Carpentry in Greco-Roman Society

As a carpenter,[105] Jesus would have been skilled in fashioning wood projects, such as furniture, tools, agricultural implements, water wheels for
irrigation, scaffolding for houses, and perhaps even ships.[106] He would
have known and used a wide assortment of tools, including axes, chisels,
drills, saws, squares, hammers, and plumb lines.[107] His skills would have
been not unlike those of carpenters of one hundred years ago.

What sort of business would a carpenter in Galilee in the first century CE have done? The traditional concept is of a simple village carpenter

"carpenter" was occasionally used for any master of an art, such as a gymnast, poet, or
physician (see LSJ). But the term in Mark 6:3 clearly is not used in that sense. Mark's
point is that because Jesus was only a carpenter, the residents of Nazareth refused to
listen to him. Otherwise the passage makes no sense.

105. Greek: τεκτων; Hebrew: חרש ; Aramaic: נגרא; Latin: *faber*.

106. See McCown, "O ΤΕΚΤΩΝ," 173–89; Furfey, "Christ as τεκτων"; and Blümner, *Technologie und Terminologie*, 2: 311–47.

107. See Wolf, "Carpenter," 539; and Burford, *Craftsmen*, 39–40.

who made mostly yokes and plows for the local peasantry.[108] According to this view, Jesus would seldom, if ever, have left the village.

The Greek historian Xenophon describes the work of a village carpenter and then compares it to the life of an artisan in a large city (evidently in a shoe factory):

> For in the small cities the same people make chairs, doors, plows, and tables, and many times this same person even builds (houses) and he is contented if in such a way he can get enough employers to feed himself. It is impossible for a man skilled in many things to do all of them well. But in the big cities because many people need each trade, one skill can support a person. And Many times (one needs) not even complete skill, but one makes men's shoes, another women's (shoes). It is possible for someone to support himself by merely stitching shoes. One divides (the parts), another only cuts out shoe pieces, and another of these workers does nothing but putting the pieces together. (Xenophon, *Cyropedia* 8.2.5)

The differences between village artisans and city artisans could be great not only in terms of job description but also in terms of economic comfort. The traditional understanding of Jesus's background has been that of the small village artisan described by Xenophon. But did Jesus's skill as a carpenter ever take him out of the village and into the city, where he learned about and participated in urban culture? If so, could his urban employment have elevated his economic status? Was Jesus a village woodworker, or did he also work in the building trade?

Traveling Artisans

Since S. J. Case,[109] an alternate view has existed regarding Jesus's background. Although Nazareth was probably a small village, it stood only three or four miles from Sepphoris, one of the largest cities in Galilee. Case suggested that Jesus as a youth had worked in the reconstruction of Sepphoris and later in the construction of Tiberias. Sepphoris had been destroyed by the Romans in 3 BCE and was then magnificently rebuilt by Antipas (*Ant.* 18.27). Since it would have taken many years to reconstruct

---

108. This is, e.g., Furfey's view ("Christ as τεκτων," 213) and Klausner's (*Jesus of Nazareth*, 233). Most recently, Miller, "Sepphoris, the Well Remembered City," 74–83, argues for this view.

109. Case, *Jesus*, 199–212.

a city such as Sepphoris, Case reasoned that a carpenter's family could have found important and lucrative work there for a sustained period of time. R. Batey has more recently taken up Case's thesis and supported it from his own work on the excavation of Sepphoris.[110]

That artisans in antiquity would travel from their home villages to work on large construction projects is well known. It is also quite plausible that Jesus and his family worked in other towns in Galilee, such as Tiberias, which began construction somewhere between 18 and 23 CE.[111] They may even have worked in Jerusalem.

There are clear examples in the Mediterranean world of artisans' traveling to distant building sites. Building temples and other public works almost always required importing craftsmen from surrounding cities. There was a general shortage of craftsmen in the building trades— carpenters, masons, sculptors—especially from the fourth century BCE on. This shortage necessitated that craftsmen travel from city to city. A. Burford cites, for example, the case of the city of Epidauros in Greece, which, to build the temple of Asclepius (c. 370 BCE), imported masons, carpenters, and sculptors from Argos, Corinth, Athens, Paros, Arcadia, and Troizen. (Argos itself had to hire Athenian masons to complete its long walls in 418 BCE.) Athens also needed carpenters and masons from Megara and Thebes to rebuild its walls in the 390's BCE.

According to Burford, this shortage of craftsmen was especially acute in the Roman period. The cities of North Africa, Asia Minor, Persia, and Palmyra imported craftsmen for their building projects. The local artisans contributed what they could. Burford affirms, "For unusual projects such as public works, no city, not even Athens, had a sufficiently large skilled labor force to do the job by itself."[112]

---

110. See the following publications by Batey: "Is Not This the Carpenter?"; "Sepphoris: An Urban Portrait of Jesus"; *Jesus and the Forgotten City*, esp. 65–82. For Sepphoris, see also Meyers et al., "Sepphoris 'Ornament of all Galilee'"; Meyers et al., *Sepphoris*; and Strange, "Sepphoris." For the history of Sepphoris, see Miller, "Studies in the History and Traditions of Sepphoris" and the monograph by the same title.

111. For the date when construction began on Tiberias, see Overman, "Who Were the First Urban Christians?," 163.

112. Burford, *Craftsmen*, 62–67; quote on 63. See also Burford, "Economics of Greek Temple Building," in which the author emphasizes the mobility of the ancient craftsmen: "Certainly, when there was a demand for them, skilled craftsmen were automatically at a premium . . . The mobility of skilled craftsmen in the ancient world thus offset the perennial shortage of skilled men in any given city" (31).

Since this was the case throughout the Mediterranean world, we should expect that in Palestine in the Herodian period artisans from surrounding cities and villages were used for large building projects. This expectation is confirmed by a passage in Josephus. Josephus relates that Herod the Great (ruled 37 to 4 BCE) made the following preparations to build his temple in 20 BCE: "He made ready 1,000 wagons which would carry the stones. He gathered 10,000 of the most skillful workers . . . and he taught some to be masons and others to be carpenters" (*Ant.* 15.390).

Josephus's description of Herod's collection and training of carpenters and builders in preparation for building his temple implies there was a shortage of artisans in Jerusalem for this massive construction project. Furthermore, according to Josephus (*Ant.* 20.219–20), the completion of the temple, which did not occur until the procuratorship of Albinus (62–64 CE), put 18,000 artisans out of work. Although Josephus's figure may be somewhat exaggerated,[113] the construction of the temple required a large force of artisans throughout most of the first century CE.

The evidence from Josephus confirms that an extensive public works project like building the temple required recruiting and importing—and even training—artisans from distant cities and employing them over long periods of time. The construction of Sepphoris and Tiberias must have required a similar contribution of skilled labor. Given the urbanization of Lower Galilee (e.g., Sepphoris, Tiberias, Magdala, Capernaum, and Scythopolis[114]) and also of the Tetrarchy of Philip (Caesarea Philippi and Bethsaida Julius), one can well imagine that an artisan in the building trade would be in demand. Since such was the case in the Greco-Roman world in general, causing artisans to move frequently from job to job, we should expect the same to have been true in Galilee. It is even possible that Jesus and his family worked on the temple in Jerusalem from time to time.[115]

---

113. A colossal project such as Herod's Temple surely required a very large force of craftsmen. Burford notes, for example (*Craftsmen*, 62), that the tiny Erechtheum in Athens needed 100 craftsmen to complete its final stages in 408 BCE. These included 44 masons; 9 sculptors; 7 woodcarvers; 22 carpenters, sawyers, and joiners; 1 lathe worker; 3 painters; 1 gilder; and 9 laborers and other unspecified workers.

114. Overman, "Who Were the First Urban Christians?"

115. Oakman, *Economic Questions*, 186–93, argues that Jesus's social contacts with people in Jerusalem indicate that he was there many times before his ministry began. Oakman points to Jesus's friends in Bethany (near Jerusalem, Mark 14:3; Luke 10:38–42; John 11:1) and to the owner of the upper room (Mark 14:12–16).

Batey asserts that carpenters were necessary for construction of public works. This construction included the erecting of scaffolding and forms for vaults, cranes, and ceiling beams.[116] Batey's assertion is confirmed not only by the examples from classical Greece listed above but also by Josephus. He celebrates the importance of carpenters for building Solomon's temple (*Ant.* 7.66; 7.340; 7.377), Zerubbabel's temple (*Ant.* 11.78), and Herod's temple (*Ant.* 15.390). Carpenters also figure prominently in building city walls (*War* 3.173).

Therefore, first, we can say with certainty that there were several continuous and massive building projects during Jesus's youth and early adulthood. Second, we can be reasonably confident that these projects necessitated the services of skilled carpenters from distant cities and villages. Jesus and his extended family could easily have worked in Sepphoris, Tiberias, and other Galilean cities, and even in Jerusalem. Opportunities were there for this family to have experienced urban culture and to have risen to the same level of economic comfort as the artisan family of Simon the temple builder.

Jesus's Standard of Living

But establishing that the possibility was there to have attained a modest level of economic comfort does not, of course, prove that Jesus's family did so. Are there any indications in the Gospels that Jesus came from an upper-level artisan family as opposed to a poor village artisan family?

Buchanan has noted[117] that Jesus is found among well-to-do people rather often. He called to be his disciples James and John, sons of Zebedee, a fishing merchant who was wealthy enough to employ day laborers (Mark 1:20). Levi the tax collector hosted a banquet for Jesus—in which they reclined at table[118]—and became a disciple (Matt 9:9–11). A certain man "of the rulers of the Pharisees" invited Jesus to dine with him

116. Batey, *Jesus and the Forgotten City*, 68–82.

117. Buchanan, "Jesus and the Upper Class," 205–6. Buchanan argues on the basis of 2 Cor 8:9 that Jesus came from a wealthy family: "He became poor even though he was rich." But Buchanan's reasons for concluding that these words refer to the historical Jesus's socioeconomic status are less than compelling.

118. Reclining while eating was a Greek practice that the Romans and others adopted. It was usually a sign of status and wealth to eat a meal while reclining on a couch. Poor people usually ate sitting upright or on mats. See Badian, "Triclinium." See also Matt 22:10–11; 26:7; Mark 6:26; John 12:2.

(Luke 14:1–6). Jairus, ruler of the synagogue at Capernaum, and a certain unnamed Roman centurion approached him (Matt 8:5; Mark 5:22–23). Zaccheus, the chief tax collector, also gave a meal for Jesus (Luke 19:1–10). Lazarus (or Simon the leper) hosted a banquet for Jesus in Bethany (Mark 14:3; John 12:2). Joanna, the wife of a court official of Antipas, was a disciple of Jesus (Luke 8:3). Nicodemus, said to be a member of the Sanhedrin, was a disciple of Jesus in secret (John 3:1–2; 7:50; 19:39). Finally, Joseph of Arimathea, who buried Jesus's body and was a disciple, is described as a member of the council and wealthy (Matt 27:57; Mark 15:43).

That Jesus could so easily move among these wealthier people suggests some experience in similar social situations and an earlier association with people of some economic means. Further, given the common urban snobbery toward the village peasants, one may reasonably wonder if a simple village carpenter would ever be the guest of such people as those listed above.

It does not follow from these texts, however, that Jesus was himself wealthy or a member of the elite class. He was only in a position to have known such people. An itinerant artisan who had experience in urban movements working for wealthy patrons could easily have become familiar with such people.

Some commentators have sought to find Jesus's teachings evidence of his urban and/or wealthy background. This evidence is, however, not convincing. Some argue that his neutral position toward Rome and his willingness to associate with all types of people prove Jesus's association with Sepphoris and other cities.[119] Others find in his use of the term *hypocrite* (a Greek theatrical term) a familiarity with the theater at Sepphoris, and in his parables about kings a firsthand observation of Antipas.[120] Still others believe that the banking and judicial system of Sepphoris informed Jesus's parables.[121] Buchanan even believes that Jesus's parables betray a wealthy background. Those parables that speak of enormous wealth (Matt 18:32–35), the investment of large sums (Matt 25:14–30), or the business practices of a large estate (Luke 16:1–9) indicate a familiarity with the affairs of the rich, maintains Buchanan.[122]

119. Cf., e.g., Case, *Jesus*, 206–10.

120. Batey, *Jesus and the Forgotten City*, 83–104, 199–234. Cf. Schwank, "Das Theater von Sepphoris," 199–206.

121. Schwank, "Das Theater von Sepphoris."

122. Buchanan, "Jesus and the Upper Class," 204–5. Buchanan states: "It is an

These items are certainly suggestive, but S. S. Miller[123] is wise to caution against accepting them as evidence. If one has already established that Jesus was well acquainted with Sepphoris, for example, then one could rightly argue that this background lies behind Jesus's actions and teachings. But it is difficult to use the argument the other way around. One can get illustrations (parables) from many sources (travelers, folk tradition, and so forth), so Jesus need not have observed, for example, Antipas in speaking about kings. Nor does it follow that he visited the theater because he used the word *hypocrite* (υποκριτης).

On the other hand, Miller's assertions about where Jesus concentrated his ministry geographically need some adjustment. Miller affirms that Jesus preached primarily at "Nazareth, Nain, Cana, and especially in the Sea of Galilee area, Capernaum, Chorazin, and Bethsaida. Noticeably missing are allusions to visits to Sepphoris and Tiberias."[124]

But Jesus is reported to have preached in his home village of Nazareth only once (Matt 13:53–58, Mark 6:1–6; Luke 4:16–30), and this effort met with opposition. The clear impression is that Jesus never preached there again. Likewise, there is only one reference to Jesus's being in Nain (Luke 7:11) and two references to his presence in Cana (John 2:1; 4:26). One hesitates to say that these places were Jesus's ministerial foci.

It does appear that Jesus concentrated on the Sea of Galilee basin. He is portrayed as living in and preaching mostly in Capernaum, which was, however, not a "rural town," but a thriving fishing-business town with a population of probably around two thousand.[125] The Gospels describe his ministry in Bethsaida and Chorazin, two other large towns, in the same terms as Capernaum (Matt 11:21–23=Luke 10:13–15). Jesus quite likely preached also in Magdala, a city Josephus said had forty thousand residents (*War* 2.608; clearly an exaggeration), since one of his most important disciples was Mary from Magdala (Matt 27:56, 61; Mark 15:40, 47; 16:1, 9; Luke 8:2; 24:10; John 19:25; 20:1, 18). Thus Jesus is often found in the cities and large towns of Galilee. He made preaching

---

impressive fact, however, that there are very few teachings of Jesus that reflect lower class associations" (204).

123. Miller, "Sepphoris, the Well Remembered City."

124. Ibid., 79.

125. Overman's estimate of 12,000 to 15,000 seems exaggerated. See his "Who Were the First Urban Christians?" 162. Miller, "Sepphoris, the Well Remembered City," 79, calls Capernaum a rural town.

ours in the countryside in Lower Galilee but concentrated mainly on the area around the Sea.

It is true that the Gospels never expressly place Jesus in Sepphoris or Tiberias. Miller affirms that this silence indicates that these cities played no significant role in either Jesus's youth or ministry.[126] Overman and Batey suggest that Jesus intentionally avoided these cities because of the danger there from Antipas and his officials.[127]

There is, however, at least one hint that Jesus preached in Tiberias. Joanna, the wife of Chuza, one of Antipas's bureaucrats, became a disciple of Jesus (Luke 8:3). As an official of Antipas, Chuza and his family would have lived in Tiberias. Joanna could have heard Jesus preach and teach in nearby Magdala or some other city, but her presence among Jesus's disciples suggests that we should keep an open mind about whether Jesus ministered in Tiberias, the capital of Galilee. And if he preached in Tiberias without the Gospels' recording it, why not also in Sepphoris?

Arguments from silence regarding geography in the Gospels should be made with great caution. These are theological works that emphasize cities and towns with symbolic importance, such as Cana, where Jesus's first miracle was celebrated (John 2:1). Thus a village which Jesus visited only once or twice may be highlighted in the Gospels because something significant happened there. Conversely, an urban center he often visited might be seldom or never mentioned because little or nothing happened of theological importance there. If Sepphoris and Tiberias were unimportant to Jesus's ministry, we may understand their omission from the Gospels. It is likely that the large Gentile populations in these two cities would have been unimpressed with a preaching artisan. All we can really say about the silence in the Gospels regarding these two cities is that the authors never expressly place Jesus there. To say anything more than that is not convincing.

Conclusion

We may say in conclusion that Jesus lived in an agrarian society that tended to be divided culturally into urban and rural, with the overwhelming majority of the population being rural. If the bias that prevailed

126. Miller, "Sepphoris, the Well Remembered City," 81.

127. Overman, "Who Were the First Urban Christians?" 167–68; Batey, "Sepphoris," 6.

throughout the ancient Greco-Roman world also existed in Palestine, the urban residents viewed the rural peasants as inferior beings. Jesus, an artisan who probably was often in urban environments, might not have been considered with the same eye of urban snobbery. Yet he had other cultural and social barriers. Artisans were usually disdained by the Greeks and Romans; the Gentile residents of the urban centers of Galilee would not have paid him much attention. On the other hand, Jews seem to have had much more respect for craftsmen.

Jesus was probably not economically destitute before his ministry. We should expect that he and his brothers worked at hard manual labor but did not want for the necessities of life. The massive building projects of Palestine—especially in Galilee—should have provided ample opportunity for work. It is even possible that his family was rather comfortable, like that of Simon the temple builder. Certain texts in the Gospels may incline us in that direction.

But in the eyes of the elite, Jesus would still have been poor. Compared to their luxurious lifestyle, he must have lived very simply and humbly. The socioeconomic distance between Jesus and the elite classes—even if he did come from a comfortable family—was enormous.

2

Leaders of Mass Movements and the Leader of the Jesus Movement

THIS CHAPTER IS AN inquiry into the leadership of peasant mass movements and the evidence concerning the social level of Jesus and other leaders in the ancient Mediterranean world. It seeks to answer two questions: (1) Is there a pattern for social origins for such leaders? (2) Does Jesus fit the pattern? Following the answers to these questions, I seek (more speculatively) to answer a third question: what was there about Jesus's background that could have facilitated his leadership? In other words, why would such large groups of people have considered a person from Jesus's socioeconomic class (that is, an artisan) a candidate for leadership?

First, I will define some terms and sketch the social structure of Herodian Palestine. This will provide the background for this investigation. Next, I will survey anthropological studies of peasant mass movements. This survey will help us place the ancient movements in a broader social context. We will find that the same pattern that existed in the ancient movements exists generally in peasant or agrarian societies. Next, I will examine cases of actual mass movements in antiquity, both in the Mediterranean world in general and specifically in Palestine. The results will show that the leaders rarely come from the peasants themselves. Finally, I will inquire whether Jesus and his movement fit the emerging pattern. My conclusion will be that they do.

Definitions

Before we proceed to the investigation, it will be helpful first to define our terms. By *mass movement* I intend to differentiate from one or two spontaneous outbursts of protest or violence. Rather, this phenomenon is a movement involving events over a more extended period of time. On the one hand, a mass movement lasts longer and is more integrated than a mob. On the other hand, it is not as well organized as a political party. Further, by the word *mass* I intend to differentiate this group from more than, say, one village. Rather, a large group involving people from outside one's extended family or village is involved. Mass movements according to my meaning may be peaceful or military, secular or religious (though in agrarian societies, certainly ancient ones, most movements of this sort were religious in some sense). Finally, these movements are by definition peasant movements since the overwhelming majority of the ancient population was made up of the rural peasantry (see below).[1]

Second, before we look at the evidence for a pattern of leadership among peasant mass movements, it will be helpful to sketch the social stratification of Herodian Palestine. A number of New Testament scholars have used as a heuristic model G. Lenski's theory of social stratification.[2] This theory analyzes societies according to economic-technological systems. His chapter on agrarian societies indicates that essentially two classes existed: upper and lower. In the upper class were the landed nobility, which for Palestine would include the rulers (king, procurator, tetrarch), the high priest, and other wealthy lay aristocrats, and the families of each of these. The upper class consisted in ancient agrarian societies of only about 1 to 2 percent of the total population according to historians.[3] We should probably expect that the upper class in Herodian Palestine was roughly the same, for it required a large percentage of agricultural work-

1. I have adapted this definition from Heberle, "Social Movements."

2. Lenski, *Power and Privilege*, 189–296. This theory is presented again in a later publication with slight modifications. See Lenski and Lenski, *Human Societies*, 166–213. For New Testament scholars who have used Lenski's model, see Fiensy, *Social History*, 155–76; Fiensy, "Jesus' Socio-Economic Background," 225–55; Saldarini, *Pharisees, Scribes, and Sadducees;* Duling and Perrin, *New Testament*, 49–56; Rohrbaugh, "Social Location of the Markan Audience"; Crossan, *Historical Jesus*, 43–46; Arlandson, *Women, Class, and Society*, 14–119.

3. See Alföldy, *Römische Sozialgeschichte*, 130; MacMullen *Roman Social Relations*, 89; Rilinger, "Moderne und zeitgenössische Vortellungen," 302; Lenski, *Power and Privilege*, 219.

ers to enable landlords to live in relative luxury, and, as Lenski shows, in agrarian societies wealth in the main was derived from land.

The second part of agrarian societies—that is the remaining 98 percent—consisted of the peasantry, artisans, merchants, and the criminal and beggar elements. Lenski offers a table that illustrates his understanding of agrarian societies.[4] The table looks rather like an upside-down toy top. The very narrow part of the top, which projects above the rest, represents the upper class. The fat part of the top represents the majority of the population: the rural peasants, and the village and urban craftsmen and merchants. A peasant was a subsistence farmer, who not only provided his own maintenance, usually by working in family units, but also, with what little surplus he produced, supported the elite class to whom he was in some way in subjection.[5] His support of the elite class came in the form of taxes or rents (or both) on the use of land. The peasants were by far the largest group, since ancient agrarian technology required about ten people in the country to produce enough food to enable one person to live away from the land.[6]

The smaller group in the fat part of the top was the group of merchants, craftsmen, and day laborers that lived in the urban centers or villages. The craftsmen or artisans composed 3 to 7 percent of the total population in agrarian societies.[7]

Toward the bottom of the upside-down top were the classes of people degraded because of illegitimate birth, occupation, or disease. At the very bottom were the so-called expendable peoples: the criminals and beggars. Lenski estimates that in most agrarian societies between 5 and 10 percent of the population belonged in this last group.[8]

---

4. Lenski, *Power and Privilege*, 284. See also his slightly altered version in *Human Societies*, 211. This table has been adapted and reproduced in numerous publications. See Fiensy, *Social History*, 158; Rohrbaugh, "Social Location," 383; Duling and Perrin, *New Testament*, 56.

5. For a more complete definition of peasant see Fiensy, *Social History*, vi–vii. See also Scott, *Moral Economy*, 157; Wolf, *Peasants*, 2–3; Foster, "What Is a Peasant?"; Powell, "On Defining Peasants and Peasant Society," 94–99.

6. See White, "Expansion of Technology," 1:143–74; de Ste. Croix, *Class Struggle*, 10. Cf. Lenski, *Power and Privilege*, 279, who says that the urban populations were 5 to 10 percent of the total. MacMullen, *Roman Social Relations*, 253, maintains, however, that 70 to 75 percent of the population in ancient Italy was peasant.

7. Lenski, *Power and Privilege*, 279.

8. Ibid., 281–83.

Thus in ancient agrarian societies approximately 90 percent of the population lived outside the city. Around 10 percent lived in cities and larger towns, including a very small percentage (1 to 2 percent) of elites, a merchant group, an artisan group (between 3 and 7 percent), and an urban day-laborer segment.

Many historians and sociologists have concluded that in addition to featuring social stratification, agrarian society was bifurcated into urban and rural populations.[9] The rural population in the eastern Roman Empire for the most part seems to have maintained their native languages and customs. On the other hand, in the cities more people spoke Greek, many were literate, and most were in touch to some degree with the great institutions and ideas of Greco-Roman society (see further below).

Leadership Patterns

Social-Science Studies of Peasantry

Studies in peasant mass movements have concentrated mainly on rebellions.[10] This emphasis may not seem at first relevant for understanding the ministry of Jesus. But one should bear in mind two considerations. First, these studies describe how leaders emerged to articulate the problems and to attempt to implement solutions for the masses. Since, as I will argue below, Jesus also led a mass movement, these leaders offer useful comparisons. Further, one must always bear in mind that religion, economics, and politics were not compartmentalized in antiquity. The mass movements surveyed below were not just political but religious as well. Sometimes the religious nature of these movements is accentuated, but even when that is not the case, one should suspect that the peasants believed that God was on their side. Whether using violent or peaceful means, most peasant mass movements have pursued goals that combine religion, economics, and politics. Thus, these other movements were not so different from the Jesus movement in form.

9. Ibid., 272–73; Alföldy, *Die römische Gesellschaft*, 10; de Ste. Croix, *Class Struggle*, 10, 13; Rostovtzeff, *Roman Empire*, 193, 346; MacMullen, *Roman Social Relations*, 46.

10. Some sociologists distinguish between rebellions (unsuccessful movements) and revolutions (which change the structure of society). Others seem to use the terms interchangeably. In this chapter, except when I quote others, the distinction will be maintained.

"By themselves the peasants have never been able to accomplish a revolution," maintained B. Moore.[11] Sociologists have observed that when peasant protest turns to rebellion, usually the movement is led by someone outside the peasantry, and that rebellions can almost never succeed in becoming successful revolutions without such leadership.[12] Who would be peasant leaders in periods of protest and rebellion? Such leaders could come from discontented intellectuals, from dissident landed aristocracy, from priests and other religious leaders, from artisans, from teachers and from village leaders.

Prior to the appearance of such leadership, peasants are not usually standing around waiting for a revolution. According to J. Migdal,[13] they may know of specific deficiencies in their relationships with the elites and want to alleviate them, but they have no vision of changing an entire system. Peasants are extremely reluctant to rebel since they always fear that their subsistence might be threatened. Further, any dissatisfaction they might have is with the particulars of their situations, not with the system as a whole. Indeed they seem to have little vision of any other possibilities. Thus peasants do not want to restructure society but simply to make their individual lives more tolerable.[14]

Therefore peasants seldom have exactly the same purpose or goals for rebellion that the leaders have. As J. C. Scott observes, "the masses are not ideologically sound."[15] Yet while they may have a different—or somewhat different—vision for the future than their leaders, they nonetheless look to them to make it all happen.

The leaders from outside the peasantry offer two services to their followers. They articulate grievances and organize for action, which has consequences beyond the peasants' immediate problems. Without outside leadership peasant goals in rebellion remain very limited. They may seize some of the landlord's grain, lead their flocks onto the landlord's meadows, or kill a tax collector. They want subsistence and lower taxes.

---

11. Moore, *Social Origins,* 479.

12. Sabean, "Markets, Uprisings"; Scott, *Moral Economy,* 173; Scott, "Revolution in the Revolution"; Mousnier, *Peasant Uprisings,* 219, 323, 327; Wunder, "Mentality," 157; Migdal, *Peasants,* 231; Chesneaux, *Peasant Revolts in China,* 6; Wolf, *Peasant Wars,* 8.

13. Migdal, *Peasants,* 248.

14. Moore, *Social Origins,* 457.

15. Scott, "Revolution in the Revolution," 97, 99.

Anything more usually requires leadership from the literate, from those of the Great Tradition (i.e., the literary, urban tradition).[16]

For example, during the German Peasants' War of 1525 one of the leaders of the uprising in the Samland was a miller.[17] Likewise the leader of the peasant movement in Russia in 1670 was a member of the upper class of old Cossacks.[18] The same can be said for rebellions in non-European peasant societies. The leader of a rebellion of miners in the Andes was a schoolteacher. Likewise the leader of the insurrection of Mexican hacienda peasants in the early part of the twentieth century was a village curate.[19]

Mainland China has experienced numerous peasant rebellions. A revolt in the seventeenth century was led by five persons, two of whom were soldiers and one of whom was from the elite class. The social origins of the other two are unknown.[20] Likewise, revolts in the nineteenth and twentieth centuries were led by ruined artisans, intellectuals, and monks, and even discontented members of the ruling class.[21]

Further, peasant rebellions often have taken a religious or millenarian meaning. Thus the German Peasants' War was cast by the miller referred to above as the "Christian men" versus the 'godless nobles'. By interpreting their plight in terms of the Christian gospel, the miller gave divine legitimacy to their concerns and so helped unite them for action. The leader of the peasants in Russia referred to above claimed for the Russian rebellion the protection of the Virgin Mary, whose will they were accomplishing. Thus the Russian rebellion conformed to God's will and was destined to restore his rightful order whereas the opponents of the peasants were on the side of Satan and his angels. Many anthropologists have noted the prevalence of millenarian ideas in these rebellions even in movements in China. Many rebels in China looked back with religious

16. The terms "Great Tradition" and "Little Tradition" were coined by Redfield. He described peasant culture as a half culture. One half is the Great Tradition, the tradition of the reflective few cultivated in schools and temples, the tradition of the philosopher, theologian, or literary man. The other half, the Little Tradition, is the low culture, folk culture or popular tradition, which is passed on among the unlettered of the village community. See Redfield, *Peasant Society,* 68–84. Cf. Foster, "What Is a Peasant?," 2–14.

17. Wunder, "Mentality," 157.

18. Mousnier, *Peasant Uprisings,* 216–27.

19. Handelman, *Struggle in the Andes,* 68; Wolf, *Peasant Wars,* 8.

20. Parsons, *Peasant Rebellions,* 6.

21. Chesneaux, *Peasant Revolts,* 16.

feeling and nostalgia to a time of primitive justice, and appealed to God for a return. Thus heaven would restore justice in a new age of peace, and light would prevail over darkness.[22] Thus, for many peasant leaders, articulating the peasants' cause has meant casting the needs and goals of the masses in religious terms.

Peasants may acquire leaders in one of two ways. An opportunist or an idealist may seize the day when he sees the situation calls for a leader. Or the peasants themselves may recruit leadership. When the latter occurs, peasants usually seek the services of a trusted official. They desire that one who has served them well in the past now perform this function.

D. Sabean[23] maintains that peasants often turn to the town market centers and to the leaders within those centers. The village artisans, priests, and officials are the brokers who mediate between peasants and the elite. These people have already established a network of both peasants and rulers. They have grown used to playing the intermediate role between the two. Thus, Sabean terms them "brokers." They can move comfortably in either world. Usually these brokers, who serve as rebel leaders, say they have been pressured by the peasantry to do so. They struggle with the tensions between loyalty to the elite and service to the peasants, and in the end choose the latter because only in that way can they remain brokers. For example, in the German Peasants' War, the mayor of a market town became a rebel leader when the peasants voted for war. He later claimed that he did not want war but went along with it when so many of the poor people voted for it, and thus he became their leader.[24] The brokers, then, often retain their structural function even in mass movements.

Thus, peasant studies of both Western and Eastern societies, both medieval and contemporary, indicate the peasant need for leadership outside the peasantry. Peasants need someone in touch with the Great Tradition, someone from the city with contacts with the elite. These potential leaders of peasant movements Sabean terms "brokers." Second, many (probably all) peasant rebellions have taken on a religious or even millenarian meaning for the peasants.

22. For the German peasants' rebellion, see Wunder, "Mentality," 157; for the Russian rebellion, see Mousnier, *Peasant Uprisings*, 216–27; for millenarianism in general, see Scott, "Revolution in the Revolution," 101–3, and Moore, *Social Origins*, 455; for China, see Chesnaux, *Peasant Revolts*, 16 and Naquin, *Millennarian Rebellion*.

23. Sabean, "Markets, Uprisings," 17–19.

24. Ibid.

The Mass Movements in the Roman Empire

A pattern similar to that of the medieval and contemporary peasant societies surveyed above is evident also in the Roman Empire. We will look at the leadership in native uprisings throughout the Roman Empire and then at the leaders of Palestine. S. Dyson[25] has argued persuasively that the following are mass movements of the native peasantry and not merely reflections of Roman politics. First, the large numbers that followed these leaders indicate generic discontent. Second, the demands for land and the complaints over taxes indicate rebellion over economic causes. The following table is largely dependent on Dyson's article:[26]

Table 2.1: Leaders of the Mass Movements in the Roman Empire (Excluding Palestine)

Leader	Social Origin
Hampsicordia and Hostus (Sardinia, 217 BCE; Livy 23.20.1–41.7)	Aristocrats
Viriathus (Spain, 150 BCE; Appian, *Iberike* 61–75; Diod. 33.1.1–5)	Shepherd
Mariccus (Gaul, 68 CE; Tacitus, *Hist.* 2.61)	Commoner?
Florus and Sacrovir (Gaul, 21 CE; Tacitus, *Ann.* 3.40–66)	Aristocrats
Vindex (Gaul, 68 CE; Dio Cassius 63.22–24)	Aristocrat
Tacfarinas (Africa, 24 CE; Tacitus, *Ann.* 2.52)	Soldier
Aedmon (Africa, 40 CE; Pliny, *HN* 5.1.11)	Freedman of King Ptolemy
Isidorus (Egypt, 172 CE; Dio Cassius 72.12)	Priest
Jonathon (Cyrene, 70 CE; Josephus, *War* 7.438)	Weaver
Boudicca (Britain, 61 CE; Tacitus, *Ann.* 14.31–37; Dio Cassius 62.2–12)	Aristocrat
Vologaesus (Thrace, 11 BCE; Dio Cassius 54.34)	Priest of Dionysus
Aristonicus (Asia Minor, 133 BCE; Strabo 14.1.38)	Illegitimate son of Royalty
Eunus (Sicily, 135 BCE; Diod. 34/35.2.5–26)	Slave
Spartacus (Italy, 73 BCE; Appian, *Civil War* 1.116–120)	Slave, former soldier

25. Dyson, "Native Revolt Patterns," 159 and 171.

26. But see also Cary, *History of Rome*, 221, 282, 36; Grant, *Social History*, 102–4; Lewis, *Life in Egypt*, 205; Crossan, *Historical Jesus*, 167.

The table indicates that practically all of these leaders, with the exceptions of Viriathus and Mariccus, came from a class other than the peasantry. Eunus, the slave originally from Syria, may have been a person also of high station before his enslavement. His leadership abilities were legendary. Most of the leaders were aristocrats from noble families. One was a deserter from the Roman army; one was a freedman of Ptolemy (we presume with considerable skill at management); two were priests; and one was a slave who had been a soldier. It is of great interest that one, Jonathon the weaver, was an artisan.

The survey of rebellions in the Roman Empire, then, is consistent with the findings of modern investigations of peasant societies. Leaders rarely came from peasants themselves. Furthermore, at least three of the leaders, Eunus, Sacrovir and Vologaesus (probably also Isidorus), sought to give their movements religious legitimacy, which, as we noted above, is often the case in peasant mass movements.

Mass Movements in Palestine

Next we survey the leaders of mass movements in Palestine. Unfortunately, more information is available from Josephus concerning the military leaders than about the prophetic leaders.[27]

Table 2.2: Leaders of Mass Movements in Palestine

Leader	Social Origin
EARLY UPRISINGS:	
Mattathias and Sons (167 BCE; 1 Macc 2.1)	Priest
Judas, son of Ezekias (4 BCE; Josephus, *Ant.* 17.271–72)	Son of a bandit
Simon (4 BCE; Josephus, *Ant.* 17.273–76)	Slave
Athronges (4 BCE; Josephus, *Ant.* 17.278–85)	Shepherd
Judas of Galilee (6 CE; Josephus, *War* 2.433)	Teacher
THE JEWISH WAR:	
Ananus (66 CE; Josephus, *War* 2.563)	Priest
Joseph ben Gorion (66 CE; Josephus, *War* 2.563)	Aristocrat?

27. In general, for comments on these leaders of mass movements, see Hengel, *Die Zeloten*; Horsley and Hanson, *Bandits*; Rhoads, *Israel in Revolution*; Barnett, "Jewish Sign Prophets."

Leader	Social Origin
Josephus (66 CE; Josephus, *Life* 1–2)	Aristocrat
Simon ben Gamaliel (66 CE; Josephus, *Life* 191)	Aristocrat
Justus of Tiberius (66 CE; Josephus, *Life* 40)	Aristocrat
John of Gischala (66 CE; Josephus, *Life* 74–76)	Merchant Class?
Simon bar Giora (66 CE; Josephus, *War* 4.504)	?
Eleazar ben Ananias (66 CE; Josephus, *War* 2.409)	Priest, Captain of the temple
Menahem (66 CE; Josephus, *War* 2.445)	Teacher
Eleazar ben Simon (66 CE; Josephus, *War* 4.225)	Priest
PROPHETIC MOVEMENTS:	
The Samaritan (37 CE; Josephus, *Ant.* 18.85–87)	?
Theudas (44 CE; Josephus, *Ant.* 20.97–98)	?
The Egyptian (55 CE; Josephus, *Ant.* 20.169–72)	?
John the Baptist (27 CE; Luke 1.5)	Priest

With the exception of those uprisings at the death of Herod the Great, most, if not all, of the groups were led by aristocrats, priests, or teachers. Simon bar Giora's origins are unknown, as are the origins of three of the prophetic leaders: the Samaritan, Theudas, and the Egyptian. It is interesting, however, that the prophet Jesus, son of Ananias, is expressly said to have been from the peasantry, but that no one followed him, and, for that matter, no one was invited to follow him (Josephus, *War* 6.300–309). He was no leader of a mass movement. Palestinian folk, then, from the meager evidence available, follow the same pattern as persons elsewhere in the empire, and follow the same pattern observable in more recent peasant societies.

Those leaders expressly said to have given religious interpretation to their movements were Judas of Galilee, the four prophetic leaders, and probably also Menahem, who made messianic—or at least royal—claims. It is not clear whether Simon bar Giora made similar claims. Yet, given the fact that many peasants see their rebellion in religious terms, as noted above, and that in first-century Palestine religion, politics, and economics were inseparably intertwined,[28] it is likely that virtually all the mass movements surveyed above were viewed as religious movements by the peasants, and thus that all of the leaders of those movements were viewed as religious leaders.

28. See Damaschke, *Bibel und Bodenreform*, 4; Redfield, *Peasant Society*, 27–28; Kautsky, *Politics of Aristocratic Empires*, 273; Wolf, *Peasants*, 277.

The answer to my first question, therefore, is that there is a pattern regarding the social origins of leaders of peasant mass movements. The pattern is that the leaders seldom come from the peasantry itself. Rather, they are discontented aristocrats, soldiers, artisans, priests, or teachers. This was the pattern for peasant societies generally, for the Greco-Roman world in antiquity, and for Palestine in the Second Temple period.

Jesus's Movement

I now ask if Jesus and his movement fit this emerging pattern. We should first of all consider it probable that large crowds followed Jesus—in other words, that Jesus had a mass movement. Both Tacitus and Josephus support the conclusion that large crowds followed Jesus. Tacitus writes:

> Auctor nominis eius Christus Tiberio imperitante per procuratorem Pontium Pilatum supplicio adfectus erat; repressaque in praesens exitiabilis superstitio rursum erumpebat, non modo per Iudaeam, originem eius mali, sed per urbem etiam . . .[29] (*Ann.* 15.44).

> The originator of this name [Christian] was Christ who was executed by Pontius Pilate during the reign of Tiberius. This pernicious superstition was repressed for a while but broke out again not only in Judea, the origin of the evil, but also throughout the city . . . (my translation)

Tacitus's statement that the superstition was "repressed" for a while only to "break out" later would seem to indicate that he thought of Jesus's following as a mass movement.[30]

The statement of Josephus is even clearer. In the (interpolated) passage about Jesus's ministry and death Josephus writes:

> Και πολλους μεν Ιουδαιους, πολλους δε και του Ελληνικου επηγαγετο[31] (*Ant.* 18.63).

> And he gained many Jews and Greeks as followers . . .

---

29. Text in Pitmann, *Cornelii Taciti.*

30. Cf. Crossan, *Essential Jesus*, vii.

31. Text in Feldman, *Josephus*, 9:50; cf. the reconstructions of Eisler (given in Feldman, *Josephus*, 9:48); Bruce, *New Testament Documents*, 110; Smith, *Jesus the Magician*, 46; and Klausner, *Jesus of Nazareth*, 55–56. All of these reconstructed versions of Josephus's interpolated text contain the words quoted above. Cf. also the Arabic text of Josephus published in Pines, *Arabic Version*, 16.

Further, Josephus's description of the ministry of John the Baptist indicates that John also had a large following. Antipas actually feared that John's followers might turn to insurrection (στασις) and believed that the crowds following John might do whatever John wanted them to do (*Ant.* 18.118). Thus on analogy with John's ministry we should expect that Jesus also had a large following.[32]

All four Gospels also attest that Jesus had a large following (Matt 4:25; Mark 5:21; 6:34; 7:17; 9:15; 10:46; 11:32; 12:12; Luke 6:17; 9:37; 12:1; John 7:31; 8:2; 12:9). Whether these are all redactional or not, at least it shows that the Four Evangelists had the impression that Jesus led a mass movement. Further, some of the gospel stories assume that Jesus had a large following. The feeding of the five thousand, for example, found in all four Gospels (Matt. 14:13–21; Mark 6:30–44; Luke 9:10–17; John 6:1–15), clearly makes no sense apart from the numbers of people present. Other scenes, especially in Mark, assume a large crowd: e.g., the story in which the roof of Peter's house is removed to lower the afflicted man to Jesus (Mark 2:1–12) and the account of Jesus's teaching from a boat because of the press of the crowd (Mark 4:1).

Finally, we must ask if Jesus would have been crucified had he not led a mass movement. Crucifixion, reserved for the worst criminals and for insurrectionists, would hardly have been the end for one teaching and leading a few score of people.[33] Therefore, I conclude that Jesus led a mass movement and that his name should be added to those leaders listed above.

Second, we should consider it probable that Jesus was an artisan, a τεκτων. Although that assertion is only found in Mark 6:22, and although in the parallel passage in Matt 13:55, he is called "the son of the carpenter," this probability remains high. All the major Greek manuscripts—except one (P[45])—and many of the early versions have the reading, "Is not this the carpenter?"[34]

Further, these words are found in a text describing Jesus's rejection at his hometown, a narrative very unlikely to have been invented by the early church. Nor is it likely that Mark would ascribe unhistorically the occupation of carpenter to Jesus especially if his gospel was written in Rome.[35] This is because the artisan occupations were not respected by

32. See Brown, *John*, 1:249–50.

33. See Hengel, *Crucifixion*, 46–50.

34. See Cranfield, *Mark*, 194–95; and Metzger, *Textual Commentary*, 88–89.

35. Many scholars agree that the tradition is correct that affirms that Mark was

the Greco-Roman upper classes (see below). Why would Mark want to invent that Jesus had been a carpenter?

The passage in Matthew ("Is not this the son of the carpenter?"), even if one were to argue that it is more accurate or authentic, actually supports the meaning of Mark since fathers usually taught their craft to their sons.[36] Therefore, if Joseph was a carpenter, then Jesus almost certainly was as well.

Finally, we have the apocryphal and patristic texts that affirm or assume that Joseph or Jesus was a carpenter. The most important patristic text is that of Justin Martyr (*Dial.* 88), who maintained that Jesus was a carpenter who made yokes and plows. The apocryphal texts include: the *Protevangelium of James*, the *Infancy Gospel of Thomas*, the *Gospel of Pseudo-Matthew*, and the *Arabic Infancy Gospel*. Several of the apocryphal texts are quite late[37] and even rely on the earlier ones. These texts seem to be an amalgam of both written and oral sources. Nevertheless, they at least testify that the church generally thought that Jesus had been an artisan.[38]

But are there any indications from the Gospels that Jesus was not one of the peasantry? G. W. Buchanan has argued[39] that Jesus is found among well-to-do people rather often. He called to be his disciples James and John, sons of Zebedee, a fishing merchant who was wealthy enough to employ day laborers (Mark 1:19–20). Levi the tax collector hosted a banquet for Jesus-in which they were said to recline at the table—and became a disciple (Matt: 9.9–11). A certain man, "of the rulers of the Pharisees," invited Jesus to dine with him (Luke 14:1–6). Jairus, ruler of the synagogue at Capernaum, and a certain unnamed Roman centurion approached him (Mark 5:22–23; Matt 8:5). Zaccheus, the chief tax col-

---

written in Rome (1 Pet. 5:13; Papias in Eusebius, *H.E.* 2.15; Clement of Alexandria in Eusebius, *H.E.* 6.14). See, e.g., Price, *Interpreting the New Testament*, 195; V. Taylor, *Mark*, 32.

36. See Burford, *Craftsmen*, 83; Klausner, *Jesus of Nazareth*, 177–78. For studies on Jesus as carpenter, see: McCown, "Ο ΤΕΚΤΩΝ"; Furfey, "Christ as τεκτων," 324–35; Fiensy, "Jesus' Socioeconomic Background."

37. For the dates, see Hennecke et al., *New Testament Apocrypha*; Vielhauer, *Geschichte der urchristlichen Literatur*; and Quasten, *Patrology*. The earlier texts are the *Prot. Jas.*, the *Inf. Gos. Thom.*, and the *Acts Thom.*, which date from the second to early third century.

38. The exception was Origen, who—in response to Celsus—tried to deny that Jesus had been a carpenter (*Cels.* 6.36).

39. Buchanan, "Jesus and the Upper Class," 195–209.

lector, also gave a meal for Jesus (Luke 19:1–10). Lazarus (or Simon the leper) hosted a banquet for Jesus in Bethany (Mark 14:3; John 12:2). Joanna, the wife of a court official of Antipas, was a disciple of Jesus (Luke 8:3). Nicodemus, said to be a member of the Sanhedrin, was a disciple of Jesus in secret (John 3:1–2; 7:50; 19:39). Finally, Joseph of Arimathea, who buried Jesus's body and was a disciple, is described as a member of the council and wealthy (Matt 27:57; Mark 15:43). These texts are spread throughout the canonical gospels and at least indicate that the Evangelists remembered Jesus as associating with the well-to-do.

That Jesus could so easily move among these wealthier people suggests some experience in similar situations and an earlier association with people of some economic means. Further, given the common urban snobbery toward the village peasants, one may reasonably wonder if a simple village carpenter would ever be the guest of such people as those listed above. It does not follow from these texts, however (*pace* Buchanan), that Jesus was therefore himself wealthy or a member of the elite class. He was only in a position to have known such people. An itinerant artisan who had experience in urban environments, working for wealthy patrons, could easily have become familiar with such people.

D. E. Oakman also argues persuasively for Jesus's itineracy and broad social contacts before his ministry.[40] Oakman notes several foci of social contacts during Jesus's ministry such as the Jerusalem–Bethlehem–Bethany area and the cities and towns around the Sea of Galilee (Gerasa, Caesarea Philippi, Chorazin, Bethsaida and Capernaum), and gives evidence that these were previously existing contacts. He also notes that Jesus is often depicted in the Gospels as associating with the wealthy. Interestingly, in the *Infancy Gospel of Thomas* 13, Joseph is reported to have made a bed for a rich patron. Thus, Oakman concludes, "might not Jesus' openness toward and knowledge of the social circumstances of the wealthy find a grounding in his previous experiences with them as a client?"[41] Thus even before Jesus began his ministry, his social circle, which served as the base of his movements during his ministry, was established.

Finally, I would add that some of Jesus's sayings are hard to explain if he is to be identified with the peasantry. Although obviously many of

---

40. Oakman, *Economic Questions*, 175–204. See also Case, *Jesus*, 202, 206, and 208, who had made many of the same observations.

41. Oakman, *Economic Questions*, 193.

Jesus's teachings appealed to the Palestinian peasants (though their interpretation of his teachings might have been different from what he intended), some of his parables betray a nonpeasant mindset. These would especially be the parables of the Wicked Tenants and the Talents.[42] The parable of the Wicked Tenants, found in all three Synoptic Gospels and in the *Gospel of Thomas* (Mark 21:1–9 and par.; *Gos. Thom.* 65), certainly exhibits a point of view that is not from the peasantry. In this parable, all too realistic in its details, the tenants refuse to pay their rent on the vineyard. Repeated attempts by the owner of the vineyard, the absentee landlord, to collect result in violence on the part of the tenants. Finally, the landlord must destroy the tenants and give the vineyard to others to rent (Mark 12:9). The wicked ones both in the Synoptic version and in the *Gospel of Thomas* are clearly the tenants. In the *Gospel of Thomas* the owner of the vineyard is called a "good man"; and in Matthew's version of the parable (21:41) the tenants are called "wicked men." Yet, as M. Hengel has shown, tenants often felt such hostility toward the landowners because the landowners were oppressive and exploitative. Such outbreaks of violence must have been rather common in the ancient agrarian economies, as the Zenon Papyri attest.[43] But Jesus tells a parable in which the wicked ones are peasant tenant farmers. This may not in itself prove that Jesus was not of the peasantry but it is surely suggestive.

The next parable is equally suggestive. In the parable of the Talents, two versions of which appear in the double tradition commonly called Q (Matt 25:14–30; Luke 19:11–27; *Gos. Naz.*), the wicked person again exhibits peasant-like behavior. The persons extolled in the canonical tradition—although both Matthew and Luke have interesting differences of detail—are those who take risks with the money entrusted to them and increase it. On the other hand, the one who buries the money entrusted to him—a behavior consistent with the peasant's reluctance to take risk[44]—is the one condemned. Interestingly, in the version of the

42. This insight was suggested to me by Professor A. Dewey of Xavier University.

43. See Hengel, "Gleichnis von den Weingärtnern." Cf. Derrett, "Fresh Light."

44. See Scott, *Moral Economy*, 18, who writes that at the core of peasant values is a very conservative outlook with respect to change of any kind. Therefore they do not view risk taking in the same light as a modern capitalist since the risk could mean excessive hardship or even death to their family. Thus they prefer old technologies, poor as they may be, which yield a consistent crop to new, unproven technologies. Peasants value survival and maintenance over change and improvement. Such economic imperatives and their concomitant value system are called by Scott the "moral economy" or "subsistence ethic." Cf. on this also Redfield, *Peasant Society*, 70–73, 137,

parable given in the *Gospel of the Nazarenes*, the three servants are called to account in a different way. One has wasted the master's money with harlots and is imprisoned; one has increased the amount entrusted to him and is rebuked; one has hidden his talent and is received with favor. This version of the parable, then, takes the point of view and value system of the peasant. Which version is closest to that of Jesus?[45] If either of the canonical versions is to be preferred, then once again Jesus has separated himself from the peasantry.

Thus I conclude that Jesus came from the artisan class. The answer to my second question is that Jesus as a leader of a mass movement fits the pattern established above for peasant movements generally, for the ancient Greco-Roman world, and for Palestine in the Second Temple period: He came from outside the peasantry.

Why Would Jesus Have Been a Candidate for Leadership?

The evidence for answering this question is less certain than above, but what I present below is at least suggestive. I submit that Jesus's networking as a carpenter enabled him to establish relationships with both peasants

---

who describes the "little tradition" of the peasants as very conservative. Scott's theory draws heavily on Moore, *Social Origins*. Scott's theoretical perspective on peasantry is followed by Migdal, *Peasants*. His theory is opposed by the political-economy theory of Popkin, *Rational Peasant* and the class-conflict theory of Paige, *Agrarian Revolution*. See the theoretical descriptions in Thilly, *Mobilization to Revolution*; and Paige, "Social Theory."

45. The scholars of the Jesus Seminar, for example (see Funk and Hoover, *Five Gospels*, 255–56, 373–74), concluded that the canonical version is very near to the actual words of Jesus. However, Malina and Rohrbaugh (*Social Science Commentary*, 150, 389); and Rohrbaugh, "Peasant Reading," 32–39, suggest that the version in the *Gos. Naz.* is the original, claiming that Westerners see erroneously in this parable "a kind of homespun capitalism on the lips of Jesus." But somebody has told the parable from the canonical and nonpeasant perspective. Was it Jesus, the Q community, or Matthew and Luke (independently of one another)? The last possibility seems remote. The differences in detail between Matthew and Luke suggest that they have worked independently and thus either used the same source or sources (in which the canonical version of our parable was found). That means, if Malina and Rohrbaugh are correct, that the Q community would have changed the parable from Jesus's original peasant-oriented version (similar to that in the *Gos. Naz.*) to the nonpeasant canonical version. But I can see no good reason for that to have been done. Since one can just as easily conclude that Jesus's parable was like the canonical version, it seems best to do so.

and the elite, with both rural and urban peoples. This networking resulting from his work in the urban centers of Galilee exposed him to urban culture, to the ideas of the Great Tradition. Therefore Jesus was a good candidate to become a broker, acting as intermediary between peasants and the elite. In other words, he articulated their needs and wants. We should not expect, however, that Jesus's goals and agenda were the same as the peasants. As I explained above, the peasants often had more limited goals than their leaders.

The crafts in the ancient world included making leather products and cloth products, pottery production, carpentry, masonry, and metal working.[46] All of these trades are attested in the sources for Palestine as well.[47]

Historians agree that most artisans worked very hard but were usually able to earn enough to live simply.[48] They were usually not wealthy, but neither were they starving. Occasionally, however, some craftsmen could attain a level of affluence if their skills were especially in demand,[49] or if they could afford slaves to mass-produce their goods.[50] Archaeologists have discovered a family of well-to-do artisans in Palestine as well, the family of Simon the Temple Builder, buried in Tomb I on Givat ha-Mivtar, north of Jerusalem.[51] This was a family of craftsmen who did hard manual labor but attained a measure of financial success since they could afford both a tomb in a rather high-priced area and ossuaries.

Artisans did not enjoy a high social standing among the Greeks or Romans. Herodotus writes that the Egyptians and other foreigners regard craftsmen as low on the social scale, and the Greeks also have accepted this attitude (2.167). Aristotle, although he allows that some of the crafts are necessary for a society (*Pol.* 4.3.11–12; cf. Plato, *Resp.* 2.396b–371e), regards the artisans as inferior beings. Artisans are much like slaves (*Pol.* 1.5.10) and they, the day laborers, and the market people are clearly inferior to other classes, even farmers (*Pol.* 6.2.7; 7.8.2.).

Xenophon also has Socrates denigrate the artisans. In some cities, says Socrates, they cannot be citizens (*Oec. 4.1–4*). The same attitude can

46. Michel, *Economics of Ancient Greece*, 170–209.

47. Klausner, *Jesus of Nazareth*, 177.

48. Burford, *Craftsmen*, 138–43; Mossé, *Ancient World*, 79; Hock, *Social Context*, 35.

49. Burford, *Craftsmen*, 141; Hock, *Social Context*, 34.

50. Mossé, *Ancient World*, 90–91.

51. Tzaferis, "Jewish Tombs," 18–22.

be found in later Greek authors such as Dio Chrysostom (see *Or.* 7,110), Lucian of Samosata (see *Fug.* 12–13), and Celsus (see Origen, *C. Cels.* 6.36) as well as in important Roman authors such as Cicero (see *Off.* 1.42 and *Brut.* 73)—although Cicero also admits that artisans are useful to the city (*Rep.* 2.22)—and Livy (see 20.2.25).[52]

This demeaning attitude toward artisans from higher-status people stemmed from the effect some artisan trades had on the body, disfiguring it or making it soft because of a sedentary lifestyle (Socrates in Xenophon, *Oec.* 4,1–4; Dio Chrysostom, *Or.* 7,110). In addition, an artisan was not considered an adequate defender of his city in contrast to a peasant farmer (Socrates in Xenophon, *Oec.* 4.1–4). We must bear in mind, nevertheless, that this was the attitude of the elite toward artisans, not the attitude of the artisans themselves or of the other classes.

But the same attitude seems not to have prevailed among Palestinian Jews. The rabbinic sources extol both manual labor (*m. 'Abot* 1:10; *'Abot R.Nat.* B XXI, 23a) and teaching one's son a craft (*m. Qidd.* 4.14; *t. Qidd.* 1.11; *b. Qidd.* 29a). Artisans often receive special recognition (*m. Bik.* 3.3; *b. Qidd.* 33a), and many of the sages were artisans.[53] Josephus also seems to have regarded artisans highly. He praises their skills in building the temples (*Ant.* 3.200; 8.76), in forming sacred vessels (*Ant.* 12.58–84) and in constructing towers (*War* 5.175). He never refers to artisans using the pejorative term "mechanical workers" (βαναυσος). It is suggestive that the only other artisan leader of a mass movement listed above, Jonathon the weaver, also had Jewish followers (see *War* 7.438).

That artisans in antiquity would travel from their home villages to work on large construction projects is well known. It is quite plausible, therefore, that Jesus and his family worked in other towns in Galilee, such as Tiberias and Sepphoris, which began construction sometime between Jesus's youth and early adulthood,[54] and perhaps even in Jerusalem.

In the first place, there are clear examples in the Mediterranean world of artisans traveling to distant building sites. Building temples and other public works almost always required importing craftsmen from surrounding cities. There was in general a shortage of craftsmen in the building trades (carpenters, masons, sculptors), especially from the

52. Hock, *Social Context*, 35–36; Burford, *Craftsmen*, 29, 34, 39–40; MacMullen, *Roman Social Relations*, 115–16.

53. Büchler, *Economic Conditions*, 50; Klausner, *Jesus of Nazareth*, 177; Krauss, *Talmudische Archäologie*, 2:249–51.

54. Overman, "Who Were the First Urban Christians?" 160–68.

fourth century BCE on. This shortage necessitated that craftsmen travel from city to city. A. Burford[55] cites, for example, the case of city of Epidauros in Greece, which, in order to build the temple of Asclepius (c. 370 BCE), imported masons, carpenters, and sculptors from Argos, Corinth, Athens, Paros, Arcadia, and Troizen. Argos itself had to hire Athenian masons to complete its long walls in 418 BCE. Athens also needed carpenters and masons from Megara and Thebes to rebuild its walls in the 390s BCE.

This shortage of craftsmen was especially acute in the Roman period, according to Burford. The cities of North Africa, Asia Minor, Persia and Palmyra imported craftsmen for their building projects with the local artisans contributing what they could. Burford affirms, "For unusual projects such as public works, no city, not even Athens, had a sufficiently large skilled labor force to do the job by itself."[56]

Since such was the case throughout the Mediterranean world, we should expect that in Palestine in the Herodian period artisans from surrounding cities and villages were used for large building projects. This expectation is confirmed by a passage in Josephus. Josephus related that Herod the Great made the following preparations to build his temple in 20 BCE: "He made ready 1,000 wagons which would carry the stones. He gathered 10,000 of the most skillful workers . . . And he taught some to be masons and others to be carpenters" (*Ant.* 15.390).

Josephus's description of Herod's collection and training of carpenters and builders in preparation for building his temple implies there was a shortage of artisans in Jerusalem for this massive construction project. Furthermore, the temple was only completed in the procuratorship of Albinus (62–64 CE), which caused, Josephus reports, 18,000 artisans to be out of work (*Ant.* 20.219–20). Thus the temple required—though perhaps Josephus's figure is exaggerated somewhat—a large force of artisans throughout most of the first century CE.

The evidence from Josephus confirms that an extensive public works project like building the temple required recruiting and importing—even training—artisans from distant cities and employing them over long periods of time. Surely the construction of Sepphoris and Tiberias required a similar contribution of skilled labor. Given the urbanization of Lower

55. Burford, *Craftsmen*, 62–67.
56. Ibid.

Galilee (e.g., Magdala, Capernaum and Scythopolis[57]) and also of the Tetrarchy of Philip (Caesarea Philippi, Bethsaida Julius), one can well imagine that an artisan in the building trade would be in demand. Since such was the case in the Greco-Roman world in general—causing artisans to move frequently from job to job—we should expect the same to have been true in Galilee. It is even possible that Jesus and his family worked on a temple in Jerusalem from time to time.[58]

R. Batey's assertion[59] that carpenters in particular were necessary for the construction of public works—erecting scaffolding, forms for vaults, cranes, and ceiling beams—also is confirmed not only by the examples from classical Greece listed above but also from Josephus. Josephus celebrates the importance of carpenters for building Solomon's temple (*Ant.* 7.77, 340, 377), Zerubbabel's temple (*Ant.* 11.78), and Herod's temple (*Ant.* 15.390). Carpenters also figure prominently in building city walls (*War* 3.173).

Therefore we can say with certainty that there were several continuous and massive building projects during Jesus's youth and early adulthood. Second, we can be reasonably confident that these projects would have necessitated the services of skilled carpenters, even from distant cities and villages. Jesus and his extended family could easily have worked in Sepphoris, Tiberias, and other Galilean cities, and even in Jerusalem. Opportunities were there for this family to have experienced urban culture and to have risen to the same level of economic comfort as the artisan family of Simon the temple builder.[60]

This observation is more important when readers realize that there was a great cultural gap between the city and the country in antiquity. As recent a historian as G. Aföldy[61] has accepted this estimate of ancient society, but he stands at the head of a long line of previous historians. The rural populations in the eastern Roman Empire for the most part seems to have maintained their native languages and customs, whether Coptic in Egypt, Celtic in Asia Minor, or Aramaic in Syria.[62] On the other hand, in the cities people spoke Greek, many were literate, and most

57. Overman, "Who Were the First Urban Christians?" 160–68.

58. Oakman, *Economic Questions,* 186–93.

59. Batey, *Jesus and the Forgotten City,* 68–82.

60. Tzaferis, "Jewish Tombs"; Haas, "Anthropological Observations."

61. Aföldy, *Die römische Gesellschaft,* 10.

62. See de Ste. Croix, *Class Struggle,* 10, 13; Rostovtzeff, *Roman Empire,* 193, 346; MacMullen, *Roman Social Relations,* 46.

were in touch to some degree with the great institutions and ideas of Greco-Roman society, the Great Tradition. This was especially true of the aristocrats but to some extent was even true of the urban poor, according to G. E. M. de Ste. Croix, since the urban poor may have "mixed with the educated" in some way.[63] Such mixing could take place in Palestinian cities not only in synagogues but in theaters, amphitheaters and hippodromes, as well as in the courts of justice.[64] Thus there was a cultural gulf between the rural peasants and even the urban poor. As L. White has observed about medieval agrarian societies, "cities were atolls of civilization . . . on an ocean of rural primitivism."[65] Thus any experience on Jesus' part in cities, any "mixing" among the urban culture of first-century Palestine could have been significant.[66]

Conclusions

Thus the answer to my first query is that there does seem to be a pattern with respect to the social origins of leaders of peasant mass movements. The common pattern, both in the Mediterranean world of antiquity and in more recent peasant societies, is that the leaders come from nonpeasant classes. These persons may be intellectuals, dissident landed aristocrats, priests or other religious leaders, artisans, teachers, or village leaders. The pattern is fairly consistent in the Mediterranean generally and in Palestine in particular.

63. De Ste. Croix, *Class Struggle*, 13.

64. In general for the benefits of the urban proletariat in living in the city, see Jones, *Greek City*, 285. For Palestine in particular, see Schürer, *History of the Jewish People*, 2:46, 48, 54, and 55. As the authors write (55) even though Josephus (*Ant.* 15.268) declared that theatres and amphitheatres were alien to Jewish custom, "it should not be assumed that the mass of the Jewish population did not frequent them."

65. White quoted in de Ste. Croix, *Class Struggle*, 10. Cf. Migdal, *Peasants*, 9, who points out that the peasant who goes regularly to the city will develop higher "information-processing capacity" and will more quickly adopt modern ways than one who stays home. The city has a strong influence on peasants for change.

66. Horsley (*Archaeology*, 43–65) challenges that Sepphoris and Tiberias were as cosmopolitan as other cities in Palestine, e.g. Caesarea Maritima and Scythopolis. He describes these cities as having "only a thin veneer of cosmopolitan culture" (59). At the same time Horsley argues that the culture of Sepphoris and Tiberias was "Roman-Hellenistic." We should probably think of the differences between the countryside and the cities, that is, between the Little Tradition and Great Tradition respectively, as more of a continuum. Some villages were more urbanized than others, and some larger towns and cities were less urbanized and cosmopolitan than others.

Second, Jesus was also a leader of a mass movement as the sources, both canonical and classical, indicate. Since he was probably an artisan, he too fits the leadership pattern for a peasant mass movement. It would, therefore, seem incorrect to term Jesus a peasant or proletarian.[67]

The most difficult question to answer (the third question proposed) is, why would an artisan have been a candidate for peasant leadership? Here I can only suggest (because the evidence is not conclusive) that Jesus as an itinerant worker met urban people and experienced urban life before his ministry. He was conversant with the Great Tradition, the ideas of the elites, and that made him better able to articulate the needs and goals of the peasants. Because Jesus was seen as an effective broker, as Sabean termed it, he would have been a candidate for a peasant leader.

What made the peasants actually follow him is, however, another matter. Doubtless, his teaching about the evils of wealth and the wealthy, and his promise of the kingdom of God, would have been what attracted them to him. Of course we must always bear in mind that the peasantry probably had a different interpretation of Jesus's words than he himself had. As J. C. Scott remarked (quoted above), peasants are seldom ideologically sound. Thus Jesus's own agenda may have been misunderstood by the masses.[68]

67. See especially Crossan, *Historical Jesus*, 421, who terms Jesus a "Peasant Jewish Cynic." For Jesus as a proletarian, see the survey in Bammel, "Revolution Theory." Bammel cites especially the work of R. von Pöhlmann (*Geschichte*).

68. Does John 6:15 recall an historical event? See Brown, *John*, 1:249–50. Brown argues that the Fourth Evangelist would not have invented a story that claimed that some people thought of Jesus as a king, especially if this Gospel was written in the midst of tensions between Rome and the church during the reign of Domitian. If Brown is correct, then this records one such difference between Jesus's vision of his leadership and the vision of the masses.

PART TWO

Galilee

3

Jesus and Debts

Did He Pray about Them?

"FORGIVE US OUR DEBTS as we forgive our debtors" (Matt 6:12). Was Jesus in his model prayer referring literally to debts or metaphorically to sins? Was Galilee in the time of Jesus plagued by widespread peasant indebtedness, and did Jesus teach about this problem? Some have assumed that the economic problem of indebtedness formed the backdrop of Jesus' ministry.[1] We have no problem, of course, in documenting that indebtedness existed, but the question is, how widespread was it among the peasants? Were a quarter of the peasants in dangerous debt? Were half or even more of the peasant farmers about to lose their land because of debt so that Jesus makes reference to the problem and preaches in favor of general debt remission?

Some scholars have cited New Testament passages to demonstrate that indebtedness was widespread in Galilee in Jesus's time. The following chart gives a list of the most often cited texts—those by Oakman, Pastor, and de Ste. Croix:[2]

---

1. See, e.g., Hanson and Oakman, *Palestine in the Time of Jesus*, 119–20 [2nd ed., 111–13]; Malina and Rohrbaugh, *Social Science Commentary on the Synoptic Gospels*, 62–63.

2. Oakman, *Jesus and the Peasants*, 11–32; Pastor, *Land and Economy*, 147–49; de Ste. Croix, *Class Struggle*, 164.

Table 3.1: Frequently Cited New Testament Texts to Support a Claim of Widespread Indebtedness in First-Century Palestine

Text (size of debt)	Oakman	Pastor	De Ste. Croix
1. (large debt)	Matt 18:23–34	Matt 18:23–34	Matt 18:23–34
2.	Matt 5:25–26 and Luke 12:57–59		Matt 5:25–26 and Luke 12:57–59
3. (large debt)	Luke 16:1–9	Luke 16:1–9	
4. (large debt)	Luke 7:41–42	Luke 7:41–42	
5.		Matt 25:27	
6. (?)	Matt 6:11–12		

In the case of the first text (the parable of the Unforgiving Servant), the debt of the first debtor (10,000 talents) is incredibly large (equal to ten times the annual income of Herod the Great [Josephus, *Ant.* 17.318–21]),[3] that of the second debtor (100 denarii) perhaps too large for a small-time peasant. The second sum would be, according to the calculations of Ariel Ben-David,[4] half the expected annual earnings of a day laborer. This text, in my opinion, witnesses to debts incurred by businessmen both large and small.

The second case (Sermon on the Mount: "Be reconciled with your accuser") describes the possibility of debtor's prison for one who does not make amends with his accuser before the trial. If he does not, he will be put into prison and not released until he has paid the last *quadrans* (Matt) or *lepton* (Luke). But I cannot tell if this is a lawsuit based on a debt, or if the judge is going to fine someone for a crime. If indebtedness is the problem, how can Jesus advise someone to be reconciled quickly with the accuser "on the way"?

The third case (the parable of the Unjust Steward) again seems to describe large debtors who are pictured as entrepreneurs. One owed 100 baths of olive oil (= 3400 liters, see Danker);[5] the second 100 cors of wheat (= 500 bushels, see Danby).[6] I estimate the average harvest for a peasant on six acres would be between thirteen and twenty-five bushels per year, depending on whether he left half of his ground fallow.[7] These are, then,

---

3. Schalit, *Herodes*, 263–64.

4. Ben-David, *Talmudische Ökonomie*, 293.

5. Danker, *Greek-English Lexicon*, 171.

6. Danby, *Mishnah*, 798.

7. Fiensy, *Social History*, 94.

sizeable sums, more (I would assume) than any sensible person would lend to a dirt-poor farmer who scratched out a living on six to ten acres.

The fourth case (the parable of the Two Debtors told after the sinful woman anointed Jesus) contains a reference to two debts, the first of which (500 denarii) would seem to be too large for a peasant but the second (50) more like a debt a peasant could acquire. In Muraba'at 18, for example (a Palestinian loan text that dates in the time of Nero[8]), the borrower borrowed 20 zuzim or 20 denarii. Thus this text could witness to indebtedness by a small businessman or a small farmer.

The fifth case (the parable of the Talents) describes indebtedness from the perspective of the lender. Lending could be a way to make money by owning money. The servant is rebuked because he did not at least make money in this way, but we do not know if this reference supports indebtedness by peasants or by entrepreneurs.

The last case is the reference in the Lord's Prayer to forgiveness of debts. This could be a prayer uttered by peasants that their monetary debts will somehow be released. Such a reading of this prayer is a distinct possibility and should not by any means be rejected out of hand. Two considerations, however, should make us hesitate. First, Luke (or someone before Luke) did not translate the presumed Aramaic word with the term ὀφειλήματα but with the term ἁμαρτία. Second, the Aramaic word *hova'* (חובא "debt"), which may have been the original word, can also be used in a metaphorical way to refer to sin or guilt, as numerous scholars have noted.[9]

Thus the New Testament references are of questionable value in arguing for a widespread peasant indebtedness in first-century Palestine. Only one reference may have a small peasant farmer in view. Even, however, if they all did refer clearly to peasant indebtedness, they could not establish our case. They are isolated references to a few cases of indebtedness. Individual documentation of debts cannot help us in our inquiry. At most they show only that debt existed. For such evidence to be of any help, we would need to be sure that we had all or most of the debt documents and know the number of peasants at any one time in Palestine.

8. See Fitzmyer and Harrington, *Manual of Palestinian Aramaic*, 136–39. The editors date the text to 56 CE. Another papyrus debt text from ancient Palestine dates to the early second century CE. These are so far the only debt documents found in ancient Palestine from around the time of the New Testament.

9. See, e.g., Jeremias, *Prayers of Jesus*, 92; Davies and Allison, *Matthew*, 1.612; Jastrow, *Dictionary*, 429; Moore, *Judaism*, 2.95.

Then we could use this evidence to establish a statistical estimate of indebted peasants. A few scattered New Testament references, however, only illustrate indebtedness; they do not prove that it was widespread.

Instead of pointing to individual cases of loans, others have sought to infer widespread indebtedness from the institution of the פרוסבול (*prosbul*). Martin Goodman[10] especially argues that the *prosbul* testifies to the growing problem of indebtedness. According to the Mishnah (*Sheb.* 10:3) the *prosbul* was enacted by Hillel (first century BCE) to counter the provision in the Torah for cancellation of debts every seven years (Deut 15:1–18; also Exod 21:2–6; 23:10–11; Lev 25:2–7). It was a legal fiction that assigned the loan to the court to collect a debt ("A *prosbul*-loan is not cancelled [by the seventh year]," *m. Sheb.* 10:3). The papyrus text 18 from Wadi Muraba'at (referred to above), dating from the year 56 CE, may illustrate the application of the *prosbul*.

Goodman maintains that the *prosbul* would have been necessary only for rich people lending to poor ones. Rich persons lending to other rich persons could count on repayment because of the pressures of social stigma and thus would not need special legislation. Goodman assumes that many peasants would have been unable to repay the loans and thus would have faced foreclosure on their farms. Thus the introduction of this legislation by Hillel in the first century BCE implies, according to Goodman, that indebtedness had become a problem.

This is an intriguing argument, but one gets the impression that the author has more assumed widespread indebtedness than proven it. If we assume there was widespread debt, then the introduction of *prosbul* can help explain it since, according to Deuteronomy 15, we would have expected all debts to be canceled. By itself, however, the *prosbul* cannot prove that peasant indebtedness was a pervasive problem by the first century CE, the time of Jesus's ministry. Just because one *can* still borrow money late in the Sabbatical Year cycle does not mean that one *will* do so. Economic pressures must cause borrowing to be widespread. Thus the *prosbul* legislation shows how the phenomenon of indebtedness was possible, but that is all.

How, then, could one establish that indebtedness was widespread? In the first place, we should admit that we have difficulty defining the expression "widespread indebtedness." We simply do not have statistics to indicate that, for example, 30 percent (a percentage that I would consider

10. Goodman, "First Jewish Revolt," 414–27.

socially very destabilizing) of the freeholding peasants of first-century Palestine were in debt and facing foreclosure. Therefore we are forced to identify "widespread" in terms of "significant social force." A significant social force would, I presume, manifest itself in social eruptions such as riots, wars, attempts at reform, or at least petitions for relief. In these cases we are dealing not with individual examples of indebtedness but with indebtedness as a collective burden that causes group action. Nor are we inferring that indebtedness was a problem on a wide scale because it fits with our understanding of rabbinic legislation. This significant social force should be a documented event or movement involving many people at once. I conclude that we would be on safe ground in identifying widespread indebtedness should we find such social eruptions.

We might first look for other examples of social eruptions that can in turn inform our search of the Palestinian materials. What would such a movement look like? In the fourth and third centuries BCE, much of Greece was a hotbed of social turmoil and class conflict. As Michael Rostovtzeff[11] has declared, the watchword of the poor in these centuries was γῆς αναδρασμος and πρεων αποκοπη (redistribution of the land and cancellation of debts). Isocrates in 339 BCE in the *Panathenaicus* (258) laments that many Hellenic cities were experiencing the twin banes of abolishing debts and redistributing lands. Written treaties of the leagues in those centuries provide evidence that aristocrats were protected from cancellation of debts, redistribution of the land, confiscation of property, and freeing of slaves. Thus there were multiple social problems and appeals for reform by the peasantry. W. W. Tarn, however, observed that the "driving force of the movement was debt."[12]

This social upheaval took place in Aetolia as well as Boeotia, but the social revolution of Achaia, especially in Sparta, is the most celebrated due perhaps to Plutarch's biography of Cleomenes III. In 244 BCE Agis IV of Sparta had attempted a social reform by canceling debts but stopped short of redistributing land. In 225 BCE, however, his successor, Cleomenes III, carried through a more thorough program of social reforms, including cancellation of debts, putting all property under the ownership of the people in common, and other measures intended to return to the austere days of old Sparta (Polybius 2.47.3; Plutarch,

11. Rostovtzeff, *Hellenistic World*, 1.141, 1376.
12. Tarn, *Hellenistic Civilization*, 121.

Life of Cleomenes).[13] Thus the social upheavals in Greece in the Hellenistic period were largely due to widespread indebtedness.

Even more relevant for our purposes are the causes of random protest and rioting because of debt burden. These riots characteristically resulted in the burning of the city archives and debt records. One such event occurred in the town of Dyme (in the northwest part of the Peloponnesus of Greece) in the latter half of the second century BCE[14]

INSCRIPTION AT DYMAE

Quintus Fabius Maximus, proconsul of the Roman people to the archons, the councils, and the city of Dymae, Greetings. The councils have declared to me about the crimes committed among you. I speak concerning the fire and the destruction of the archives [αρχεια] and the public documents [τα δημοσια γραμματα]. The leader of the entire confusion was Sosus Tauromeneus who also had written laws contrary to the form of government given to the Achaeans by the Romans. These things we have recounted in part in Patrae to the present magistrate. Those who perpetrated these actions seem to me to have been fabricating the worst sort of situations and riots among the Greeks. After hearing the true arguments of the accusers, I judged Sosus guilty of the following crimes: Impeding social interaction among us and trying to bring about cancellation of debts [χρεωκοπιας] as well as hindering our freedom and purposes. Sosus was both the leader of these events and a writer of laws intended to destroy our form of government. I have accordingly handed him over for execution.[15] Similarly, Formiscus, one of the artisans, who cooperated in the burning of the archives [αρχεια] and the public documents [το δημοσια γραμματα], since he also confessed,

13. Rostovtzeff, *Hellenistic World*, 1.208–9; 2.611–12.

14. See Rostovtzeff, *Hellenistic World*, 2.757, who dated the inscription to 116 BCE and Dittenberger, *Sylloge Inscriptionum Graecarum*, 271, who dated it to 139 BCE The Greek text is in Dittenberger.

15. The previous three sentences are a paraphrase. The more literal translation is as follows: "For not only for things that are at home to a lack of social interaction with one another and to bringing about a cancellation of debts; but also for things which are foreign to the freedom common to the Greeks and to our purpose, I, the accusers having presented true arguments, judged Sosus, the leader of the events and the writer of laws to destroy the present way of government, to be guilty and have delivered him over for execution."

as well as Timothy, who wrote the laws along with Sosus, since he appeared less guilty, I ordered to be taken to Rome.[16]

The masses, led by a reformer who has made new laws and by two of his accomplices, rose up in a rage and started a riot. The riot evidently degenerated into an angry destruction of property, and in the course of the events, the record offices [αρχεια] with the documents kept in them were burned up. Fabius Maximus, the proconsul, affirms that they were surely intending to destroy the records and contracts and thereby achieve a self proclaimed cancellation of debts.

Josephus also narrates a story of an archive that burned in 70 CE in Antioch of Syria. This fire burned the market, the record offices, the archives [αρχεια], and the basilicas. A defector from Judaism named Antiochus accused the local Jews of setting the fire, but after an investigation, it was discovered that the fire had been started by those with more economic motives. Some people suffering from indebtedness had wanted to alleviate their burden by burning the public records (*War* 7.60–61).

Thus one can discern a pattern. There were times and places where indebtedness became so pervasive and burdensome that leaders might offer cancellation of debts and other benefits in an effort to secure their own power. At other times crowds of debtors might in the heat of anger or after calculation burn down the hated record office with those documents demanding payment on their loans

By my judgment such events indicate widespread indebtedness. If we can find any similar events in first-century Palestine, we can safely conclude that indebtedness was a pervasive problem. As is well known, Josephus does narrate one clear case of such an event in Palestine. In 66 CE during the Feast of Wood-Carrying, the sicarii ("dagger carriers") and others broke forth into the upper city and set on fire the houses of Ananias the high priest and of Agippa I and Bernice. Then the mob turned to the public buildings:

> After these things, they began to carry the fire to the archives [αρχεια], being zealous to destroy the contracts of those who had loaned money and to cancel [αποκοψαι] the collection of debts. (*War* 2.427)

Josephus speculates at this point that the Sicarii hoped to win to their side a multitude [πληθος] of debtors.

16. Dittenberger, *Sylloge*, 3:684.

Thus both the act of burning the archives (similar to those at Dyme and Antioch) and Josephus's reference to a multitude of debtors compel us to conclude that Judea in the years leading up to the war of 66–73 experienced ubiquitous peasant resentment. Since such outbreaks indicate only the boiling point in a gradually heating cauldron of resentment over spreading indebtedness, it is probable that the problem had existed for some time. The sicarii ("dagger carriers") knew well about this resentment and directed the rage of the mob toward the archives and their hated documents of indebtedness. I conclude that Judea, like many of the Greek cities, saw more and more peasants burdened by debt at least in the years or decades before the war.

However, as an interpreter of the New Testament, I want to know if this rising indebtedness in Judea can be also assumed as background for the ministry of Jesus in Galilee. Here I hesitate to answer in the affirmative since I can give no evidence for it. Although Josephus also narrated an attempt by revolutionary forces in 67 CE to burn Sepphoris (*Life* 376), where we presume the archives would have been stored at that time (*Life* 38), he says nothing about any specific attempt to destroy debt documents. Indeed, the wording sounds more as if he regarded it merely as an attempt to loot the houses of the wealthy. Even if we were to grant this as a case of debt-document burning in Galilee, what should we conclude about how long indebtedness had been a problem? Was indebtedness also a problem forty years prior to this event, when Jesus was teaching and preaching? There is simply no way to answer that question based on the evidence. Therefore, I cannot conclude that pervasive indebtedness existed in Galilee in the earlier part of the first century CE and that it served as historical and economic backdrop to the ministry of Jesus. Thus attempts to interpret Jesus's words based on a presumed, pervasive peasant indebtedness may be mistaken.

4

The Ancient Galilean Economy

A Model

WHY ARE THERE CHAPTERS about the ancient economy in a book about the Christian origins? It is because the economy affects every other aspect of life (family, religion, community, work, health, and politics). Further, there are numerous direct references and allusions to economic issues in the New Testament. Scholars are now realizing that we cannot understand the New Testament without some attention to the subject.

Yet the subject would be too broad for a general survey through the entire New Testament. One could with profit write about the economic teachings in the epistles or the Apocalypse (book of Revelation). But for the purposes of this chapter, we will focus on the ministry of Jesus in Lower Galilee. Such a focus will give our treatment more unity and at the same time will handle what has been a growing debate: Was the ancient economic system like that of modern Western capitalist societies? Were the economic conditions driving the peasants toward starvation? Or was Lower Galilee so prosperous that the economic boom floated all boats, so to speak? Did Jesus criticize the ancient economic system? We can not answer these questions fully, but perhaps we can give some of the information upon which conclusions should be based. We will return to these three questions at the end of the chapter.

We will divide the inquiry into two parts. First, we will describe the ancient economy generally. That is, we will describe the economy for the Mediterranean world and Palestine (including Idumea, Judea, Samaria, and Galilee) as a whole. Second, we will turn specifically to Lower Galilee, and there we will present and explain our economic model.

The Ancient Economy in General

The study of economics has to do with "the production of goods and services, the distribution of these among members of society, and the consumption of goods and services."[1] The economy includes, then, not only the farm crops and handcrafted goods (pottery, for example) but also human labor and who gets to make the most use of these items. Was one group privileged and another deprived? If so, which one was the favored one?

There are three descriptors in the main that one should discuss in reference to the ancient economy. It was agrarian, it was aristocratic (ruled by a dominant political group), and it was a peasant society. We will take each of these in order.

Agrarian

The first thing we should say about the ancient economy of the Mediterranean and Middle Eastern regions is that it was agrarian. This observation is so common as to be beyond dispute.[2] An agrarian economy was based on land ownership and farm production. This fact implies two corollaries. First, agrarian economies were one step up from horticultural economies. The latter were capable of supporting small communities of gardeners who used primitive tools such as the hoe. Agrarian economies saw much more land cultivated (by the plow) and could support large cities. Second, the way to acquire wealth in an agrarian economy was to acquire more land. There was not much else a person could do with wealth but buy land. One could invest in trading and shipping, but it was risky. The culturally acceptable and economically less risky investment was land. People wanted land and the more the better. A fair-sized estate of 200 acres could make the owner very wealthy.

1. Beals and Hoijer, *Anthropology*, 450.

2. Rostovtzeff, *Large Estate*, 270; Lenski, *Power and Privilege*; Finley, *Ancient Economy*; Bedford, "Economy of the Near East"; Malina and Rohrbaugh, *Social Science Commentary*, 3–6; Oakman, *Jesus and the Peasants*; Davies, "Hellenistic Economies," 77.

An agrarian economy was marked by certain common features. Lenski[3] lists twelve main characteristics, but we might coalesce these into three: First, agrarian societies were controlled by monarchs who gained and held power by their military. They imposed their will on their subjects (and enriched themselves) usually by brutal force. Thus, the economy almost always produced a certain political reality as well. Second, due to technological advances, diversity of labor, and improved trade, there was a collective surplus of food beyond what was needed merely to subsist. Most of the surplus, however, was siphoned off by the rulers. Third, since there was a surplus, urban communities could exist and the population in general could increase. In most agrarian societies about one-tenth of the population lived in urban centers, the rest in small villages that worked the land.[4]

Aristocratic

Ancient agrarian societies tended to be structured around two groups: the takers and the givers. These societies, then, were mostly empires ruled by an aristocratic class. J. H. Kautsky defined the aristocracy as those persons who, while not laboring on the farms themselves, benefit from the farm produce by controlling the peasants' surplus.[5] The aristocrats did not engage in physical work and usually did not even live on the farms. Rather, as absentee landlords, they lived in the cities and demanded rents and taxes from the peasants. Jesus reflected this system in his parable in Mark 12:1–8. In this parable an absentee landlord has planted a vineyard and left tenant farmers to take care of the crop and harvest the grapes. At harvest time he sends his servants to collect his share (usually one-third to one-half of the crop). The tenants are surly and angry toward the landlord and beat the servants. They evidently thought their lives were too miserable to pay the rent.

The number of these aristocrats was always small in agrarian societies. Most historians estimate that only about 1 percent of the population was in this class.[6] The surplus was simply not large enough to support a

3. *Power and Privilege*, 192–210.

4. Lenski, *Power and Privilege*, 200; Mann, *Sources of Social Power*, 264; Saller, "Framing the Debate," 236; Fiensy, "Jesus' Socioeconomic Background," 235; Malina and Rohrbaugh, *Social Science Commentary*, 7.

5. *Aristocratic Empires*, 79–80.

6. MacMullen, *Roman Social Relations*, 89.

greater number of wealthy persons. That percentage would mean that Lower Galilee, with a total population of around 175,000, had between 1,500 and 2,000 aristocrats. Most, if not all, of these persons lived in one of the two main cities: Sepphoris or Tiberias. Some of their houses in Sepphoris have been excavated.[7]

Some of the aristocrats in the Roman Empire controlled huge tracts of farmland. We read of farms comprising, for example, 75,000 acres in Egypt and one whopping estate of 270,000 acres in Spain.[8] Such farms required a large labor force and must have produced huge harvests for the owners and controllers of the land. Of course most of the elites had somewhat smaller farms of a few hundred acres.

There certainly were large estates in Palestine as well.[9] But were there such large farms specifically in Lower Galilee (the area from Nazareth on the south to the northern tip of the Sea of Galilee) where Jesus came from? So far the archaeological evidence says no.[10] Yet, on the Great Plain, just south of Nazareth, there is both literary and archaeological evidence that large estates had been in existence already for three hundred years by the time Jesus was born. Jesus had only to look over the Great Plain from the edge of the Nazareth ridge to view some of these vast farms.

Perhaps Jesus's observation of these estates furnished material for many of his parables. As mentioned above, Mark 12:1–8, the parable of the Tenants, refers to a vineyard with tenant farmers, an absentee landlord, and several slaves who were sent to collect the rent. In order to support several tenant farmers, the vineyard must have been quite large.[11] Luke 16:1–12 speaks of debts of one hundred measures of oil and one hundred measures of wheat, which would have required at least a medium-sized estate to produce.[12] The same conclusion can be made with respect to the parable of the Talents (Matt 25:14–30=Luke 19:11–27), the parable of the Debtors (Luke 7:41–43=Matt 18:23–34), and the parable of the Unforgiving Servant (Matt 18:21–35). These parables speak of large sums of money that imply great wealth. In the ancient economy one could possibly become wealthy as a merchant, but the overwhelming majority of

7. Fiensy, *Jesus the Galilean*, 39–40.

8. Finley, *Ancient Economy*, 99; MacMullen, *Roman Social Relations*, 38; Hitchener, "Advantages of Wealth," 213.

9. Fiensy, *Social History*, 21–73.

10. Fiensy, *Jesus the Galilean*, 43.

11. Hengel, "Gleichnis," 1–39.

12. Herz, "Grossgrundbesitz," 98–113.

wealthy people acquired their wealth through land. Thus great wealth implies large estates.

Still others of Jesus's parables depict scenes on a large estate. The parable of the Rich Fool (Luke 12:16–21), for instance, describes an estate owner hoarding grain in a manner reminiscent of accounts in Josephus (*Life* 71–72, 119) about the granaries "of Caesar" in Upper Galilee and of the granary of Queen Bernice on the Great Plain. Luke 17:7 refers to a man's servant plowing his field for him. Matthew 20:1–15 narrates about a landowner who has so much land he must hire day laborers to work it. Luke 12:42–43 alludes to a wealthy man who has a bailiff to run his estate. Matt 13:24–30 describes a farm that requires several slaves to work it. Finally, Luke 15:11–32 pictures an estate with day laborers and slaves. Clearly Jesus was familiar with what happened on these huge farms, but archaeologists have not found evidence for their existence in Lower Galilee itself.

Peasant

Another way of describing agrarian societies, instead of in terms of empire and the elite class, is from the perspective of the largest number (90 percent) of their inhabitants: the peasants. Peasants were "rural cultivators whose surpluses are transferred to a dominant group of rulers that uses the surpluses both to underwrite its own standard of living and to distribute the remainder to groups in society that do not farm."[13]

The peasants and the ruling elites viewed the land and its labor in a very different way. The ruling class regarded their land and the peasants as income for themselves;[14] the peasant saw his land and work as the means of feeding his family and not as a business for profit.[15] Peasants worked for subsistence. They were not trying to become wealthy or even comfortable. They wanted to feed themselves.

Peasants labored on their land as family units (when they were freeholders or tenant farmers). Those bound to a piece of land also were bound to their families. But when they became landless (a horrible plight in an agrarian society unless one knew a craft), they also tended to lose family bonds. Day laborers and agricultural slaves, then, were at most

13. Wolf, *Peasants*, 3–4.

14. Ibid., 13.

15. De Ste. Croix, *Class Struggle*, 210–11; Redfield, *Peasant Society*, 27–28.

risk for loss of subsistence. Land means, to a peasant, family bonding in addition to guaranteed subsistence.

All peasant societies have been and still are marked by a radical bifurcation in which a small group of aristocrats stands over against the mass of agriculturalists. The aristocrats see their taxes and rents as their due; the peasants see them as one more burden placed on their labor and their land.[16] Consequently, peasant protests were common. In Egypt, for example, the papyri attest to peasants frequently going on strike and threatening to move to another location because of unfair treatment and, thus, being beaten and coerced to stay on the landowner's estate.[17] In Syria, the inscriptions witness to about the same: The tenant farmers are forced to pay more rent than the agreement had stipulated, they file a complaint with an official, and they are beaten and tortured for filing the complaint.[18]

The peasant surpluses, extracted in rents and taxes, kept the wealthy in their accustomed style of living and also fed the landless merchants, craftsmen, and day laborers, many of whom lived in the cities. From the point of view of peasants, life was a continual challenge to juggle the demands of the powerful on their farm produce with the subsistence needs of their families.[19] Improved technology and farming methods gave them a small surplus, but the surplus was gobbled up by the powerful and ruthless ruling class.

Lower Galilee: The Model

To assist us in visualizing the ancient economy with special reference to Lower Galilee in the first half of the first century CE, we will present a model. The model we will use as a heuristic visualization of the economic system is based on that of J. K. Davies.[20] Davies's model stresses the flow of goods and services as the key to understanding how the economy worked. The direction of the flows and the relative size of the flows (see the arrows) quickly inform us as to what the economy was doing. Especially telling is that we see the unidirection (one-way) flows or uneven

16. Fiensy, *Social History*, vii.

17. Rostovtzeff, *Large Estate*, 76, 80, 85–86.

18. De Ste. Croix, *Class Struggle*, 214–15.

19. Wolf, *Peasants*, 15.

20. "Linear and Nonlinear Flow Models," 150.

reciprocity. For example, note the one-way flow from the villages to the temple in Jerusalem; and the uneven flow (uneven reciprocity) between the villages and Antipas, the tetrarch or ruler of Galilee. In other words, the village peasants received nothing economic in return for their tithes to the temple in Judea. Likewise for their rents and taxes, paid to Antipas and other aristocrats, the peasants received certain government services, such as protection, which probably did not seem like an equal exchange to them.

Readers will first notice that the oval shape of the flowchart is intended to represent the economic unit of Lower Galilee. Lower Galilee formed an economic system because of politics and geography. Politically, Lower Galilee was under the control of the tetrarch, Antipas. In the ancient world, economics were not divorced from politics since the political leader was personally enriched by and held dominance over the economy. Therefore, sociologists often use the term *political economy* in describing ancient economies.[21]

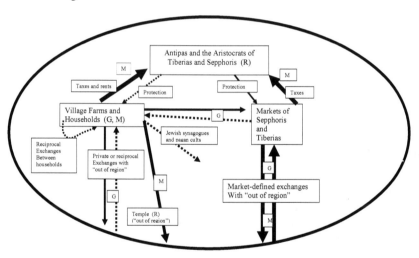

Flow Chart of Resource Movement, Lower Galilee First Century CE (After Davies,"Linear and Nonlinear," 150)

Geographically and topographically Lower Galilee is differentiated from Upper Galilee (the region from the northern tip of the Sea of Galilee to Lebanon). Upper Galilee is more mountainous and remote and, therefore, was more isolated in antiquity. Lower Galilee is more open to travel and thus in antiquity saw a more vigorous trading activity.

21. Hanson and Oakman, *Palestine in the Time of Jesus,* 99–129 [2nd ed., 93–121].

Second, note the multitude of economic relationships the average village peasant had. A peasant might trade with other family members or with fellow villagers ("Reciprocal Exchanges Between Households"). These would be equal exchanges of goods or services. One would trade, for example, a basket of figs for a basket of grain, or a jar of olive oil for a handcrafted tool.

A peasant might also trade outside the village ("Private or reciprocal Exchanges with 'Out of Region'") or at the "Markets of Sepphoris and Tiberias," whether trading surplus farm produce or handmade crafts. Two villages from Lower Galilee are now becoming, because of archaeological excavations, known as major exporters of common pottery. Likewise, two other villages produced and marketed a significant amount of stoneware vessels. These exchanges might have been made at the market centers in the two largest cities of Lower Galilee, Sepphoris and Tiberias, or they might have been done in market centers outside Lower Galilee. For example, the pottery manufactured in Kefar Hananya has been found in towns and villages in the Golan.[22]

The peasant villager was also obligated to send tithes, wave offerings, and temple taxes to the temple in Jerusalem. The villager received nothing economic (in the physical sense) in return for this flow of goods. But, as J. K. Davies points out, there are "non-physical flows" that play a role in the economy.[23] For example, a person who donated a sum of money to a village might receive back only the nonphysical flow of increased honor. Yet the honor made the act of charity entirely worth it. Therefore, it is probably incorrect (even ethnocentric!) to maintain that the Galileans resented having to send tithes to the Judean temple. It ignores the value of sacred space in ancient culture[24] and, thus, misses the value of the nonphysical flow of blessing that returned to the village peasant. Nevertheless, I have chosen not to represent nonphysical flows in the model.

Finally, the peasant was compelled to pay a portion of farm produce to the tetrarch or the absentee landlord. The amount of the tax paid to Antipas is debated, but if we assume that it was at least 12 percent, we will not be too far off. The amount of rent the tenant farmers paid to the landlords ranged from one-fourth to one-half of the crops.[25] In return (notice

22. Fiensy, *Jesus the Galilean*, 51.
23. "Linear and Nonlinear Flow Models," 142.
24. Fiensy, *Jesus the Galilean*, 189–91; Eliade, *Sacred and Profane*, 28.
25. Fiensy, *Social History*, 81, 99.

the difference in the width of the arrows) the village peasant received from their tetrarch and other aristocratic overlords what I have abbreviated "protection."[26] By this term I mean the various government services such as laws, peace, rituals, ceremonies, and even medical advice.[27] Was it a fair trade? I doubt that the village residents thought that it was, but they were helpless to change anything.[28]

Four features in the model need explanation. First, note the different width of the arrows. The greater the width, the higher the volume of the flow of goods and services. The different "bandwidths" (Davies's term) thus illustrate uneven exchanges, such as the exchange between the villagers and the aristocracy just described. The fattest widths represent the greatest flow (to markets, to aristocrats); the thinner solid arrows represent somewhat less flow (to, for example, the temple); the thinnest solid arrows represent private exchanges; and the broken lines represent the least amount of flow.

Second, the points labeled *M* represent what Davies calls "motors." Motors are impulses or motivations that keep the flow going. I can think of four: First, there was the drive to accumulate wealth that propelled the aristocracy. They wanted more land, more surplus, bigger houses, and more luxury goods. The parable of the Talents/Minas, found in Matt 25:14–30 = Luke 19:12–27, illustrates this motor very well. In the story (the details of which are somewhat different in Matthew and Luke) the servant who did not increase the investment of his master states that he knows the master (i.e. the aristocratic absentee landlord) is a severe person who demands a profit (Matt 25:24/Luke 10:21). The aristocrats were driven by the will to acquire. A second motor was the desire for the village peasant to provide subsistence for his or her family. The will to feed one's family can propel one to the most intensive labor and thus to greater production of goods. Thus, the prayer "give us our bread" (Matt 6:11/Luke 11:3) represents a real anxiety. One's daily bread (or "bread of tomorrow") was often in jeopardy. A third motor was the wish that those at the market centers would trade goods of one kind either for goods of another kind or for money (coins). Finally, there was the value especially among the Jewish people for their sacred space, the Temple. This value kept goods flowing to Jerusalem.

---

26. Davies' term, "Linear and Nonlinear Flow Models," 150.

27. Edwards, "Socio-Economic and Cultural Ethos," 62.

28. Cf. Lenski, *Power and Privilege*, 206.

The third item to be explained in the model is what Davies calls the "gates" (=G). Gates are "impediments to the rapid flow and exchange of resources, goods and services."[29] The gates in the economy of Lower Galilee in the early first century CE would be farming technology and methods. In other words, the primitive methods and technology would have limited the productivity of the land. The method is illustrated in the parable of the Sower (Matt 13:1–9 / Mark 4:1–9 / Luke 8:4–8). The sower or planter simply cast the seeds on the ground in a rather careless fashion, some of which fell on unproductive soil. Many of the seeds were eaten by the birds, and only a few of them germinated. Another gate to the ancient economy of Lower Galilee was the means of transport of goods (by pack animal). The Good Samaritan was evidently a small merchant or trader carrying goods on his donkey (Luke 10:34) for trade in Jericho. But a donkey can carry only so much, and the distance between markets made it impossible to trade every day. On the other hand, by this measure, taxes, such as taxes on transportation (see Levi in Mark 2:14) and taxes on land, are not gates in the economic sense since they force the flow of goods even though the peasants might have regretted and resented them. Sociologically speaking, taxes were a hardship and probably most of the time hated by the peasants. But economically speaking, they served a different function.

Readers will also note the reservoirs (=R). These are the places of resource accumulation and thesaurization (treasure building). Although Davies concedes that poor peasants can participate to a limited extent in reservoir building (by, for example, a small coin stash under the floor of their house), the significant reservoirs were with the temples and the governing elites. Thus in the model the reservoirs are with Antipas and the aristocrats in Galilee and the temple in Jerusalem. Jesus told a parable about an aristocrat who built up a sizeable reservoir (Luke 12:13–21). The story reminds one of the granary or barn that Queen Bernice owned in the village of Besara (=Beth Shearim), located in the northwest corner of the Great Plain (Josephus, *Life* 119). Josephus indicates in his narrative that the queen owned (in 67 CE) several villages in the area (and the land adjacent to them) and had collected from them her hoard of grain for her barn(s) in Besara. Since Bernice was a descendant of Herod the Great, this granary and the large estate it served probably were inherited from him. Is it possible that Jesus even had King Herod in mind when

29. Davies, "Linear and Nonlinear Flow Models," 151.

he represented him as a greedy hoarder whose life was at last required of him by God? That Jesus did not approve of hoarding (=reservoirs) is also seen in his admonition to his disciples against thesaurization (Matt 6:19–21/Luke 12:33–34).

Finally, note that Davies gives great emphasis to the market exchanges. He stresses the villages' exchanges within themselves, the villages' exchanges with the major market centers (for us, Sepphoris and Tiberias), and the exchanges between the major market centers in the region with those out of the region. Although some historians hesitate to affirm a market economy in Lower Galilee,[30] I accept this characteristic especially in light of recent archaeological discoveries. Archaeologists have revealed that at least four villages were producing and marketing their wares for the rest of Lower Galilee and even beyond: Kefar Hananya, Kefar Shikhin, Bethlehem of Galilee, and Kefar Reina.

The pottery of Kefar Hananya and Kefar Shikhin was already well known from the rabbinic sources (*m. Kelim* 2:2; *b. BM* 74a; *b. Shabb.* 120b). Now, archaeologists have established that the tiny village of Kefar Hananya (located on the border between Lower Galilee and Upper Galilee) exported its common pottery up to twenty-four kilometers away into Galilee and the Golan. Further, they maintain that 75 percent of the first-century common tableware excavated at Sepphoris so far (cooking bowls) were made in Kefar Hananya. In addition, 15 percent of the storage jars or kraters discovered thus far in Sepphoris originated in the nearby village of Shikhin. The Shikhin storage jars account for the majority of pottery of that type in Galilee.[31]

The process by which these conclusions were made is called neutron activation analysis. The scientific test allows the excavators to determine the chemical content of the clay used in making the pottery. The clay content of many of the wares found in the villages and cities of Galilee indicates that much of the pottery came from the area of Kefar Hananya and that many of the large jars came from the tiny village of Shikhin (1.5 kilometers from Sepphoris).

Further, archaeological discovery has brought to light two quarry workshops in Lower Galilee—one in Bethlehem of Galilee (just southwest of Sepphoris) and the other in Kefar Reina (just east of Sepphoris). These

---

30. Oakman, *Jesus and the Peasants*, 84–97; Horsley, *Archaeology*, 66–87.
31. Fiensy, *Jesus the Galilean*, 51.

villages were major producers of stone cups and other vessels. Stoneware has been discovered throughout Galilee in twelve villages and cities.[32]

The conclusions usually drawn from these discoveries are (1) the cities with their rich people must not have exploited the peasants who lived in the villages but rather must have given them opportunities for marketing their goods and thus increased their economic situation; (2) the villages not only engaged in farming but had industries as well. Thus, the socioeconomic effects of the increase in marketization are often *assumed* to have been positive. Some archaeologists believe that increased marketization must have brought unprecedented prosperity to Lower Galilee.

But economists speak a word of caution. Karl Polanyi's analysis of the transformation from a subsistence economy to a market economy is a classic.[33] Much of what he wrote has to do with the "Great Transformation" that took place in Europe during the industrial revolution, but his insights are also informative for our period.

Polanyi notes that when societies depart form a subsistence economy for a market economy, there are both economic and social consequences. Economically, subsistence is abandoned in favor of gain: "for the motive of subsistence that of gain must be substituted."[34] At first this change might seem beneficial. But what if the market begins to pay less than one's goods had been worth when one traded in reciprocal exchanges? Now one is at the mercy of the going market price both for goods and for labor: "A market economy . . . is an economy directed by market prices and nothing but market prices."[35]

The irony could become that subsistence is actually threatened. Polanyi stated that in traditional ("primitive") societies starvation was not a threat unless the whole community starved at the same time since one could always count on help from the relatives and neighbors (which must be reciprocated later): "There is no starvation in societies living on the subsistence margin."[36] But a market economy pays individuals the going rate for both goods and labor and, therefore, in down cycles human labor might be devalued if indeed one can even find a day's work.[37] This

32. Ibid., 51–52.

33. Polanyi, *Great Transformation*.

34. Ibid., 41.

35. Ibid., 43.

36. Ibid., 163.

37. Cf. Lenski, *Power and Privilege*, 206.

condition is reflected in one of Jesus's parables (Matt 20:3), in which day laborers must sell their labor in the market each day. But many of them find no takers for their labor.

Further, Polanyi noted the social effects of marketization. The increase in the value of markets tends to negate traditional institutions (such as family, neighborhoods, and religious convictions).[38] Everything now has a market price, and these old associations are not valued very highly.

How advanced was the market economy in Lower Galilee in the time of Jesus and Antipas? I think it had started down the road described by Polanyi but had not advanced very far. The stresses were beginning in my judgment but were not yet causing a "Great Transformation"—to use Polanyi's expression—but only a small transformation (indeed, there was no great transformation anywhere in antiquity). There is no evidence for such a seismic socioeconomic transformation in the first half of the century. It may be, however, that later the change did develop sufficiently to help aggravate the desire for war in 66 CE.[39] Although the ancient economy saw no transformation like the industrial revolution, it still witnessed from time to time economic stresses that were a milder form.

To Jesus are attributed words of rebuke aimed at religious leaders (sometimes they are scribes, and other times Pharisees) for wanting a "greeting in the market place" (Matt 23:7; Mark 12:38; Luke 11:43, 20:46). Was at least part of Jesus's irritation at religious leaders who craved to be greeted in public based on the fact that it was in the markets of Sepphoris and Tiberias that the peasants were being taken advantage of? Instead of helping the plight of the peasants, perhaps the leaders basked in their social stature and overlooked injustice right under their noses.

Conclusion

Let us now return to our questions. Was the ancient economic system like that of modern Western capitalist societies? No, the ancient system was agrarian and not industrial. It was based on the essential bifurcation of its society into aristocrats and peasants. It is, therefore, confusing

38. Polanyi, *Great Transformation*, 163.
39. See Fiensy, "Jesus and Debts."

to interpret economic references in the New Testament from a modern perspective.[40]

Were the economic conditions driving the peasants of Lower Galilee toward poverty, even starvation? No, there is no evidence that the economy in Lower Galilee was causing great social upheaval. The system, however, was against the peasant agriculturalist. It was hard just to survive, let alone to thrive or get ahead in that kind of economic world. Yet, during the time of Jesus and Antipas, we see no great stress on the economic life of the average villager. That may have come later, just before the war of 66–73 CE.

Was rising tide of Lower Galilean prosperity so great that it floated all boats, so to speak? That was not exactly so. There was a vital economy. The goods were flowing as the model shows. The agricultural society was also developing vibrant markets for locally handcrafted goods such as pottery and stoneware. Yet marketization, as it develops over time, can turn on the individual worker and place stress on both subsistence and traditional institutions. It may well have been better for the average farmer in Lower Galilee than in the rest of Palestine during the time of Jesus and Antipas. But Galilee's day was coming.

Did Jesus criticize the ancient economic system? He criticized not the system so much as the dominant partners of the system: the aristocrats. Consider the following:

> How difficult it is for one who has wealth to enter the kingdom of God (Mark 10:23 and par.; *Gos. Naz.*; Shepherd Herm *Sim.* 9:20:1–4)

> It is easier for a camel to go through the eye of the needle than for a rich person to enter the kingdom of God (Mark 10:25 and par.)

When Jesus talked about rich persons in such a critical way, he was referring to those 1,500 to 2,000 aristocrats living in Sepphoris and Tiberias. He said nothing we know of about the system as such. But he could be stingingly critical of the wealthy men and women who controlled it.

---

40. Cf. Morris and Manning, "Introduction," 21.

5

The Nature of the Galilean Economy in the Late Second Temple Period

The Sociological–Archaeological Debate

IN RECENT YEARS A rather heated disagreement has arisen among two groups benefiting from the heritage of the social sciences with respect to the socioeconomic conditions of Galilee in the first century CE: These are, namely, archaeologists in one group and biblical scholars utilizing social-science models in the second. Although the discipline of anthropology claims the subdisciplines of both archaeology and cultural anthropology under its umbrella, some archaeologists seem critical of those seeking guidance from social-science—specifically cultural-anthropology—models. They ask, should we use the social-science models to guide us and help us interpret the historical and archaeological data? and often answer no.

The hesitation is understandable. Certainly social-science models can be used in an unhelpful way. One gets the impression from some works that the ancient data are almost irrelevant. If the social-science critic says peasant society had certain features, then those features must have been there in first-century Galilee as well. The New Testament scholar using social-scientific models can be so model-driven that the model becomes the evidence, or, in other words, the scholar works deductively instead of inductively from evidence.

But some archaeologists may have also overreacted to the use of social-science models. Thus we have charges that certain scholars' works are nothing but "myth and legend" and the claim that Galilee was an egalitarian society, a rather remarkable claim for any first-century region.[1] But as the crowd of social-scientific New Testament scholars responds, "the material remains do not interpret themselves."[2] The stones do not actually speak; interpreters must speak for them. Although one must be cautious in applying sociological theories to the study of ancient society, some helpful insights can nevertheless result from such attempts. If the sociological model has been informed by ancient sources and is judiciously eclectic in its selection of modern sociological theory, we can be reasonably assured that we are not guilty of merely molding the past to fit the present.

On the other hand, to ignore macrosociology or cultural anthropology is to invite ethnocentrism and anachronism.[3] The social sciences urge the historian to listen to the side largely muted by the texts: the side of the poor and oppressed.[4]

A major point of contention is the extent of the exploitation of the lower classes by the elites of Galilee. Here we must divide the discussion into two parts. Our first question is, how poor or exploited were the rural people (i.e., the freeholding farmers) as a whole? The second question will be, to what extent was there a landless rural proletariat? This chapter will survey how each method of interpretation—one relying on

1. Overman, "Jesus of Galilee," 67–73; and Groh, "Clash," 29–37.

2. See the analyses of Horsley, "Historical Jesus," 91–135; Oakman, "Archaeology of First-Century Galilee," 220–51; and Freyne, "Archaeology and the Historical Jesus," 129. See also the critique of Horsley in Meyers, "Archaeological Response," 17–26.

3. The failings of ethnocentrism and anachronism are the principal fears of the members of the Context Group. See Neyrey, "Preface," xxiii; and Malina, "Rhetorical Criticism," 17.

4. See the use of Lenski, *Power and Privilege,* 189–296 and Lenski and Lenski, *Human Societies,* 166–213 in Crossan, *Historical Jesus,* 44–45, who also has used Lenski's work as a check against viewing Jesus's world through uninformed, ethnocentric spectacles. Crossan writes: "One can obviously debate Lenski's master-model in whole or in part, but I accept it as a basic discipline to eliminate the danger of imposing presuppositions from advanced industrial experience on the world of an ancient agrarian empire." For other New Testament scholars who have used Lenski's model see Fiensy, *Social History,* 155–76; Fiensy, "Jesus' Socioeconomic Background"; Saldarini, *Pharisees, Scribes, and Sadducees*; Duling and Perrin, *New Testament,* 49–56; Rohrbaugh, "Social Location of the Markan Audience"; Arlandson, *Women, Class, and Society,* 14–119; Neyrey, "Luke's Social Location of Paul."

archaeology, another utilizing sociology—has concluded regarding these questions, and how each attempts to reach a conclusion.

Question 1: How Close to the Subsistence Minimum and How Exploited Were the Freeholding Farmers of Galilee in the First Century CE?

Here the sociologist New Testament scholars differ sharply from the archaeologists of Galilee. The former tend to expect trouble. They see the problem in the agrarian economic system itself. The latter answer, "Your conceptions do not harmonize with the material remains."

We will see that there are three main views with respect to this question: 1) The social-science interpreters claim that Galilee was in or approaching *economic crisis*. 2) The archaeologists maintain that Galilee experienced during the time of Jesus and Antipas *economic prosperity*. 3) Others (myself included) conclude that there was *economic stasis* and hold that while there is no convincing evidence that Galilee experienced unprecedented prosperity during this time, neither is there compelling evidence for economic crisis.

Arguments for Economic Crisis

Those using social-science perspectives and finding economic duress in Galilee in the time of Jesus and Antipas refer to the following lines of evidence: Their social-science model usually presents conditions of class conflict and economic stress for the non-elites. Their model also stresses the burden of taxes; the model assumes the ubiquity of debt; and their model will explain that the invention of money (monetization) made the economic situation worse for the village farmer.

THE SOCIOLOGICAL MODEL

Douglas Oakman is a good example of a New Testament scholar using the social-science models. Oakman argues that historians are too often guilty of "inductive positivism," which masks ideological bias. "Clear [sociological] models," he maintains, "help to overcome bias and social obfuscation . . . Critically selected models allow data to speak in relationship to a larger picture, transforming it into compelling evidence."[5] Oakman proceeds to develop his model (based on that of Talcott Parsons), which states that the elites made up 10 percent of the population, controlled every aspect of society by their political power, and extracted taxes from the non-elites. He suggests that the peasants were usually on the verge of starvation, were angry over taxation and indebtedness, were losing their land at an alarming rate, and were resentful of both the Galilean and the Judean elites.

On the one hand, we need the models. As K. Hopkins observes,

> The model is a sort of master picture, as on the front of a jigsaw puzzle box; the fragments of surviving ancient sources provide only a few of the jigsaw pieces.[6]

Models help us sketch out the social, economic, or cultural picture, much like an artist's reconstruction of an archaeological ruin. Without some kind of model, we are left only to talk about the individual pieces. Models may also help us examine our own bias both in selecting the sources to examine and in interpreting them. The best way to think about a social-science model is to regard it as a working hypothesis, a sort of template on which one places data. As the social-science interpreters repeatedly remind us, we need to reflect on the social-science models because they can guard against twin errors of "ethnocentrism and anachronism."[7]

But on the other hand, any good historian must always be ready to affirm, edit, or reject the hypothesis based on the data. With the model must come diligence to validate its assumptions or to discard them when the evidence demands it. The problem with the application of many of these models for the social-science critics is that the model has become the evidence. Thus, one cannot simply state that because a condition exists in a model (e.g., debt or burdensome taxes), therefore the same condition must have been there in Galilee in the time of Jesus and Antipas.

---

5. Oakman, *Jesus and the Peasants*, 246.

6. Hopkins, "Rome, Taxes, Rents and Trade," 191.

7. See Neyrey, "Preface," xxiii; Malina, "Rhetorical Criticism," 17; Neyrey and Stewart, "Healing," 201; Malina and Neyrey, "Ancient Mediterranean Persons," 258.

TAXES

R. Horsley, one of the New Testament scholars using the social sciences, argues that Galilee was under economic stress. To reach this conclusion, he adds up the tally, as most sociologists do. Antipas needed extra funds to build his two cities (first Sepphoris in 4 CE, then Tiberias in c. 20 CE). He needed to support his bureaucrats/retainers and of course keep himself and his family in their accustomed lifestyles. The only way to increase income would be to raise taxes: "Peasants were under intense economic pressure of indebtedness. Families and even village communities were disintegrating under the pressure."[8] Ekkehard W. Stegemann and Wolfgang Stegemann accept the estimate that the resident of ancient Palestine under Herod the Great paid between 12 percent and 50 percent of their crops in taxes. They describe the tax obligation as "an unbearable burden."[9]

A number of these scholars seem to assume that under Antipas the Galileans continued to pay the tax at the same rate as under his father, and that this included a tax to Rome as well as to the Jewish ruler. More recently, Fabian Udoh has challenged the conclusion that the Galileans paid a tax to Rome in the time of Jesus and Antipas.[10] Further, when historians look at the building projects of a ruler and assume that they were paid for entirely from taxes, they may be making a methodological error. Rulers also used proceeds from their large estates. While it appears that Horsley may be partly correct, the tax burden may not have paid for all the building projects of Antipas and therefore may not have been as great as he (and Stegemann and Stegemann) has opined.

DEBT

Some have assumed that the economic problem of indebtedness formed the backdrop of Jesus's ministry.[11] We have no problem, of course, in documenting that indebtedness existed, but the question is, how widespread was it among the village farmers? Were 25 percent of them living

8. Horsley, "Jesus and Galilee," 65.

9. Stegemann and Stegemann, *Jesus Movement,* 119.

10. Udoh, *To Caesar,* 118–90.

11. See, e.g., Hanson and Oakman, *Palestine in the Time of Jesus,* 119–20 [2nd ed., 111–13]; Malina and Rohrbaugh, *Social Science Commentary,* 62–63.

in dangerous debt? Were half or even more of the freeholding farmers about to lose their land because of debt so that Jesus makes reference to the problem and preaches in favor of general debt remission?

Some scholars have cited New Testament passages to demonstrate that indebtedness was widespread in Galilee in Jesus's time.[12] Others have sought to imply widespread indebtedness from the institution of the *prosbul* (the provision created by Hillel to allow for loans even toward the end of the Sabbatical Year cycle).[13] But as I have argued elsewhere,[14] citing New Testament texts to prove widespread indebtedness is unsound methodology. Many of the debts alluded to in the parables are clearly exaggerations (e.g., owing ten thousand talents); further, one cannot determine that the scattered allusions record for us a widespread problem. The use of the *prosbul* (*m. Sheb.* 10:3) to prove widespread indebtedness is also unconvincing. Its existence only proves that people could go into debt; not that they did go into debt. The hard fact is that in spite of an almost universal appeal to debt as a major economic stress in the Galilee of Jesus and Antipas, we have little evidence that it was a serious social problem.

MONETIZATION

Still others offer that the invention of coins—money—brought hardship on the village farmer:

> Peasant families are forced to get money by selling or borrowing. They now have to hold a token in place of real goods but cannot eat a token. Village exchanges are now "converted" into the form of balanced reciprocity accountable in money.[15]

The assumption in such concerns is that under Herod the Great and his son Antipas the use of coins as means of payment, instead of trading goods in kind, increased dramatically. One way of checking this

12. Oakman, "Jesus and Agrarian Palestine"; Pastor, *Land and Economy,* 147–49; de Ste. Croix, *Class Struggle,* 164; Stegemann and Stegemann, *Jesus Movement,* 134, 426. The texts they cite are Matt 5:25–26, 40, 42; 6:11–12; 18:23–34; Luke 4:18; 7:41–42; 16:1–9.

13. Goodman, "First Jewish Revolt."

14. Fiensy, "Jesus and Debts," and above, pp. 59–66.

15. Hanson and Oakman, *Palestine in the Time of Jesus,* 125 [2nd ed., 116–17]. See also Arnal, *Jesus and the Village Scribes,* 138.

assumption is by simply counting coins. Morten Jensen, following Danny Syon, has reported recently that no increase in coinage is detectable in the Herodian period. Coins were not minted during this time at a faster rate than before.[16] Thus, monetization seems to have played no significant role in the economic plight of the villagers in the time of Jesus and Antipas.

The survey of evidence above has indicated that there is no sound reason for concluding that Galilee in the first century CE—at least during the rule of Antipas (4 BCE—39 CE)—was experiencing economic stress and crisis.

Arguments for Economic Prosperity

The archaeologists advance three lines of evidence to maintain that the villagers were not exploited: The evidence of industry in some of the Galilean villages (especially the pottery distribution from Kefar Hananya and Shikhin), the houses of Galilean villages (especially Yodefat and Khirbet Qana), and the luxury items found in some of the villages.

Industry

The pottery of Kefar Hananya and Shikhin was already well known from the rabbinic sources (*m. Kel.* 2:2; *b. BM* 74a; *b. Shab.* 120b). Now, D. Adan-Bayewitz and I. Perlman have established that the tiny village of Kefar Hananya (located on the border between Lower Galilee and Upper Galilee) exported its common pottery up to twenty-four kilometers away into Galilee and the Golan. It is also clear that 75 percent of the first-century common tableware excavated at Sepphoris so far (cooking bowls) were made in Kefar Hananya. Further, 15 percent of the storage jars or kraters discovered thus far in Sepphoris originated in the nearby village of Shikhin. The Shikhin storage jars account for the majority of pottery of that type in Galilee.[17] These conclusions were made based on neutron-activation analysis.

The conclusions often drawn from this analysis are (1) the cities with their rich people must not have exploited the rural folk who lived in the villages but rather must have given them opportunities for marketing

16. Jensen, "Rural Galilee," 43–67 (esp. 63).

17. Strange et al., "Excavations at Sepphoris: Part I."

their goods and thus increased their economic situation; (2) the villages not only engaged in farming but had industries as well, and these industries elevated the economic life of the village residents. [18]

These are very interesting results from hard archaeological work. We must urge some caution, however, when we *interpret* the data. The material remains certainly suggest that there could have been a thriving industry in Galilee, which the cities supported. Yet, Oakman responds that "it is much more likely (based on his sociological model) that powerful interests controlled the two pottery villages . . . and that the distribution of these products reflects rather the outcome of monopoly than of a free market."[19] In other words, when the data are filtered through his model, a different picture emerges.

Another representative of the social-scientist New Testament scholars, R. Horsley, believes that since a redistributive economic system was in play in Lower Galilee (instead of a market economy), the archaeological evidence with respect to Kefar Hananya and Shikhin cannot indicate village prosperity and egalitarianism. The widespread distribution of the pottery is more a result of taxation.[20] Again, the assumed economic system drives the interpretation.

Finally, G. Lenski (the macrosociologist), who often stresses the exploitation of the "peasantry" by the elites of the cities, observed that there was a steady flow of goods from the peasant villages into the urban centers in most agrarian societies. In return, the villagers received certain political, cultural, religious, and financial services along with commodities, such as salt, that they could not produce themselves. Lenski calls the relationship between the villages and cities "symbiotic" but with "overtones of parasitism." It is parasitic, explains Lenski, because the peasants are not in a position to bargain with the elites concerning the amount of the surplus they must deliver and concerning the compensation for their goods. But the relationship is not purely parasitic since peasants volunteer to come to the urban centers to market their goods.[21] The point

18. See Adan-Bayewitz, *Common Pottery,* 23–41, 216–36; Adan-Bayewitz,"Kefar Hananya, 1986," 178–79; Adan-Bayewitz and Perlman, "Local Trade," 153–72; Strange, "First-Century Galilee," 41; Edwards, "Urban/Rural Relations," 169–82; Edwards, "Socio-Economic and Cultural Ethos," 53–91; Meyers, "Jesus and His Galilean Context," 57–66.

19. Oakman, "Archaeology of First-Century Galilee," 232.

20. Horsley, *Archaeology,* 70–83.

21. Lenski, *Power and Privilege,* 206.

is that merely citing the material remains may not necessarily answer the question. The remains can agree with what the sociologists have already said about agrarian societies. But the sociologists have a different interpretation of the data.

Industries are also in evidence from two other villages: Yodefat (or Jotapata) and Khirbet Qana (sometimes alleged to have been the Cana of the New Testament). These villages were producing goods beyond their own domestic uses. In other words, they were engaged in trade. They each had small industry (dove raising, olive-oil production, and wool dying at Cana; pottery manufacture and oil production at Yodefat).[22]

Y. Magen's work on stoneware production has also developed this evidence. He brought to light two quarry workshops in Lower Galilee—one in Bethlehem of Galilee (just southwest of Sepphoris) and the other in Kefar Reina (just east of Sepphoris). These were major producers of stone cups and other vessels. Stoneware has been discovered throughout Galilee as well (in twelve villages and cities).[23] Again, sociologists may dispute whether the trade was locally owned and initiated or was part of a broader governmental, elite-controlled network.

HOUSES

The second line of archaeological evidence that would seem to challenge the sociological view is the excavation the houses of Yodefat and Khirbet Qana. Residents lived in modest but decent houses, some of which were more finely constructed than others. At Khirbet Qana there were three types of houses, representing evidently three tiers of economic prosperity in the village. One large house in Yodefat had rather elaborate frescoes in a style similar to those in the Herodian palace at Masada and in the houses of the wealthy in Jerusalem.[24] There was little evidence that houses had been abandoned because of economic stresses. Thus, the residents of these two villages, on the whole, lived more modestly than residents of

22. Richardson, *Building Jewish,* 57 71; Hixon et al., "3 D Visualizations," 195–204; Adan-Bayewitz and Aviam, "Jotapata, Josephus, and the Siege," 131–65; Edwards, "Khirbet Qana," 101–32.

23. Magen, *Stone Vessel Industry,* 160.

24. Aviam, "Yodefat," 18–19.

Sepphoris, but they were not destitute, and, as a matter of fact, some were obviously prospering.[25]

We might also compare these two villages with two others: Nazareth and Capernaum. So far, the excavations under the two churches in modern Nazareth have revealed that it was an agricultural village. There are granaries, pits, vaulted cells for storing wine and oil, and oil presses.[26] Only a slight trace of the houses has been left, leading one archaeologist to suggest that the houses must have been made of fieldstones and mud.[27] These villagers do not seem to have been as prosperous as those at Yodefat and Khirbet Qana, judging solely from the housing. Yet the presence of so many food installations argues that they also were not starving.

Capernaum was a medium-sized fishing and agricultural village. The private houses were built of undressed basalt fieldstones with large courtyards surrounded by small house-rooms, the largest of which is 7.5 x 6 meters.[28] There are no houses such as those at Khirbet Qana and Yodefat, and certainly none discovered thus far with elaborate and expensive frescoes. Yet the houses were more than adequate and do not betray economic duress.

LUXURY ITEMS

Sharon Matilla has argued that the presence of luxury good in houses in Capernaum suggests economic prosperity. The excavators have turned up Early Roman glassware, Rhodian jars (dating from the Hellenistic to the Early Roman periods), and red-slipped tableware (Eastern Terra Sigilata A) from the first century BCE.[29] These goods, some of which are elegant and many of which are imported (the Rhodian jars and red-slipped ware) are not what one expects to find associated with the houses of poor persons. Although the houses of Capernaum are not of noteworthy construction, the luxury goods are striking.

25. Richardson, *Building Jewish*, 57–71; Hixon et al., "3-D Visualizations," 195–204; Adan-Bayewitz and Aviam, "Jotapata, Josephus, and the Siege"; Edwards, "Khirbet Qana"; Matilla, "Jesus and the 'Middle Peasants'?" 291–313 (esp. 310).

26. Bagati, "Nazareth, Excavations."

27. Reed, *Archaeology*, 132.

28. Corbo, *House of Saint Peter*, 35–52; Strange and Shanks, "House Where Jesus Stayed"; Loffreda, "Capernaum."

29. Matilla, "Revisiting Jesus' Capernaum."

Another interesting small find that supports the view that the village residents were not extremely poor—although this find is not exactly a luxury item—is the Herodian lamp. These lamps were undecorated and formed on a wheel, and their nozzles were hand pared with a knife. By an examination of the chemical composition of the lamps and lamp fragments found in several sites in Judea and the Golan (Masada, Qumran, Gamla) and especially in sites in Galilee (Yodfat and Sepphoris), it has been determined that a high percentage of these lamps were manufactured from clay from the Jerusalem vicinity. The lamps are especially frequent in the ruins of Jewish centers. Ninety-four percent of the Early Roman lamps from Yodfat, 93 percent of those from Gamla, and 80 percent of those examined from Sepphoris were manufactured from Jerusalem-area clay. The knife-pared lamps began appearing in the first century BCE, at about the same time that the stoneware vessels began to appear. Although there is local clay in most of these areas from which to manufacture lamps, the locals preferred lamps made from Jerusalem clay.[30] Thus, the locals preferred to import their lamps, and perhaps to pay a higher price than for locally produced lamps, in order to fulfill (evidently) a religious purpose.[31]

Thus, a look at all of these sites presents us with ruins from villages sometimes with houses clearly of upper-level or wealthy villagers, sometimes with less prosperous houses, but also certainly not with the remains of starving or destitute persons. We conclude from these archaeological remains that the villagers were not on the verge of either starvation or bankruptcy. The results from the eight villages[32] suggest strongly that the rural residents of Galilee were not destitute. The freeholding farmers were not starving. As a matter of fact, some were doing rather well in Galilee.

30. See Berlin, "Jewish Life before the Revolt," 417–70 (esp. 434–36); Adan-Bayewitz et al., "Preferential Distribution of Lamps," 37–85 (esp. 47).

31. Magness, *Stone, Dung, Oil and Spit*, 65: "I believe that the motivating factor was a desire to avoid the figured images." Magness adds that the price of these wheel-made lamps would at least have been equal to the mold-made lamps. But in addition, of course, one had transportation costs and perhaps toll costs when crossing borders. Adan-Bayewitz et al. opine that the lamps "may have had some socio-religious or ritualistic significance." One use, they suggest, was in lighting the house for the Sabbath meal. (Adan-Bayewitz et al. "Preferencetial Distribution of Lamps," 75). Thus, the Jews from these villages and from Sepphoris preferred lighting this lamp made from clay from the holy city of Jerusalem.

32. Kefar Hananya, Shikhin, Khirbet Qana, Yodefat, Nazareth, Capernaum, Kefar Reina, and Bethlehem of Galilee.

That conclusion, of course, does not mean that the freeholding farmers were not exploited in some fashion. The mere increase in population in the cities (Sepphoris and Tiberias each with eight thousand to twelve thousand people)[33] required more food to be brought in from the countryside. In the ancient world there was only so much food to go around. Thus the increased urbanization put stress on the farmer. Only the relatively small sizes of the cities kept the urbanization from turning into a really serious danger for the Galilean farmers.

Question 2: Was There a Landless Rural Proletariat of Destitute Persons on the Brink of Disaster?

The conclusion that the rural freeholders in Lower Galilee were not destitute brings us to our second question. Were there significant numbers of rural persons who no longer lived on a farm, as freeholders, and who, therefore, existed in dire circumstances? What percentage of the population in Galilee lived in extreme poverty?

Let us consider the usual figure for extreme poverty given for the empire in general. This figure is based on statistics from other societies. Ramsay MacMullen notes that in Europe in the fourteenth and fifteenth centuries, one-third of the population lived in "habitual want." According to MacMullen, the person living in "habitual want" "devoted the vast bulk of each day's earnings to his immediate needs and accumulated no property or possessions to speak of."[34] Was Galilee in the time of Jesus and Antipas similar?

Some using-social science models have argued—or assumed—that Galilee was dominated by large estates: "Estates grew and tenancy increased as economies of scale for cash crops were created."[35] This statement implies that Galilean farmers were losing their land, either settling

---

33. These are the figures of Reed, *Archaeology*, 117. Meyers suggests 18,000 for Sepphoris and 24,000 for Tiberias ("Jesus and His Galilean Context," 59). Overman, "Who Were the First Urban Christians?" offered 30,000 to 40,000 for Tiberias and 30,000 for Sepphoris. Horsley, *Archaeology*, 45, maintained that both cities together had a population of 15,000. If we adhere to the general rule that 10 percent of the population in the ancient world lived in the cities (see below), then a population of 175,000 for Galilee, accepted above, needs around 10,000 or fewer in each of the two cities.

34. MacMullen, *Roman Social Relations*, 93.

35. Crossan and Reed, *Excavating Jesus*, 70.

in as oppressed tenant farmers or being evicted and becoming a shiftless proletariat. Nevertheless, Richard Horsley, another social-science interpreter, rejects the view that there were large numbers of rootless people forced off their land. Instead he insists that the pressure of taxation was affecting families and villages but had not yet built up to the economically dangerous level. Thus, not even Horsley argues for a large population of destitute persons.[36]

On the other hand, Dennis Groh, from the archaeologists' group, maintains that we have been too influenced by Marxist historians, who invented the ancient tension between cities and villages, between elites and rural peasants. We do not find evidence, he insists, in Galilee of great distance between the rich and the poor. Galilee, he concludes, was a "largely egalitarian society (at least in external appearance)."[37]

But even some of the archaeologists have pondered the price for building the cities of Galilee. Thus E. Meyers notes that the fertile lands in the valleys near Sepphoris, which had once been used for subsistence of the villagers, had to be transformed into places where products were grown on a larger scale. Cities became "centers of consumption."[38] Jonathan Reed admits that the shift from a traditional to a commercialized, agrarian society placed economic strain on the Galilean peasants.[39] Douglas Edwards allowed that "the Roman empire may have been born on the backs of its peasants," but insisted that the peasants received in turn: laws, protection, peace, rituals, ceremonies, and medical advice.[40]

The markers of stress on the peasantry could be of two kinds. We might find *archaeological* evidence in pathological examination of skeletal remains from Galilean tombs. Ian Morris[41] suggests in his study of ancient Athens that one could examine skeletal remains to determine nutrition, stature, mortality, and morbidity. This information might serve as evidence for an undernourished and impoverished proletariat. But since he finds too little of this sort of evidence, he turns to the remains of houses to calculate the standard of living. Likewise, in Galilee, so far, not

36. Horsley, "Jesus and Galilee," 65.
37. Groh, "Clash," 29–37, quotation on p. 32.
38. Meyers, "Jesus and His Galilean Context," 62.
39. Reed, *Archaeology*, 96.
40. Edwards, "Socio-Economic and Cultural Ethos," 62.
41. Morris, "Archaeology, Standards of Living," 91–126, esp. 107.

enough of the skeletal remains have turned up.[42] We might find further archaeological evidence in poorly constructed houses throughout Lower Galilean villages. That could mean that the village residents simply had no time or resources to build anything better. But the meager evidence we have thus far argues the other way. The evidence presented above concerning the villages of Khirbet Qana and Yodefat indicates no such conditions. Even the simple dwellings of Capernaum and Nazareth were not houses of destitute persons.

The *historical* evidence might also be of two kinds: it would have to show as probable both the rise of large estates and the rise of social upheaval in Lower Galilee. First, if we could show that there was increasing movement toward large estates, it would demonstrate at the same time that farmers were losing their land. Loss of land by a sizeable minority of rural folk would create horrible stress. But no evidence exists to date (either archaeological or literary) for the growth of large estates in Galilee outside the Great Plain. It appears that the large estates had been in existence on the Great Plain for centuries before the time of Jesus and Antipas. But the settlement of Galilee was too recent. Since it had only taken place in the last century before Jesus and Antipas, most farmers were still small freeholders.[43]

Many historians conclude that there is no evidence for large estates in Galilee in the early first century CE.[44] Presumably, they mean that we have found no incontrovertible archaeological evidence, or no smoking-gun material remains like those at Qawarat bene Hassan in Samaria or at Horvat Eleq on the Ramat Ha-Nadiv ridge near Caesarea Maritima. Qawarat bene Hassan was a village, occupied from the Hasmonean through

---

42. See Smith et al., "Skeletal Remains," 118, who report that the remains of some children in a fourth-century tomb suffered from an iron and protein deficiency that could be based on either socioeconomic conditions or disease. Of course the problems are this is in Upper Galilee and three centuries after Jesus and Antipas. More relevant are the remains of well over two thousand persons found at Yodefat. The bones of around twenty-five of these individuals were examined for morbidity and the findings were that these persons were "healthy." (Oral report given by Mordecai Aviam at the 2008 Society of Biblical Literature in Boston, MA.). See further on the skeletal remains at Yodefat, Aviam, "Yodefat/Jotapata," 121–33.

43. See Fiensy, *Jesus the Galilean*, 42–45.

44. There is one tantalizing reference in Josephus, *Life* 71–73, which concerns John of Gischala's attempt to seize the imperial grain stored in Upper Galilee. This grain could be the harvest from an imperial large estate. But it could also be merely the taxes on small freeholders. See the discussion in Rostovtzeff, *Roman Empire*, 664 n. 32; Hoehner, *Herod Antipas*, 70; Alt, *Kleine Schriften*, 2:395; and Fiensy, *Social History*, 55.

the Herodian periods, located approximately forty kilometers southwest of Shechem. The village had between 175 and 200 family holdings with farm plots marked off by stone walls. The total area covered by the farm plots was 2000 acres. On a hill overlooking the village was a complex of storage buildings, strong towers, cisterns and a residential area. The archaeologist who surveyed this site, Shimon Dar, reasoned that this complex of buildings represented the fortified granary of the owner of the village. Also adjoining the farm plots is a building of massive stone blocks of Herodian style, which the locals call the Citadel of Herod. Dar opined that this palace served the owners of the large estate as their country villa. Thus, we have at Qawarat bene Hassan a village of tenant farmers whose landlord owned two thousand acres.[45]

The estate on the Ramat Ha-Nadiv ridge controlled 2,500 acres, according to Yizhar Hirschfeld. On the estate was a complex of buildings, one of which had 150 rooms and was decorated in elaborate marble panels. This was clearly the estate of a very wealthy person. On the other side of the ridge there was another ruin connected to the first one by an ancient road. This was a more modest construction, which Hirschfeld concluded was the agricultural center of the estate. Unlike with the estate of Qawarat bene Hassan, there was no village associated with it. The agricultural workers must have lived in the complex, perhaps as slaves, or traveled there each day to work as day laborers.[46]

Clearly then, these were large estates of two thousand acres or more, worked by tenant farmers in the first case and agricultural slaves or day laborers in the second case. These archaeological remains are what I meant above by smoking-gun evidence. No remains like these are evident yet in Lower Galilee.[47] There is simply no historical-archaeological evidence for large estates in Galilee in the time of Jesus and Antipas.[48]

Second, if we could cite incidents of rural protest or social upheaval, it would demonstrate that there was stress on the villagers. There were

---

45. Dar, *Landscape and Pattern*, 230–45, and figures 115, 124, and 130.

46. Hirschfeld, "The Early Roman Bath and Fortress"; Hirschfeld, *Ramat Hanadiv Excavations*: and Hirschfeld and Feinberg-Vamosh, "A Country Gentleman's Estate."

47. But an estate was identified in Upper Galilee, albeit from an earlier time. See Herbert and Berlin, "New Administrative Center."

48. See Fiensy, "Did Large Estates Exist?" Cf. the essay of Kloppenborg, "The Growth and Impact of Agricultural Tenancy," whose detailed survey of sources that document large estates in Palestine in the late second Temple to Mishnaic period gives no evidence for them in Galilee.

military uprisings in 4 BCE, at the death of Herod the Great (Judas the son of the bandit Hezekiah; *War* 2.56; *Ant* 17.271–72), and when Judas of Gamla in 6 CE began a resistance movement that Josephus calls the Fourth Philosophy (*War* 2.118; *Ant* 18.3–9). After these incidents, which are not clearly protests over economic stresses, there is no protest until the Great War of 66–73 CE. So it does appear that the economic situation had deteriorated since the "Galileans" tried to burn down the city of Sepphoris "which they hated" (Josephus, *Life* 375). But this happened thirty-five to forty years after Jesus's death. The period of Antipas and Jesus does not exhibit markers of peasant stress but appears to have been peaceful.[49]

Yet, there must have been a price to pay for the increased urbanization and building. Horsley allows that the peasants were not yet being thrown off their land. Meyers, Reed, and Edwards concede that the building of the cities put strain on the peasant way of life. Perhaps that is as far as we can go. During Jesus's ministry, the rural folk might have been feeling pressured in taxes but were still able to keep up.

Thus, MacMullen's figure of one-third of the population living in habitual want may be out of line for Antipas's Galilee. Neither the archaeological remains nor the literary texts support a huge, rural, and half-starving proletariat. That there were some destitute persons, however, is a reasonable assumption (see Luke 14:21–23). Even in modern prosperous economies these persons can be found. But it may be that the conditions in play elsewhere in the Roman Empire in the first century CE—and even in Judea—were not duplicated in Galilee. Certainly the average Galilean farmer or artisan was poor compared to the elite classes, but was not destitute and did not live in habitual want. I doubt if one-third of the population was in that state.

Two Conclusions and a Suggestion

1. The rural freeholders, although presumably under some stress from the urbanization, were still able in the time of Jesus and Antipas to cope (i.e., hold on to their land and feed themselves). I think that situation may have gradually changed into a more critical economic condition just before the war of 66 CE.

49. See Fiensy, "Jesus and Debts." Cf. Jensen, "Rural Galilee" 49.

2. Although Lower Galilee was not an egalitarian society, there was, on the other hand, no large, landless rural proletariat. At least there is no evidence for such conditions.

3. Finally, I suggest that it is wise to begin with a sociological model as a heuristic structure for the data. This procedure helps to avoid the assumption that our own economic system was in play in the ancient world. Yet, the model must remain open to validation and emendation as new evidence for a particular region warrants. The model must be refined by a continual process of comparison with the historical and the archaeological data.

6

Did Large Estates Exist
in Lower Galilee in the First Half
of the First Century CE?

LARGE LAND-ESTATES, SOME OF them huge even by modern standards, were a phenomenon in the Early to Late Roman period. One in Spain was allegedly 270,000 acres; one in Italy topped 226,000 acres, and an estate in North Africa was 75,000 acres.[1] Such economic cities-unto-themselves required a skilled manager, a suitable physical plant to store the produce, and, of course, a large and dependable workforce. No estate approaching these sizes existed in Palestine/Israel in the late Second Temple period, but there certainly were estates of 2000 to 3000 acres.

Since the publication of Johannes Herz's "Large Estates in Palestine at the Time of Jesus" in 1928, it has been assumed that Jesus's parables were alluding to real economic conditions in Lower Galilee.[2] Whether historians have accepted that all, or even most, of these parables originated from the historical Jesus, they nonetheless have seen in the parables genuine reflections of economic life in Palestine/Israel. Specifically, several of Jesus's parables assume that there were large agricultural estates in ancient Palestine/Israel. Certainly these estates were not as large as the celebrated ones listed above, but they were large enough to require tenant farmers, agricultural slaves, and bailiffs to care for the landowner's

1. See the references in Fiensy, *Social History*, 23; and Stegemann and Stegemann, *Jesus Movement*, 43.

2. Herz, "Grossgrundbesitz," 98–113.

farm. Luke 16:1–7 speaks of debts of one hundred measures of oil and one hundred measures of wheat, which would have required at least a medium-sized estate to produce. Herz maintained that one would have needed 160 olive trees and forty acres of wheat to lend such a sum.[3] Of course, these numbers may only be scenery, but the fact that they can be used in a story otherwise quite believable and ordinary shows that they are not out of line with experience.

The same sort of conclusion can be drawn from the parable of the Talents (Matt 25:14–30/Luke 19:11–27), the parable of the Debtors (Luke 7:41–43/Matt 18:24–34), and the parable of the Unforgiving Servant (Matt 18:21–35). These parables speak of large sums of money, which imply great wealth. In the ancient economy one could become wealthy as a merchant, but the overwhelming majority of wealthy persons acquired wealth through land.[4] Thus, great wealth usually implies large estates.

Still other parables depict scenes on a large estate. The parable of the Rich Fool (Luke 12:16–21), for instance, describes an estate owner hoarding grain in a manner reminiscent of an account in Josephus (*Life* 119) about the granary of Queen Bernice. Luke 17:7 refers to a man's servant plowing his field for him. Matthew 20:1–15 narrates about a landowner who has so much land he must hire day laborers to work it. Luke 12:42–43 alludes to a wealthy man who has a bailiff to run his estate.

Based on the New Testament, Josephus, and the Talmud, several scholars attempted to describe how these ancient large estates looked and worked.[5] Mark 12:1–12, the parable of the Tenants, received special treatment from Martin Hengel. This parable refers to a vineyard with tenant farmers, a landlord, and several slaves who were sent to collect the rent. Hengel, following leads by Herz, Albrecht Alt, and Victor Tcherikover,[6] sought to illustrate how this parabolic estate must have been understood by reference to the third-century BCE Zenon papyri. The estate of one Apollonius in Beth Anath (in Galilee?) was said to have had eighty

---

3. Ibid.

4. Fiensy, *Social History*, 21–73; Stegemann and Stegemann, *Jesus Movement*, 42–44.

5. Hengel, "Das Gleichnis"; Alt, *Kleine Schriften*, 2:384–395; Klein, "Notes on Large Estates" 1/3, 3–9; Klein, "Notes on Large Estates" 3/4, 109–16; Derrett, "Fresh Light," Krauss, *Antoninus und Rabbi*, 18; Applebaum, "Economic Life in Palestine," 631–700 (esp. 658); Kippenberg, *Religion und Klassenbildung*, 118; Freyne, *Galilee*, 164–65; Charlesworth, *Jesus within Judaism*, 39–48; and Horsley, *Galilee*, 210–14.

6. Tcherikover, "Palestine under the Ptolemies."

thousand vines plus fig trees and probably grain fields. Hengel surmised that eighty thousand vines required forty acres (seventeen hectares) and could support twenty-five workers and their families. He thought that this size was about right for the hypothetical estate of Mark 12. Thus, Hengel thought he had demonstrated the plausibility of the parable of Mark 12, and with it an important feature of the late Second Temple Galilean economy, in finding in an actual estate many of the same elements as in Mark 12.[7]

Other historians have also concluded that Jesus's parables (whether all of them were actually uttered by the historical Jesus or not) and other indications from the New Testament Gospels were alluding to real economic conditions in Lower Galilee. They have supplemented the evidence for the large estates in the New Testament Gospels with reference to Josephus and the rabbinic literature.[8]

The presence or absence of medium to large estates (anything from fifty acres to thousands of acres) in Lower Galilee affects one's evaluation of the economic conditions. The conclusions that these estates existed and that they were large estates drives the argument in favor of exploited peasants. The presence of large estates in Lower Galilee at the time of Jesus would imply that landlords lived from the labor of others (i.e., tenants, day laborers, or slaves). We might infer from this condition that some peasants have been deprived of their land.[9] Such a situation could result in economic disaster for a potentially growing rural proletariat. But if there were no—or relatively few—large estates, or if they were actually on the smaller end of the spectrum, or if there were more than enough land for everyone even with the presence of large estates, then it implies that most peasants still lived on their own land and controlled their own economic destiny. The discussion of large estates in Galilee in the first century CE is not the only issue to be used in determining the economic conditions of the common people, but it is one of the very important ones.

Some historians have stated that there is no evidence for large estates in Galilee during the ministry of Jesus.[10] On the other hand, some

7. Hengel, "Das Gleichniss," 1–39.

8. Jeremias, *Jerusalem*, 96; Hanson and Oakman, *Palestine in the Time of Jesus*, 116–19 [2nd ed., 108–11]; Stegemann and Stegemann, *Jesus Movement*, 111.

9. The larger the estate, the larger the workforce needed and, thus, the greater number of farmers that must have been expelled from their small farms.

10. See for example: Horsley, *Galilee:* "Most of the evidence for [large landowners]

of those using the social sciences to inform their New Testament studies have assumed that they existed since this conclusion is suggested by their macro-economic model. One work, for example, states, "Estates grew and tenancy increased as economies of scale for cash crops were created."[11]

Large Estates on the Great Plain

The statement that "there is no evidence for large estates in Lower Galilee" is certainly not true if we include the Great Plain in Galilee. The sources sometimes include the Great Plain (or Valley of Jezreel or Plain of Esdraelon) in Lower Galilee and sometimes not (include: *m. Git.* 7:7; Josephus, *War* 3.48; exclude: *War* 3.35, 1 Macc 12:49).[12] But perhaps the question of whether the Great Plain technically fell within the borders of Galilee is irrelevant. The Plain certainly lay close enough that it could have affected the economy of Lower Galilee.

The Great Plain with its huge area of 141 square miles (or 90,496 acres)[13] has a long literary history of references to large estates. In 44 BCE the Roman Senate reaffirmed the right of the Hasmoneans to private ownership of it:

> And the villages in the great plain[14] which Hyrcanus and his ancestors formerly possessed—it pleases the Senate for Hyrcanus and the Jews to have them according to the terms they had before. (*Ant.* 14.207)[15]

Since the Hasmoneans (in 44 BCE) and their forefathers for generations before that possessed the villages of the Plain, evidently the

---

... locates them not in Galilee but in Judea, Samaria, the coastal plain, the Great Plain, or the *har ha-melek*" (214); Ben Witherington in a blog entry: "It is time ... to stop talking about large estates in Galilee swallowing up all the land of the small land holders in Galilee" (http://blog.beliefnet.com/bibleandculture/); and Chancey, "Disputed Issues in the Study of Galilee": "There is no evidence for large estates in Galilee."

11. Crossan and Reed, *Excavating Jesus*, 70.

12. See the discussion in Frankel, "Galilee," esp. 879.

13. According to Abel, *Geographie*, 1:91.

14. But to what do the words "great plain" refer? Most have believed that they refer to the Plain of Esdraelon or Valley of Jezreel. But Fabian Udoh (*To Caesar*, 60–68) has more recently argued that this plain is the Plain of Sharon on the coast. At least, however, the remaining evidence indicates that the Plain of Esdraelon became a (series of) large estate(s).

15. Text is from Marcus, *Josephus*, 7:558.

ownership extended back at least to the early first century BCE (perhaps to before that). Albrecht Alt[16] suggested that the ownership extended to the Ptolemies, was passed on to the Seleucids and then to the Hasmoneans. The discovery of the Hefzibah inscription in the eastern part of the plain, which attests to ownership (or perhaps only the usufruct) of the entire Scythopolis Plain by an official of Ptolemy around the year 200 BCE, supports Alt's hypothesis.[17] Later, Herod the Great (25 BCE) settled his veterans in the western part of the Plain at Gaba (*Ant.* 15.294; *War* 3.36) indicating that he owned the lands there. Still later, we read of Bernice, sister of Agrippa II, who owned a granary at Besara (Beth Shearim; *Life* 119). One final bit of evidence that the Great Plain was owned entirely by members of the elite is that Josephus himself was granted lands there by Vespasian after the war (*Life* 422). The entire Plain, or much of it, had become the personal property of Emperor Vespasian. Thus, apparently, the Great Plain was owned as a private estate by royal families from at least the Hasmonean era but probably from the Ptolemaic era.[18]

There is clearly literary and inscriptional evidence to support the Great Plain's being owned or used as a large estate (or a series of large estates). But is there archaeological evidence? An archaeological survey has located 117 wine presses on the southern edge of the Great Plain, scattered from the village of Jenin to the ruins of Megiddo (about fifteen kilometers in distance). Some of these were undoubtedly constructed (cut into bedrock) long before the time of Jesus but were apparently still in use in the early first century CE. Others were added to the ancient presses during the age of Jesus and Antipas. So many presses in so small an area may indicate a large-scale wine-producing industry controlled by one agency. In other words, the presses may have belonged to an estate devoted to wine production.[19]

Thus, there is literary and some archaeological evidence that the western part of the Great Plain was a royal estate at least since the Herodian (and possibly the Hasmonean) era. It passed from Herod the Great to his heirs. Later it was passed to the Roman emperor, Vespasian. Yet did the development of this estate result in the peasants losing their land? It did not if the estate first became a royal domain under the Hasmoneans

---

16. Alt, *Kleine Schriften*, 2:384–95.

17. See Landau, "Greek Inscription"; and Taylor, *Seleucid Rule*.

18. See Fiensy, *Social History*, 28–31.

19. Ahlström, "Wine Presses and Cup-Marks."

(or even before their era) and before the Judeans settled in Galilee (after its annexation by Aristobulus in 104–103 BCE). Thus, no Jewish peasants were evicted in order to give way to the elite owner(s) of the Great Plain.[20]

But were there large or medium-sized estates elsewhere in Galilee? The remainder of this chapter will assay the evidence. I will reach the conclusion, based on both literary and some archaeological data, that medium-sized estates existed in the Bet Netofa Valley of Lower Galilee (the valley just north of the Nazareth ridge) during the first half of the first century CE. As to whether the presence of these estates caused catastrophic economic changes for a growing body of peasants we cannot say with any certainty. This seems doubtful, for reasons I will present shortly.

Two Archaeological Examples of Large Estates outside Galilee

As has been stated above, some historians confidently affirm that there is no evidence for large estates in Galilee in the early first century CE.[21] Presumably, they mean that we have found no incontrovertible archaeological evidence or no smoking-gun material remains like those at Qawarat bene Hassan in Samaria or Horvat Eleq on the Ramat Ha-Nadiv ridge near Caesarea Maritima. Qawarat bene Hassan was a village, occupied from the Hasmonean through the Herodian periods, located approximately forty kilometers southwest of Shechem. The village had between 175 and 200 family holdings with farm plots marked off by stone walls. The total area covered by the farm plots was two thousand acres. On a hill overlooking the village was a complex of storage buildings, strong towers, cisterns, and a residential area. The archaeologist who surveyed this site, Shimon Dar, reasoned that this complex of buildings represented the fortified granary of the owner of the village. Also adjoining the farm plots is a building of massive stone blocks of Herodian style, which the locals

20 It may have resulted in loss of land if the area came under royal ownership only in the Herodian period. It depends on how we interpret the expression "The Great Plain." See above.

21. There is one tantalizing reference in Josephus, *Life,* 71–73, which concerns John of Gischala's attempt to seize the imperial grain stored in Upper Galilee. This grain could be the harvest from an imperial large estate. But it could also be merely the taxes on small freeholders. See the discussion in: Rostovtzeff, *Roman Empire,* 664 n. 32; Hoehner, *Herod Antipas,* 70; Alt, *Kleine Schriften,* 2:395; and Fiensy, *Social History,* 55.

call the Citadel of Herod. Dar opined that this palace served the owners of the large estate as their country villa. Thus, we have at Qawarat bene Hassan a village of tenant farmers whose landlord owned 2,000 acres.[22]

The estate on the Ramat Ha-Nadiv ridge controlled 2,500 acres, according to Yizhar Hirschfeld. On the estate was a complex of buildings, one of which had 150 rooms and was decorated in elaborate marble panels. This was clearly the estate of a very wealthy person. On the other side of the ridge there was another ruin connected to the first one by an ancient road. This was a more modest construction, which Hirschfeld concluded was the agricultural center of the estate. Unlike with the estate of Qawarat bene Hassan, there was no village associated with it. The agricultural workers must have lived in the complex, perhaps as slaves, or traveled there each day to work as day laborers.[23]

Clearly then, these were large estates of two thousand acres or more, worked by tenant farmers in first case and by agricultural slaves or day laborers in the second case. These archaeological remains are what I meant above by smoking-gun evidence. No remains like these are evident yet in Lower Galilee.[24] But should one conclude then that there were no large estates there? Let us consider what evidence does exist, both literary and archaeological.

The Bet Netofa Valley

I here suggest that the Bet Netofa Valley was also a series of large estates owned entirely by the elites, most of whom may have lived in Sepphoris. Six clues or lines of evidence support this conclusion:

1. The pattern in evidence elsewhere in Second Temple Palestine/Israel

2. The evidence from Josephus

3. The rabbinic references to Eleazar ben Harsom

4. The Joseph ben Simai story

5. The remains of three buildings in Shikhin

22. Dar, *Landscape and Pattern*, 230–45, and figures 115, 124, and 130.

23. Hirschfeld, "Early Roman Bath"; Hirschfeld, *Ramat Hanadiv*; and Hirschfeld and Feinberg-Vamosh, "Country Gentleman's Estate."

24. But an estate was identified in Upper Galilee, albeit from an earlier time. See Herbert and Berlin, "New Administrative Center."

6. And the remains of houses in Sepphoris

The Pattern of Estate Ownership

The pattern in antiquity was for the best lands to be owned by kings and other elites. All land in principle and the best land in fact belonged to the monarchs and their aristocratic allies.[25] Such a pattern is well attested under the Ptolemies and Seleucids in the Hellenistic period for Egypt and Syria, and this pattern included the territory we call Palestine/Israel.[26] The large estates in the Jericho Valley and on the Great Plain are examples of this land ideology at work. We can trace a history of royal ownership of these prime agricultural lands that began no later than the Hellenistic period and perhaps in the Persian period.[27] We, therefore, would naturally presume that the Bet Netofa was also owned by a few aristocrats and not divided up into small peasant farm plots of five to ten acres.

Josephus's References to "Asochis"

Second, hints of the economic importance of the Bet Netofa are found in Josephus. During the high-priesthood of Alexander Janneus (103–77 BCE) Ptolemy Lathyrus sacked a village he called Asochis (long identified as the equivalent of the Talmudic village of Shikhin[28]), capturing "about a myriad persons and a great deal of other (things)" (περι μυρια σωματα και πολλην ετεραν ελαβε λειαν): i.e., booty (*Ant.* 13.337; cf. *War* 1.86). We might question whether the town of Asochis ever held ten thousand inhabitants, but the capture of "other things," evidently plunder, suggests this was an important town economically. Later, Josephus made Asochis his headquarters during the Jewish War (*Life* 207, 233, 304). Josephus writes that the entire valley (which the rabbinic literature called the Bet Netofa) was in his day named after this town (thus, the Plain of Asochis; *Life* 207). The name Plain of Asochis is evidence of the importance of the village of Asochis. Further, during the war, although nearby Sepphoris

---

25. Fiensy, *Social History*, 23.

26. See Hengel, *Judaism and Hellenism*, 1:19–20; Klein, "Notes on Large Estates" 1/3, 3; Tcherikover, *Hellenistic Civilization*, 13; Bell, *Egypt*, 44; Tarn, *Hellenistic Civilization*, 187; Rostovzeff, *Large Estate*, 66; and Horsley, *Galilee*, 207–14.

27. Fiensy, *Social History*, 25–31.

28. See Avi-Yonah, "Shihin or Asochis"; Jacobs and Ochser, "Sihin."

was opposed to the war and indifferent to Josephus, the inhabitants of Asochis strongly supported him as commander of the rebel forces in Galilee (*Life* 232).

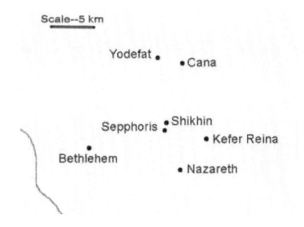

Figure 6.1: Lower Galilee Centered at Sepphoris

The village's support for both the war and Josephus in contrast to the opposition in Sepphoris suggests that the inhabitants of Asochis did not have the same economic standing as those in Sepphoris even though there was a great deal of plunder to be had there. They thought they had less to lose and more to gain from revolution. Further, since Josephus made Asochis his military headquarters, we are inclined to see Asochis as an administrative center and perhaps a granary or storage depot. Military commanders tended to bivouac where there was an amble supply of food for the troops.[29] This historical information and the inferences one can draw from it suggest that Shikhin/Asochis was a village like Qawarat bene Hassan, owned by elite families of Sepphoris who also owned the entire Bet Netofa Valley (or Plain of Asochis), and that Asochis/Shikhin was populated by tenant farmers who did not share their landlords' view of the war.

29. See Dar, *Landscape and Pattern*, 219–20, 233.

Rabbinic References to Eleazar ben Harsom

Third, the rabbinic literature[30] confirms this inference when it remembers Eleazar ben Harsom, the wealthy priest and alleged owner of one thousand villages in Judea, Samaria, and Galilee, as the owner of the village of Shikhin and claims the taxes from this village (and two others in Galilee) were so heavy they had to be carried to Jerusalem (where Eleazar lived?) in a wagon (*Lam. Rab.* 2.2//*y. Ta'an.* 4.5; 69a):

Lam. Rab. 2.2	*y. Ta'an.* 4.5; 69a
There were 10,000 cities on the Har Ha-Melek. R. Eleazar ben Harsom owned one thousand of them . . . The taxes of three of these cities, Kabul, Shikhin and Magdala went up to Jerusalem . . . Shikhin (was destroyed) because of sorceries.[31]	There were 10,000 cities in the Har Ha-Melek. R. Eleazar ben Harsom owned a thousand of them . . . The taxes of three of them , Kabul, Shikhin, and Migdol Zebiiah, went up to Jerusalem in a wagon . . . Shikhin was destroyed because of sorceries.[32]

The fact that Eleazar owned[33] the village of Shikhin/Asochis (or part of it) means that it was a tenant village and administrative center for a

30. Since the now-classic works of Jacob Neusner, the use of rabbinic literature in writing history has received greater scrutiny. His method of evaluating the date of a legal ruling (e.g., *From Politics to Piety*, 92–96) has been further refined by the next generation of scholars: e.g. Strack and Stemberger, *Introduction to the Talmud*, 56–61; and Instone-Brewer, *Prayer and Agriculture*, 30–40. But we should point out with respect to the use of rabbinic materials in this investigation the following: 1) Neusner was mainly interested in identifying the date of sayings attributed to the pre-70 Pharisees (see *Rabbinic Traditions*), but we are not attempting to achieve this goal. 2) We are not explaining a New Testament theological concept by appeal to rabbinic theology. 3) The economic condition of ownership of villages is attested in other sources such as Josephus and the Hefzibah inscription. Thus, the economic information in these rabbinic texts fits nicely with the nonrabbinic information. 4) The general idea that these rabbinic citations contribute (that Shikhin was an estate center) is at least implied in the texts from Josephus. Thus under these circumstances, it seems appropriate to listen to the voice of the rabbinic texts.

31. Text is from *Judaic Classics*.

32. Text online: "Talmud Yerushalmi."

33. Eleazar would have "owned" the entire village (or probably only a part of the village) in the sense that he owned much of the land around the village and charged the resident tenant farmers rent. The concept of owning a village was quite common in antiquity (See Fiensy, *Social History*, 29 n. 54a). Monarchs rewarded their favorite

large landed estate. The "taxes" could be taxes owed to Rome or could be the rent owed to Eleazar by the tenant farmers. (I think it was the latter.)

It is difficult to decide exactly when Eleazar lived. Some think his villages were destroyed in the war of 66 CE,[34] others in the Bar Cochba war of 132 CE.[35] I think it more likely that it was destroyed in 66 CE since its destruction would fit in well with Josephus's information about the pro-revolt spirit of the village.[36] Their disdain for the pacifist Sepphoreans and adulation for the Jewish general, Josephus, would have made them a target for Roman destruction. Either way (whether the village was destroyed in the Great War or the Bar Cochba war), the text quoted above seems to establish that the Bet Netofa Valley was a large estate or a series of medium estates.

Further, the Talmud claims that Eleazar inherited the tenant villages from his father (*b. Yoma* 35a).[37] Thus, Shikhin was a tenant village at least one generation before Eleazar's time. This consideration takes us back into the first half of the first century CE if, in fact, this village was destroyed in 66 CE. Since Eleazar, and his father before him, owned the village (or part of it), then the residents were tenant farmers and the village was the center of an estate or several estates.

---

administrators with villages and lands. This practice was also found in Palestine/Israel as is demonstrated by the Hefzibah inscription, several references in Josephus, and rabbinic texts. But even if we accept the assertion of Horsley (*Galilee*, 202, 331) that there was no private property ownership in Palestine/Israel, the situation does not change much. Whether Eleazar actually owned part of this village or only had the usufruct from it seems to me to amount to much the same thing.

34. Büchler, "Die Schauplätze," 143–205 (esp. 191).

35. Schlatter, *Die Tage Trajans*, 55–56. Jeremias, *Jerusalem*, 97, agreed with Schlatter. See the discussion in Safrai, "Eleazar ben Harsom."

36. The parallel with the town of Magdala (also said to have been owned by Eliezer ben Harsom and to have been destroyed) is helpful. Josephus reported that Titus and Vespasian sacked Magdala (*War* 3.497–502). There may also be archaeological confirmation of the town's destruction. See de Luca, "Urban Development." The author speaks of "dramatic events of the First Jewish Revolt (66–67 A.D.) described by Josephus, to which many stratigraphical evidences of destruction and abandonment can be related."

37. See also the reference in *Eccl. Rab.* 4.8 to a Gebini ben Harsom who inherited a fortune from his father. Is this the same person as Eleazar or a descendant of Eleazar?

The Joseph ben Simai Story

Fourth, there is a rabbinic story, repeated in four texts, of a Joseph bin Simai in Shikhin, who is said in Babylonian Talmud to have been an administrator (Greek loanword: επιτροπος) of "the king." A fire started in the courtyard of Joseph who lived in Shikhin, and (evidently Roman) soldiers from the military camp (i.e. the *castra*[38]) in Sepphoris came to put it out. Most historians want to date this event somewhere between the two wars (Jewish War of 66–73 CE and Bar Cochba of 132–135 CE), perhaps in the 80s or 90s of the first century.[39] There is evidence for a small military unit both during the Jewish War of 66 CE and on into the second century CE (see table below).[40]

What the parallel stories indicate is that Joseph was a wealthy person: 1. He sent expensive rewards to the soldiers and the governor for responding to his fire. 2. He was evidently an important person since the soldiers rushed to Shikhin from Sepphoris (a distance of 1.39 km[41]) to put out his fire. Though some have doubted that he truly was an administrator of "the king" or have debated which king this would have been (either Agrippa II or Emperor Vespasian[42]), Joseph was at least an important person and a person of wealth.

---

38. A *castra* (a Latin loanword) was a Roman military camp. See Jastrow, *Dictionary*, קסטרא; Lewis, *Latin Dictionary*, *castrum*; and Miller, *Studies*, 40–41, 55.

39. See especially Miller, *Sepphoris*, 33.

40. Ibid., 41.

41. According to the conclusions of Strange et al., "Excavations at Sepphoris: Part I," 216–27 (esp. 216). See also the second part of the study in Strange et al., "Excavations at Sepphoris: Part II."

42. See the discussion in Miller, *Sepphoris*, 37–40. There is a Talmudic reference to a steward (*'epitropos*) of Agrippa (clearly Agrippa II) in *b. Sukkah* 27a. Was this Joseph ben Simai? Miller thinks not (40).

t. Shabb. 13:9	b. Shabb. 121a	y. Shabb. 16.7	Deut. Rab.
A case: A fire started in the courtyard of Joseph ben Simai in Shikhin. And men from the *castra* in Sepphoris came to put it out. And he did not permit (them) . . . On the passing of the Sabbath he sent to them a *selah* and to the governor (υπαρχος,[43] or is it *praefectus* Prefect?[44]) who was over them 50 dinars.[45]	Baraita: A case: A fire started in the court- yard of Joseph ben Simai in Shikhin. And men from the *castra* of Sepphoris came to put it out because he was an administrator (επιτροπος) of the king.[46]	A case: A fire started in the courtyard of Jose ben Simai in Shikhin and the men from the *castra* of the Sepphoreans came down to put it out. And he did not allow them. He said to them, "Allow the tax collector to collect his debt" . . . After the Sabbath passed, he sent to every one of them a *selah* and to the governor (υπαρχος, or is it *praefectus* Prefect?) he sent 50 dinars."[47]	A case: In the days of Jose ben Simai who was from Shikhin a fire started in his courtyard on the Sabbath. And the *quaestor* of Sepphoris came out and went down to put it out and he (Jose) did not permit them.[48]

I suggest that Joseph was an estate overseer, perhaps of royal lands.[49] It may well be that, as was the case with the Great Plain (see above), Vespasian confiscated what was already a large estate or series of large estates. But at least these parallel texts suggest that some of the Bet Netofa was given over to wealthy families and that Shikhin was the administrative center, perhaps also used as their granary, and that Joseph ben Simai was one of the bailiffs of the estate(s). Thus, a history of references suggests that the Bet Netofa and its ruling village (Shikhin/Asochis) was a large estate or series of large estates.

From the literary evidence it seems that most if not all of the Bet Netofa valley was owned by a few elites—among them Eleazar ben

43. Jastrow, *Dictionary*, איפרכא

44. Miller, *Sepphoris*, 40–41.

45. Text from Zuckermandel, *Tosefta*.

46. "Six Orders of the Talmud Bavli."

47. "Talmud Yerushalmi."

48. Text in Miller, *Sepphoris*, 33.

49. See the suggestion of Miller, *Sepphoris*, 39: "The word *'epitropos* in this case may very well refer to a steward or guardian of the king's possessions and not to an administrator or official in charge of the area."

Harsom and, most likely, the Sepphoris aristocrats. During the Great Jewish War (66–73 CE), Shikhin was pro-revolt while Sepphoris was pro-Roman. Shikhin was, therefore, destroyed along with Eleazar's holdings. Between the wars, there was a Roman garrison in Sepphoris, which came to the aid of Joseph ben Simai when a fire started. The estates of Bet Netofa Valley had by then been confiscated by "the king"—I think Vespasian (and his heirs)—just as he had confiscated them in the Great Plain after the war. He employed a Jewish administrator, Joseph ben Simai,[50] to oversee his estates in the valley.

Archaeological Remains of the Village Identified as Shikhin

Fifth, the archaeological remains of Shikhin may offer interesting suggestions as to the function of at least part of the village. The team headed by James Strange, Denis Groh, and Thomas Longstaff surveyed the site in 1988, which they identified as Shikhin-Asochis.[51] Their intention was to examine the physical remains and the topography to see whether that particular location was a likely site for the ancient village of Shikhin-Asochis. They concluded that it was and have shown that the large vessels crafted there were in use throughout Galilee.

But is it also possible that Shikhin-Asochis was an agricultural center where the large-estate overseers or bailiffs resided, and where grain was stored? The survey team reported the ruins of three buildings that could arouse some interest: One (locus 88006) was 10 m. long and had walls from .8 m to 1 m thick.[52] The total width is unknown because of the partial destruction of the site, but it was preserved for a width of 5 m. A second (88022) was 8.5 m long (measured by the cut bedrock foundation).[53] A third (88027) had walls .5 m thick and was preserved for a length of 6.2 m (thus it may have been longer).[54] These building sizes and wall thicknesses are rather large for a typical one- or two-room village house but not elaborate enough to have been the residences of well-

50. We know he was Jewish, of course, not only by his name but also because this story is told in the rabbinic literature to illustrate Joseph's piety toward the Sabbath.

51. Strange et al., "Location and Identification of Shikhin: Part I"; and Strange et al., "Location and Identification of Shikhin: Part II."

52. Strange et al., "Location and Identification of Shikhin: Part II," 173.

53. Ibid., 175.

54. Ibid.

to-do families. While the archaeological remains do not form proof, the remains make it is at least plausible that these remains come from what were the dwellings of estate overseers, their administrative buildings, or their storehouses and granaries. Other constructions of similar dimensions and wall thicknesses have been identified as one of these three possibilities at sites such as Hirbet Basatin in Samaria,[55] Caesarea Maritima,[56] and Bethsaida.[57] Final acceptance of this hypothesis could only follow actual excavation of the site.[58]

The Houses of Sepphoris

Sixth, there is other archaeological evidence for the Bet Netofa having been a series of large estates, albeit that this evidence is indirect. I refer to the houses in the residential section of Sepphoris (the Western Domestic Quarter), with their multiple rooms, courtyards, fresco paintings, and mosaic floors. These houses must have been built from some source of wealth. The most likely source was agriculture, and the nearest prized land is in the Bet Netofa Valley.[59]

55. Dar, *Landscape and Pattern*, 25, identifies "Building 1" at Hirbet Basatin, with dimensions of 10m X 8 m and 1.2-m-thick walls, as the residence of the owner. He identifies "Building 4" with dimensions of 17m X 8 m, and divided into at least three rooms, as storehouses.

56. Patrich, "Warehouses and Granaries." Patrich reports the dimensions of several *horrea* (i.e., warehouses): the "Mithreum horreum": 30 m X 5 m; "corridor horreum": 15.5 m X 1.8 m; a "dolia hall" (i.e., storehouse for *pithos* jars): 15.9 m X 4.5 m.

57. Arav, *Bethsaida*, 35–50. Arav reports that three of the gate chambers were granaries and the fourth was a storage building. Each gate chamber measured around 10 m X 3 m. The dimensions of the storage rooms at Qawarat Bene Hassan, were, however, much larger (Dar, *Landscape and Pattern*, 219–20). The Hirbet Firdusi at Qawarat Bene Hassan consisted, among other buildings, of six or seven store buildings, each 30 to 40 meters long and 5 to 10 meters wide. These large store buildings compare with those at Masada and Pergamum according to Dar (220).

58. "I think that your suggestions are plausible ones but until some scientific excavation can be undertaken it seems to me that your speculation is just that: a plausible hypothesis that could be tested by excavation in the vicinity of the remains (some of which are only places where bedrock has been cut to provide a foundation for the structure above). I certainly would not say that your speculation was unfounded (the size of the structures may well suggest something other than a house); instead I would say that they are plausible but unproven." Private correspondence with Thomas R. Longstaff, 19 October 2009. The village of Shikhin is now under excavation, albeit in the early stages. See Strange, "Excavations at Shikhin."

59. Meyers, "Jesus and His Galilean Context," 57–66 (esp. 62) notes that the fertile

Thus, six lines of evidence converge to lead me to conclude that the Bet Netofa was owned entirely or mostly by the elite families of Sepphoris before the war, including by Eleazar ben Harsom, and after war by Emperor Vespasian and his heirs.

Calculating Estate, House, and Population Sizes

We can further check this conclusion by arguing backwards. Since only around 1 percent of the population could live in leisured wealth,[60] if we calculate the total population of Galilee at 175,000,[61] that means there were perhaps somewhere between 1,500 and 2,000 elites in Galilee. Let us say for the sake of the calculation that there were 1,750 elites. If we divide this number by two (since there were only two cities in Galilee, Sepphoris and Tiberias—and almost all elites lived in cities), we would expect around 875 elite persons in Sepphoris to have been supported by the Bet Netofa Valley. That number would equal, if we follow Arieh Ben-David's suggestion for typical family sizes[62] (six to nine persons per family, or an average of 7.5 per family), approximately 116 wealthy families. The total land area in the Bet Netofa (using F.-M. Abel's figures[63]) was around 6,348 acres. If we divide these acres by the figure of 116 families, we have an average of 54 acres per family. These elites then owned medium-sized estates. Hans Dohr maintained that in the Roman Empire small estates ranged from ten to eighty *iugera* (or six to fifty acres); medium estates from eighty to five hundred *iugera* (or 50–315 acres); and large estates over five hundred *iugera*, or 315 acres.[64] But a gentleman could live comfortably from a medium estate. There are plenty of examples of these sizes

lands in the valleys near Sepphoris, that had once been used for subsistence of the peasantry, had to be transformed into places where products were grown on a larger scale. Cities became centers of consumption.

60. For the percentage of elites in the agrarian societies of the ancient Mediterranean basin, see MacMullen, *Roman Social Relations*, 89; Rilinger, "Moderne un zeitgenössische Vorstellungen," 299–325 (esp. 302); Alföldy, *Römische Gesellschaft*, 130; and Scheidel, "Stratification, Deprivation and Quality of Life," 40–59 (esp. 42). Cf. Lenski, *Power and Privilege*, 228, who gives a similar figure for other agrarian societies.

61. See Meyers, "Jesus and His Galilean Context," 59; and Hoehner, *Herod Antipas*, 53. Hoehner prefers the figure 200,000, and Meyers prefers 150,000 to 175,000.

62. Ben-David, *Talmudische Ökonomie*, 45. Ben-David based his estimate on tomb and village sizes.

63. Abel, *Geographie*, 1:91.

64. Dohr, *Die italischen Guthöfe* (cited in White, *Roman Farming*, 385–87.)

of estates providing a good income. At Pompeii landowners had usually estates of around sixty-three acres[65] or one hundred *iugera*. Cato wrote that this size was about right for the farm of a gentleman, which would include vineyards, willow plantations, olive orchards, meadows, grain fields, forests, and acorn woods (Cato, *De Agricultura* 1.7). Cato further observed that a farm of one hundred *iugera* would require about sixteen workers.[66] The estate at Beth Anath described in the Zenon papyri was around forty acres.[67] Interestingly, J. Herz estimated one of the estates alluded to in the Gospels as a forty-acre estate.[68] These would not have been extremely wealthy families compared to the land barons of the Roman Empire but nevertheless well-off in comparison with the average freeholding farmer of Palestine/Israel.

We must stress at this point that these calculations are only to illustrate the possibilities for elite income based on the nearest excellent arable land. But wealthy folk were known in the ancient world to possess multiple farms scattered in several locations throughout the Greco-Roman world.[69] It is possible, therefore, that some of the Sepphorean aristocrats owned farms not only in the Bet Netofa Valley but also elsewhere in Palestine (like Eleazar ben Harsom) and, possibly even, beyond Palestine.

65. Day, "Agriculture in the Life of Pompeii." Day calculated that at Pompeii the 63-acre estate of vineyards would produce an annual income of 36,000 denarii (183–84). Stegemann and Stegemann (*Jesus Movement*, 44) calculated that a farm of 60 acres used mostly for wine growing would have produced about 800 denarii per acre or 48,000 denarii per year. If we accept the lower estimation of Day, then 50 acres could produce an annual income of 28,569 denarii. If we further calculate 250 denarii per year as the rough equivalent of the minimum wage in the United States (=$15,000), then this sum would equal in US economy $1,714,140. Thus the ancient elites of Sepphoris would be lower upper-class in terms of modern American economic standing. Of course, calculations that compare ancient wealth with modern are notoriously precarious. All this calculation shows is the relationship of the ancient day laborer to those of the lower upper class.

66. See Stegemann and Stegemann, *Jesus Movement*, 29.

67. See Hengel, "Die Gleichnis," 13. Hengel maintained that the estate of Apollonius at Beth-Anath in Galilee, which had 80,000 vines, would require about 40 acres and 25 workers.

68. Herz, "Grossgrundbesitz," 100.

69. See, e.g., Herodes Atticus of Athens in the second century CE, who owned estates not only near Athens but at Marathon, on the island of Euboea, at Corinth and other places in the Peloponnesus, and in Egypt. Malania the Younger in 404 CE sold off estates in Italy, Sicily, Spain, and North Africa. See Finley, *Ancient Economy*, 101, 102, 112; and Stegemann and Stegemann, *Jesus Movement*, 43.

The suggestion that the elites of Sepphoris were, for the most part, families of modest wealth also harmonizes with what archaeologists have noticed about the houses in the Western Domestic Quarter of Sepphoris. They are nice but not as elaborate as those discovered in the Jewish Quarter of old Jerusalem. If we compare the houses of the aristocrats of Sepphoris—those of the "western domestic quarter" whose inhabitants according to Eric Meyers, were "well-to-do aristocratic Jews"[70]—with aristocratic houses of Jerusalem, we notice some striking differences. The houses in Sepphoris were certainly nice by ancient standards. They had multiple rooms and a courtyard. Many had fresco paintings, and some had mosaic floors. Several were multistoried. They were impressive for their time and place. But compared with the Jerusalem houses (excavated in the Jewish quarter of the old city), they were modest. For example, the "Great Mansion" of Jerusalem had a living area of 600 square meters while a large house of Sepphoris (labeled 84.1) had an area of 300 square meters. The size difference alone is remarkable. Further, the small finds in the aristocratic houses of Sepphoris indicate modest wealth. Bone instead of ivory was used for cosmetic applications. Aristocrats in Sepphoris employed common pottery, not fine ware. They imported no wines.[71] Thus based on the evidence of the houses from first-century Sepphoris discovered so far—Tiberias has not been excavated adequately for such an assessment—we would have to say that the extreme distance between the elites and lower class, found elsewhere in the Roman Empire, and evidently in Judea, was diminished in Galilee. While there certainly was an economic distance between the two groups, it was not as great as in other regions.

Conclusion

The following scenario seems to me plausible: Before the war of 66 CE the elites of Sepphoris and others such as Eleazar ben Harsom owned most if not all of the land in the Bet Netofa Valley. Eleazar owned lands in the valley, as is stated in the rabbinic literature. That other aristocrats of Sepphoris owned estates in the Bet Netofa is a reasonable inference from their house sizes. Shikhin may have been the administrative center

70. Meyers, "Roman Sepphoris," 321–38 (esp. 322).

71. See Meyers, "Problems of Gendered Space"; and Avigad, "How the Wealthy Lived."

of these estates, housing the estate bailiff(s). That Josephus made it his headquarters suggests that a supply of grain was at hand in the years 66–68 CE, and, therefore, we might rightly surmise that the village was the granary of the estates. The plundering of this village a century and a half earlier also suggests that it had already been a storage center for large estates during the reign of Alexander Janneus. Shikhin was, unlike Sepphoris, pro-revolt and was destroyed during the war. After the war, the estates of the Bet Netofa were confiscated by Vespasian, as were those of the Great Plain. Between the wars there was a Roman military camp in Sepphoris. When a fire started in Shikhin, the soldiers came to put it out. Joseph ben Simai was the Jewish administrator of Vespasian's (or his successor's) estate at that time.

To sum up, medium-sized estates (but not large estates) did exist in the Bet Netofa Valley in the first half of the first century CE. The elites of Sepphoris, however, were not as wealthy as those of Judea and elsewhere in the empire. Their estates must have been more modest, based on the size of the Bet Netofa Valley. The domestic quarters and the small finds within those quarters confirm that the residents were families of modest wealth. Therefore I would hesitate to affirm that the small farmers (or peasants) were being overly exploited by increasingly wealthy persons. That social dynamic was perhaps developing slowly but not yet in full bloom (though elsewhere in Palestine/Israel it seems to have been already a reality). Further, the assertion that the villages of Hananya and Shikhin were thriving pottery factories and that this economic tide lifted all boats must be viewed with some caution.[72] If Shikhin was, in addition to a pottery manufacturing center, an administrative center for estates of the Sepphorean aristocrats, the residents may not have prospered as much as some historians have suggested.[73] Some of them may have been tenant farmers living in an estate administrative center like Qawarat bene-Hassan.

---

72. See Adan-Bayewitz, *Common Pottery*, 23–41, 216–36; Adan-Bayewitz, "Kefar Hananya, 1986"; Adan-Bayewitz and Perlman, "Local Trade"; Strange, "First-Century Galilee," 39–48 (esp. 41); Edwards, "Urban/Rural Relations"; Edwards, "Socio-Economic and Cultural Ethos"; and Meyers, "Jesus and His Galilean Context."

73. It is interesting that the two pottery villages, Hananya and Shikhin, are singled out in the Talmud as those especially needy during famine years. During years of want, the poor from these villages would wait at dusk at the Sabbath limit where two benefactors would hand out dried figs to them (*b. 'Erub.* 51b).

Finally, the picture one could visualize based on the Gospels' parables and other indications seems to be largely inaccurate for Lower Galilee. The large estates implied in some of these parables were not, as far as the evidence has shown thus far, a reality for Galilee in the time of Jesus. One could doubtless travel just south of Nazareth and see them on the Great Plain, but there is no evidence for the two-thousand- to three-thousand-acre estates north of the Plain.

7

Assessing the Economy of Galilee in the Late Second Temple Period

Five Considerations

"IT WAS THE BEST of times; it was the worst of times." Charles Dickens is not the only one that can write this way. This observation also summarizes what the historians of Galilee in the late Second Temple period have written lately. Yet, these scholars do not make this observation in order to point out the varied nature of conditions. Scholars seem divided into two groups, and each group concludes only one side of the Dickensian paradox: Either Galilee knew the best of times (i.e., economic prosperity and even an egalitarian society), or it witnessed the worst of times (i.e., increasing indebtedness, land losses, and exploitation of the peasants).

It is small wonder that we can read such drastically differing analyses. Each side works with different data, different methodologies, and different assumptions. It reminds me of the story of the sight-impaired persons who discovered an elephant. One person grabbed the tail and said, "This is a rope with which the wealthy of Galilee were strangling the poor." Another felt the elephant's leg and exclaimed, "This is a tree trunk, strong and stout, like the Galilean economy in the Late Second Temple period."

So where do we go from here? I would like to survey five considerations for assessing the economy of Galilee in the late Second Temple period. The five considerations have helped me to strike a position midway between the polar opposites. I see the economic situation in Lower Galilee in the late Second Temple period as (so to speak) young. It had not yet developed into an oppressive society but was perhaps moving in that direction. The five considerations are

1. The current broader academic environment, specifically the studies of the ancient economy among classical historians.

2. The differences, as I see them, between Galilee and other Israelite territories (especially Judea). I observe three important economic distinctions.

3. The chronological distinctions. Were the years 6–44 CE the same as 45–66 CE? In particular, was indebtedness the same in both of those periods?

4. The fragmentary nature of the data, especially archaeologically.

5. The function of social-science models.

Consideration 1

In the discipline of classical history, they are now in the post-Finley era. Two significant collections of essays have been published recently, one in 2002[1] and one in 2005.[2] Each volume received the same title: *The Ancient Economy* (the title Moses Finley had also used[3]), but they could better have been titled *The Study of the Ancient Economy in the Post-Finley Era*. These two recent collections contain essays that assess the legacy of the great historian, sometimes positively, more often critically.

As these authors see it, there are now four (overlapping) approaches to the study of the ancient economy. First, we have the *formalist* position vs. the *substantivist* position. Finley (a substantivist) opined that the ancient economy was based more on status and civic ideology than supply and demand. Economic development was constrained by elite values. For Finley, economic behavior is "embedded in a network of social relationships that determine values, attitudes, and actual behavior."[4]

---

1. Scheidel and von Reden, *Ancient Economy*.
2. Morris and Manning, *Ancient Economy*.
3. Finley, *Ancient Economy*.
4. Scheidel and von Reden, *Ancient Economy*, 1–8.

The formalists, on the other hand, maintain that the economic sphere was separate from social relations. They question whether the "elite mentality" played such a significant role in the ancient economy. They now are focusing more and more on trade as an important part of the ancient economy. They find economic growth in the Roman Empire because the empire's structure encouraged markets and trade. These historians of the ancient economy maintain that Finley underestimated the power of markets and exchange.[5]

The second polarity is the *primitivists* vs. the *modernists*. Finley , a primitivist, maintained that the so-called market economy was no more than four hundred years old, and thus the modern discipline of economics could be no older. Modern economics textbooks are essentially about modern market economies and thus are of little value in understanding the ancient economy,[6] Modernist Michael Rostovtzeff, however, assumed that "modern capitalistic development differs from the ancients only in quantity and not in quality."[7] Modernists in general affirm that economics is the study of "laws that hold true between humans and goods . . . They apply in all periods of history and to all forms of society."[8]

We might with benefit allow Finley and Rostovtzeff to represent the two sides. One classical economist has summarized their differences as follows:

> Primitivist versus modernist, no-trade versus long-distance trade, autarky versus integrated markets, technological stagnation versus technological progress, no economic growth versus growth, non-rationalist traditionalist versus rational individualists.[9]

It looks to me like those who view Galilee in late Second Temple period as prosperous (mostly archaeologists) are formalists and modernists (like Rostovtzeff). Those who view Galilee as poor and exploited (mostly those using social-science models) are substantivists and primitivists (like Finley). The assumptions are quite different and thus, the conclusions, the picture of the whole, if you will, must be different. But both

5. Ibid.
6. Meikle, "Modernism," 236.
7. Ibid., 239.
8. Ibid., 236.
9. Saller, "Framing the Debate," 224.

sides can benefit by listening in on the conversation among the classical historians.

As far as my own intellectual pilgrimage is concerned, I should say that I have been a loyal disciple of Finley for some time, but now I am exploring the significance of market exchange. In this context, I present an economic model in this volume (chapter 4). There is room in that model for both potential exploitation of the poor and potential economic success depending on the specific conditions as indicated by the data.[10]

Consideration 2

When constructing a picture of the Galilean economy in the late Second Temple period, we should make geographical distinctions. Too many of us—and I confess my error here as well—have treated Palestine/Israel as one economic unit. There is a sense in which that can be done. All territories were once under Herod the Great; most of the residents were Jewish. One could even treat Palestine and Syria as an economic unit with some success (as Heichelheim has done[11]). They were under the same Roman oversight. But this should be done only to a point. Failure to look at Galilee as separate from Judea/Idumea/Samaria masks significant differences. I can think of three distinctions that should always be kept in mind.

Different Histories

Judea/Idumea/Samaria came under direct Roman rule in 6 CE; Galilee not until 44 CE. This fact means that the former three territories were taxed directly by Rome from then on. Were their taxes greater than in Galilee? Probably both areas had the *tributum soli*. The rate of the tax on the soil may have increased in Judea. It may have included both a tax on annual produce and a flat tax on land.[12] In addition to the *tributum soli*, the Romans may have added the *tributum capitis* or poll-tax (i.e., head-tax), though that is now disputed.[13] This tax was levied in Syria

10. Fiensy, "Ancient Economy and the New Testament," 199. See pp. 67–80 of this volume. The model I used was developed from Davies, "Linear and Nonlinear Flow Models," 150.

11. Heichelheim, "Roman Syria," 121–257.

12. Udoh, *To Caesar*, 222.

13. Ibid., 237, 241. But see Millar, *Roman Near East*, 110, who writes, "We have to

(according to Ulpian, *Digest*) on every male between the ages of fourteen and sixty-five, on every female between twelve and sixty-five. For Judea this tax *might* have been one denarius per person (based on Mark 12:13–17). Or it could have been one denarius plus a percentage of the movable property, i.e. animals, slaves, ships, and wagons,[14] There were also house taxes and duties on produce brought into Jerusalem (*Ant.* 18.90, 19.299).[15] The point is, taxation seems to have been a greater burden in Judea than in Galilee. Whether it was so much greater as to lower the standard of living significantly in Judea *vis a vis* Galilee, is the question. We know that in 17 CE Judea appealed to Tiberius for tax relief (Tacitus, *Ann.* 2.42[16]). Thus, direct taxation from Rome seems to have contributed to a lower standard of living.[17]

Different Economies

Galilee was more recently settled than Judea and therefore had a newer economy. There are three hypotheses at present as to the origin of the Galileans. Some have suggested that they were the remnants of the old Israelites, those left behind when the elites were deported in the eighth century BCE. Others offer that these folk were converted Ituarians, Gentiles who became Jews when Aristobulus conquered the territory in the late second century BCE. Finally, a third group of historians posits that the people of Galilee were Jewish colonists (from Judea) who settled in Galilee after Aristobulus annexed the territory for Judea. The data from archaeological surveys support the third view. The surveys indicate an

---

assume that both a land tax (*tributum soli*) and a 'head-tax' were payable [in Syria]." He bases his conclusion on the third-century-CE evidence from Ulpian and the Roman jurist Paul.

14. Fiensy, *Social History*, 100–101. Udoh (*To Caesar*, 222) thinks that the taxes on movable property, if they were assessed, would have been added to the *tributum soli*.

15. Udoh, *To Caesar*, 238.

16. Tacitus described Judea and Syria as *fessae*, "exhausted," by taxes. See Finley, *Ancient Economy*, 90. Cf. Josephus, *War* 2.85–86; *Ant.* 17.204–205, 306–307 who reports that the people of Palestine/Israel complained about the taxes levied by Herod the Great

17. "Taxes distort prices and thus the decisions of households and firms" (Mankiw, *Principles of Macroeconomics*, 9.) The author means that a centralized economy—one controlled by the government by heavy taxation—is the opposite of a free-market economy. Thus observations based on free markets may not apply to the ancient Palestinian economy if the taxation was unusually burdensome.

absence of Galilean settlements for over a century after the conquest by the Assyrians (thus ruling out hypothesis #1). Further, the reign of Alexander Jannaeus (103–77 BCE) coincides with an increase in population (thus suggesting #3). Most archaeologists and historians now support hypothesis number 3.[18] The implications of a young economy are very significant. Even if we accept that it was inevitable in the ancient economy that the rich became richer and the poor, poorer, that more and more land was being concentrated in the hands of fewer and fewer elites, that peasants tended to go into debt during lean years and then to lose their land through foreclosure, these forces were probably not yet well developed in Galilee. They may have been moving in that direction (we can still debate that issue) but were still years from producing those results. The economy was too young in the first half of the first century CE.

Different Levels of Wealth

Finally, we can see a gap in the the level of wealth between the aristocrats of Galilee and the elites of Judea. If we compare the houses of the aristocrats of Sepphoris—those of the "western domestic quarter," whose inhabitants, according to E. Meyers,[19] were "well-to-do aristocratic Jews"—with aristocratic houses of Jerusalem, we notice some striking differences. The houses in Sepphoris were certainly nice by ancient standards. They had multiple rooms and a courtyard. Many had fresco paintings and some had mosaic floors. Several were multistoried. They were impressive for their time and place. But compared with the Jerusalem houses (excavated in the Jewish quarter of the old city), they were modest. For example, the "Great Mansion" of Jerusalem had a living area of 600 square meters while a large house of Sepphoris had an area of 300 square meters. The size difference alone is remarkable. Further, the small finds in the aristocratic houses of Sepphoris indicate modest wealth. Sepphorian aristocrats bone instead of ivory for cosmetic applications. They employed common pottery, not fine ware. They imported no wines.[20] Thus, based on the evidence of the houses from first-century Sepphoris discovered

18. Reed, "Galileans," 87–108; Meyers et al., "Meiron Excavation Project," 1–24; Aviam, "Galilee," 453; Aviam, *Jews, Pagans and Christians,* 41–49; and Freyne, "Archaeology and the Historical Jesus," 133–34.

19. Meyers, "Roman Sepphoris," 322.

20. Meyers, "Problems of Gendered Space," 51; Avigad, "How the Wealthy Lived."

so far (Tiberias has not been excavated adequately for such an assessment) we would have to say that the extreme distance between the elites and lower class, found elsewhere in the Roman Empire, and evidently in Judea, was diminished in Galilee. While there certainly was an economic distance between the two groups, it was not as great as in other regions.

Consideration 3

We must always consider chronology when we present a unified understanding of the Galilean economy in the late Second Temple period. This caveat is especially important with respect to the question of debt. Was peasant indebtedness widespread in Galilee? Was it at about the same level throughout the years 6–44 as it was from 45 to 66? Did it surge after direct Roman rule? Or did it gradually increase throughout these two periods? I think some scholars have assumed a more or less uniform percentage of debtors throughout the first century CE. Therefore, the invention of the *prosbul* in the first century BCE and the attack on the debt records in Jerusalem in 66 CE serve as backdrop—as historical parentheses really—to the ministry of Jesus. These two events are believed to prove that indebtedness was a major economic problem in the first century CE. Consequently, any text from the Gospels that refers to debts must confirm this conclusion.[21]

But this historical method is imprecise. We need careful definitions of what constitutes widespread indebtedness and hard evidence for it. Elsewhere I have argued[22] that the only valid evidence we have—barring the future discovery of enough data to do a statistical analysis—is a social eruption in protest of debts. Social eruptions (i.e., riots, wars, attempts at reform, and petitions for relief) imply a group effort by persons who are at their wits' end with frustration. Where we have social eruption over debts, we have indebtedness as a significant economic factor.

The only case of such a social eruption was in Jerusalem in 66 CE during the Feast of Wood-Carrying when the Sicarii broke into the upper city and set on fire the houses of Ananias the high priest and Agrippa II. Then the mob turned to the public archives to burn the debt records (*War*

---

21. Goodman, "First Jewish Revolt"; Oakman, *Jesus and the Peasants*, 11–32; Pastor, *Land and Economy*, 147–49.

22. Fiensy, "Jesus and Debts"; also above, pp. 59–66.

2.427). Josephus speculates at this point that the Sicarii hoped to win to their side a multitude of debtors.

Thus both the act of burning the archives and Josephus's reference to a multitude of debtors compel one to conclude that in the years leading up to the war of 66–73, Judea experienced ubiquitous peasant anger. Since such outbreaks mark only the boiling point in a gradually heating cauldron of dissatisfaction over spreading indebtedness, it is likely that the problem had existed for some time. The Sicarii knew well of this resentment and directed the rage of the mob toward the archives and the hated documents of indebtedness. A plausible conclusion, then, is that Judea, like many of the Greek cities in the Hellenistic period (highlighted by Rostovtzeff[23]), saw more and more peasants burdened by debt, at least in the years or decades before the war.

There are two problems with using this event as backdrop for the ministry of Jesus: First, this took place in Judea, not Galilee (see consideration #3 above). Second, even if we should use this event as also describing Galilean economics, what should we conclude about how long indebtedness had been a problem? Was indebtedness also a problem forty years prior to this event, when Jesus was teaching and preaching? There is simply no way to answer that question based on the evidence. Therefore, one cannot conclude that pervasive indebtedness existed in Galilee in the earlier part of the first century CE and that it served as historical and economic backdrop to the ministry of Jesus.

Consideration 4

The nature of the data is fragmentary. This fact should both cause us to be cautious in our conclusions and to press for more data of the appropriate type. The central question in the "economy wars" (i.e. the debates between some Galilean archaeologists and some of those New Testament scholars utilizing social-science models) is about the standard of living of the Galilean folk in the late Second Temple period. Was the standard of living rising, falling, or remaining the same? It is a law of modern economics that standard of living is tied to productivity.[24] Standard of living may be defined not only as the acquisition of possessions but also as nutrition levels and longevity.[25] Only when a society produces more goods

---

23. Rostovtzeff, *Hellenistic World*, 1:141.

24. Mankiw, *Principles of Macroeconomics*, 11–12.

25. Ibid. Here we might add a note of gratitude to Douglas Oakman, who was

and services does standard of living go up. But how does one find data in archaeological remains to inform us about productivity?

Ian Morris[26] calls for studies of the ancient folk to determine their stature, nutrition, mortality, morbidity, and housing. He asks for more attention to floral, faunal, and pollen remains to determine diet. In the end, he laments the general lack of information in most of these areas and settles on housing alone to make his case that the standard of living increased in Greece from the eighth to the third centuries BCE. His study of three hundred houses indicates, remarkably, that house sizes increased five- or sixfold in that span, and he concludes that there must have been "a dramatic improvement in the standard of living." Therefore, Morris rejects Moses Finley's ancient-economy model in which there was "essentially static economic performance."[27] Morris's study is most interesting, and I agree with his call to see more data on the skeletal remains (to determine stature, nutrition, morbidity and mortality) before I conclude that the standard of living for most persons improved in Lower Galilee. There are still questions I have about primarily using housing as the measure for standard of living: Have poorly constructed houses left any traces? Were not most houses do-it-yourself constructions like the log cabins of the American frontier? To what extent do house sizes reflect cultural as opposed to economic factors?

It seems to me that those arguing for a prosperous Galilee in the late Second Temple period focus, as Morris does, mostly on constructions, especially houses, and secondarily, on market opportunities. I know of no studies like Ian Morris's with respect to Galilee, but it is common to cite the nice houses in Gamla, Khirbet Qana, and Yodefat, as evidence that the peasants were not poverty-stricken, but that, on the contrary, the economy was booming. The houses are well constructed and did not seem to have deteriorated because of inability to maintain them.[28]

There also may have been more industry in Galilee than elsewhere in Palestine/Israel during this period, indicating more market exchange. The pottery of Kefar Hananya and Kefar Shikhin has been featured in

calculating average daily caloric intake for the ancient Palestinian people before most New Testament scholars even thought about it. See Oakman, *Economic Questions*, 58–59. Another New Testament scholar who considered this important issue was Jeremias, *Jerusalem*, 122–23.

26. Morris, "Archaeology," 107.

27. Ibid., 123, 107.

28. Richardson, *Building Jewish*, 57–71. See also pp. 132–42 of this volume.

studies of D. Adan-Bayewitz and I. Perlman[29] and in studies of J. Strange, D. Groh, and T. Longstaff.[30] Mordecai Aviam rightly stresses the olive-oil industry of Galilee;[31] Y. Magen has reported on stone-vessel factories in Galilee;[32] and J. Strange notes the availability of roads and travel in Galilee.[33]

The conclusions often drawn from this analysis are (1) The cities with their wealthy elites must not have exploited the peasants who lived in the villages but rather must have given them opportunities for marketing their goods and thus improved their economic opportunities. (2) The villages not only engaged in farming but had industries as well, and these industries elevated the economic life (the standard of living) of the village peasants.[34]

One should not discount this evidence. These data are part of what is needed for us to understand the Galilean economy. But as Morris observes, we need more examination of human remains. I realize in Israel this is much more difficult than in Greece. But some attention to analysis of bones, asking whether there was a protein or iron deficiency, if done in several sites, could be quite revealing.

One reason to ask for human pathological data is because of data from the Meiron excavation report. Although some of the houses were nice—one elaborate one was dubbed the "Patrician House"[35]—there were interesting results in the examination of the skeletal remains. First, there was a high rate of child mortality.[36] Second, a pathological examination of the children's skulls revealed that most had protein and iron deficiencies. The examiners concluded that these deficiencies were caused either by disease or "socioeconomic conditions" (i.e., poverty). In other words, the

29. Adan-Bayewitz and Perlman, "Local Trade"; and Adan-Bayewitz, *Common Pottery*.

30. Strange et al., "Location and Identification of Shikhin, Part I."

31. Aviam, *Jews, Pagans and Christians*, 51–57.

32. Magen, *The Stone Vessel Industry*.

33. Strange, "First-Century Galilee," 39–41.

34. See Adan-Bayewitz, *Common Pottery*, 23–41, 216–36; Strange, "First-Century Galilee," 41; Edwards, "Urban/Rural Relations," 169–82.

35. Meyers et al., *Excavations at Ancient Meiron*, 50–72.

36. See Hachlili and Smith, "Genealogy," 67–71, esp. 69. The children from 0–19 years of age in the Meiron tombs represented 47 percent of the total. This is roughly the same as the average percentage of children of that age in Greek tombs (49 percent) but much higher than for the tombs of Jericho (39 percent, a first-century-CE tomb) and two tombs in Jerusalem (43 percent, also from the first century).

children may have been malnourished.[37] So the presence of nice houses does not necessarily indicate how equitable the economy was and thus may not reveal the overall standard of living. This case is intriguing since Meiron was a village in Galilee, but also ambiguous since this village tomb was used from the first century BCE until the fourth century CE.[38]

Some recent skeletal examinations have been done by M. Aviam in his excavations of Yodefat. At the SBL meeting in Boston in 2008 he reported on an examination of around twenty-five skeletons out of the 2,500 found at the site. He reported that they all "looked healthy."[39] This report is enormously helpful. But we need to enlarge the sample size to feel comfortable about any statistical results.

Neither housing construction nor evidence of trade is sufficient—though, again, these are important clues—as the determiner of the Galilean standard of living. But there is a kind of construction more helpful in determining standard of living. Again—if we are to live by the principles of modern economists—standard of living rises only if productivity rises. Thus finding some nice houses does not alone settle for us the efficiency of the economy (i.e., the size of the pie) or the equity of the economy (i.e., the size of the slice of pie the average family received).[40] But there may be a type of construction that would be more relevant. If we could show that family grain silos were increasing in size in the first century CE, that would go a long way toward settling this issue.

Consideration 5

Understanding the function of social-science models should make us more judicious in our use of them. Like economists, sociologists and anthropologists construct models to assist them in interpreting the data. I. Morris and J. G. Manning observe:

> While humanists tend to work from a specific body of texts and to focus on particulars, economists tend to begin from

37. Smith et al., "Skeletal Remains" in Meyers et al., *Excavations at Ancient Meiron*, 110–20. There were 197 individuals in this tomb. Ninety-five of them were under age 18. Seventy percent of the 95 persons were younger than five years.

38. One must be cautious even in assessing the nutritional evidence from human remains. Cereal-based economies in general could result in deficiencies even though there might be enough food to eat. See MacDonald, *What Did the Ancient Israelites Eat?*, 80–87.

39. Aviam, "Economy and Social Structure."

40. Mankiw, *Principles of Macroeconomics*, 5, 11.

propositions, drawing out logical implications that can be op-
erationalized . . . The data are there to test the hypothesis, not to
be enjoyed or understood in their own terms.[41]

We might substitute in this quotation Galilean archaeologists for
humanists and social-science interpreters for economists. Those New
Testament scholars utilizing the social-science models operate similarly
to the economists in the quotation. They appropriate an existing model
and investigate its efficacy in explaining a text in the New Testament.
They ask, Can the disparate data be better understood if they are unified
by the construction of a sociologist or anthropologist? They tend to work
more deductively (though they prefer the term "abduction"[42]) while the
archaeologists work more inductively.

I would like to propose five caveats to those using the social-science
models, or to those refusing to use such models.

1. The model should not be based on only one social theory (e.g.,
   functionalism, class conflict, Marxism) but should be eclectic.

2. The model should have been informed by a study of ancient societies. Models based only on abstractions from contemporary societies
   may be anachronistic.

3. The model should be cross-cultural. Models formulated from observations only from Western Europe or the United States may not
   be relevant to the ancient economy.

4. The model should not become "proxy data." This term is used by
   classical historians for comparing ancient societies with "relevantly
   similar" contemporary ones.[43] Proxy data, as I understand them,
   are hypothetical scenarios not supplied by the ancient evidence but
   by "likelihood, analogy, or comparison."[44] For example, someone
   reasoned that Pompeii did not sell much wine outside its own city
   limits by calculating the amount of grain needed to feed its citizens.[45]
   I would say, these methods are interesting and show us possibilities
   but should not be trusted as hard evidence.

   Thus when New Testament scholars assume that more and
   more land in Galilee was being gobbled up by the wealthy, and that,

41. Morris and Manning, *Ancient Economy*, 29.
42. See, e.g., Neyrey, "Preface," xxii.
43. Cartledge, "The Economy (Economics) of Ancient Greece," 17, 21, 22.
44. Andreau, "Twenty Years," 39.
45. Ibid.

therefore, the average peasant was on the verge of losing his land, we may justifiably ask for evidence. One recent work, for example, states, "Estates grew and tenancy increased as economies of scale for cash crops were created."[46] We can agree with this statement if one is speaking in general about the ancient Greco-Roman world or even about Palestine/Israel as a whole. But we need to know whether there is hard data (archaeological or literary) that show that there were large estates in Lower Galilee and that these estates were both increasing in size and multiplying.

5. On the other hand, those rejecting social science models out of hand need to sound a cautionary note. We do need the models.

As K. Hopkins observes:

> The model is a sort of master picture, as on the front of a jigsaw puzzle box; the fragments of surviving ancient sources provide only a few of the jigsaw pieces.[47]

Models help us sketch out the social, economic, or cultural picture, much like an artist's reconstruction of an archaeological ruin. Without some kind of model, we are left only to talk about the individual pieces. Models may also help us examine our own bias both in selecting the sources to examine and in interpreting them. The best way to think about a social-science model is to regard it as a working hypothesis, a sort of template on which one places data. Any good historian must always be ready to affirm, edit, or reject the hypothesis based on the data.

Thus Sean Freyne has used the model of Thomas Carney, a kind of threefold barometric reading, to conclude that economic changes were happening in first-century-CE Galilee. These three "elements" help Freyne to focus his research and to organize his data. They assist him in getting beyond what he calls the "intuitivist" approach (the "hit or miss aspect") which leaves one open to unstated biases.[48]

We all approach the data with some sort of a priori. The classical historians now challenging Finley's primitivist economic theory approach the evidence with modernist theory. It is not a question of whether one will use a model, but of which model consciously or not one will select. As the social-science interpreters repeatedly remind us, we need to reflect

46. Crossan and Reed, *Excavating Jesus,* 70.
47. Hopkins, "Rome, Taxes, Rents and Trade," 191.
48. Freyne, "Herodian Economics," 23, 46. See also Carney, *Shape of the Past.*

on the social-science models because they can guard against twin errors of "ethnocentrism and anachronism."[49]

I offer one example. When one archaeologist claims that Galilee in the time of Jesus was, "a largely egalitarian society,"[50] and that New Testament scholars who think otherwise have been influenced by Marxist historians who invented the ancient social tensions, it gives one pause. The term *egalitarian* might apply to fifth-century-BCE Athens but not to very many other places. Even there we find slaves and noncitizens. Egalitarianism is a modern concept that has been anachronistically imposed on late Second Temple Galilee.

Those who argue for economic prosperity and even egalitarianism in first-century Palestine/Israel need to remember the Jewish War of 66–73 CE. Neither did it sprang to life overnight, nor was it only about religion. In Judea at least, if we can credit Josephus's account, there was a simultaneous class war alongside the war against the Romans. During the procuratorship of Felix (52–60 CE), certain bands of ruffians looted the houses of Jewish nobles, killing their owners (*War* 2.264). Once war broke out in 66 CE, a full-scale campaign against the wealthy followed, begun by the Sicarii, the Zealots, and the followers of Simon bar Giora (*War* 2.426–28, 652; 4.140–45, 315, 327, 335, 358; 5.309, 439–41, 527–32). Elsewhere, when we see uprisings in the Roman Empire (or anywhere else for that matter), we naturally assume that socioeconomic factors played at least some role. The question is, of course, was Judea at that time significantly more stressed economically than Galilee?

Conclusion

In the last thirty years remarkable gains have been made in understanding Galilee in the late Second Temple period. This is a credit both to fine archaeological work and to the study of the insights of the social sciences. We must continue to use all the resources available as we advance this pursuit. I, for one, intend to drink from both wells in assessing Lower Galilee in the late Second Temple period. I have enjoyed immensely sampling the mineral waters of each camp. But neither well alone seems to quench my thirst. Mixed together, however, they form a refreshing draft that strengthens one to move forward in the quest.

49. See Neyrey, "Preface," xxiii; Malina, "Rhetorical Criticism," 17; Neyrey and Stewart, *Social World*, 201; Malina and Neyrey, "Ancient Mediterranean Persons," 258.

50. Groh, "Clash," 32.

8

Domestic Space and
Standard of Living

Does the Size of a House Indicate
the Wealth of the Family?

SCHOLARS OF CLASSICAL HISTORY are going through a revolution in their thinking about the ancient economy. In particular, they are debating the usefulness of certain classicists' (e.g., Moses Finley's[1]) assumptions and methods for understanding and researching the Greco-Roman world. Those studying the economy of Galilee in the late Second Temple period are also involved in this debate but often not aware of its counterpart among classical scholars.

The current quest for the historical Galilee is a study in contrasts: 1) Some look at Galilee through the lenses of cultural anthropology and macrosociology; others look at Galilee through the lenses of archaeology and reject the use of social theories. 2) Some maintain that the relations between rural villages and the cities were hostile; others propose that the relationship was one of economic reciprocity and goodwill. 3) Some suggest that Galilee was typical of other agrarian societies—with poor peasants who lived in the rural areas, and exploitative wealthy people who lived mostly in the cities; others respond that life was pretty good for everyone in Galilee and that it was an egalitarian society. By those arguing for a prosperous Galilee a great emphasis has been placed on

1. Finley, *Ancient Economy*.

domestic space. This chapter will highlight this area of disagreement at play in the study of the economy of the Roman Empire which also plays a role in the current debate over the historical Galilee.

House Sizes and Standard of Living

Since the days of Moses Finley it has been a given in many academic circles that the ancient economy was essentially stagnant. The overall level neither improved nor, for that matter, deteriorated throughout antiquity. Finley believed that the ancients were limited not only in technology but in their ideology and thus the economy was doomed to stagnation. [2]

But of late that doctrine is being challenged. R. Bruce Hitchener,[3] in two essays, has pointed to a significant increase—from the first century CE until the third century CE—in olive-oil production, in planting larger vineyards, in livestock raising, in cereal cultivation, and in the harvesting of marine resources. This was a period of increased population and the growth of cities. Hitchener maintains that the economy and standard of living improved dramatically.

Ian Morris has also argued for an increase in the standard of living in the Early Roman to Late Roman periods. He has observed that archaeology is undermining what had been called the Finley orthodoxy. Morris calls for studies of the ancient folk to determine their stature, nutrition, mortality, morbidity, and housing. He asks for more attention to floral, faunal, and pollen remains to determine diet.[4] In the end, however, he laments the general lack of information in most of these areas, and settles on housing alone to make his case. The archaeological remains of houses demonstrate to him that the standard of living increased in Greece from the eighth to the third centuries BCE. His study of three hundred houses indicates, remarkably, that house sizes increased fivefold in that span and he, therefore, concludes that there must have been "a dramatic improvement in the standard of living." Table 8.1 demonstrates Morris's evidence. Morris gives both the mean and median sizes of the houses for each period. He distrusts using simply the mean sizes since a few very large houses in the fourth century would skew the evidence. But even considering

2. Morris, "Foreword," xxix. For the Finley "orthodoxy" see xxiv and xxxv and n. 46.

3. Hitchener, "Olive Production"; Hitchener, "Advantages of Wealth and Luxury."

4. Morris, "Archaeology," 107.

mostly the median sizes, the increase in size is remarkable. Therefore, Morris rejects Moses Finley's ancient-economy model in which there was "essentially static economic performance."[5]

Table 8.1: Morris's Evidence for the Rise in Standards of Living in Greece from 800 BCE to 300 BCE[6]

PERIOD	MEAN SIZE OF HOUSES	MEDIAN SIZE OF HOUSES
800–700	53 m²	51 m²
c. 700	69 m²	56 m²
700–600	53 m²	45 m²
600–500	92 m²	67 m²
500–400	122 m²	106 m²
400–300	325 m²	240 m²

Morris's study of housing size is most interesting, but I have questions about primarily using domestic space as the measure for standard of living: First, can space alone (i.e., square meters) be a sufficient indicator of standard of living? Here I intend to raise three issues connected to the domicile that should be noted. Second, I agree with Morris's call to see more data on the skeletal remains (to determine stature, nutrition, morbidity and mortality) before I conclude that the standard of living for most persons improved in, e.g., Lower Galilee. The general health (or lack of health) should conform to housing evidence. Third, I offer the question, to what extent do house sizes reflect cultural as opposed to economic factors? Here I will raise two issues. Fourth, I ask were not most houses do-it-yourself constructions like the log cabins of the American frontier? If a family builds the house themselves, they may make it any size they please. We will return to these questions later.

Keeping these questions in mind, I here first follow Morris's lead in comparing housing sizes in Palestine between the Hellenistic and the Byzantine eras to determine if the size (in square meters) of the domestic space increased. By "domestic space" I mean not only the buildings under roof but the courtyards as well. I intend also to ask if the increase/

5. Ibid., 123, 107.
6. Ibid., 110.

decrease or essential stasis of housing sizes is an effective indicator of standard of living.

Did Domestic Space Increase?

Our base of data will be the work of Yizhar Hirschfeld,[7] who gathered dimensions on more than fifty houses spanning the Hellenistic to the Byzantine periods. The tables presented here are based mostly on his work. We must offer several cautions before we look at these results. First, one may ask if Hirschfeld's sample size is adequate. Analyzing fifty-plus houses is certainly not as satisfying as Morris's analysis of over three hundred houses. Second, one may ask about Hirschfeld's selection of the houses he has described. How and why did he select the houses included in his monograph? Thus, one cannot claim to be comparing Hirschfeld's results with equal sampling given by Morris. Yet this work does offer at least a preliminary comparison. The advantages of choosing Hirschfeld's data include that he presents us with a widely spread assortment of houses from the Golan, Upper Galilee, Lower Galilee, Samaria, Judea, and the Negev; second, Hirschfeld's houses cover the periods from the Hellenistic through the Byzantine (and five houses from later periods), which is exactly the time period of interest to me in my investigation of the standard of living in Galilee in the late Second Temple Period. Thus, Hirschfeld is comprehensive in scope if not exhaustive.

Table 8.2 gives the mean and median house sizes by archaeological periods[8] (in imitation of Morris's example in Table 8.1[9]). The difference between Hirschfeld and Morris is that Morris gave only housing dimensions of those portions "probably roofed." Hirschfeld included the courtyards as well, a significant difference. According to these figures, the Early Roman period saw the largest house sizes on average. There is no evidence of house sizes gradually improving, as Morris found in his study. Based on this comparison, if one wants to tie standard of living to average house sizes, the standard of living fluctuated rather freely in ancient Palestine. If we follow the median sizes (preferred by Morris),

7. Hirschfeld, *Palestinian Dwelling*.

8. Hell: 333–37 BCE; ER: 37 BCE—70 CE; MR: 70–250 CE; LR: 250–363 CE; Byz: 363–640 CE.

9. Morris, "Archaeology," 108.

there was a decline in standard of living from the Early Roman period through the Late Roman period.

Table 8.2: Average Size of Palestinian Houses by Period[10]

ARCHAEOLOGICAL PERIOD	MEAN SIZE OF HOUSES[11]	MEDIAN SIZE OF HOUSES	SAMPLE SIZE
Hellenistic	297 m²	925m²	5 houses
Early Roman	761 m²	1425m²	13 houses
Middle Roman	380 m²	1065m²	11 houses
Late Roman	180 m²	190m²	6 houses
Byzantine	348 m²	460m²	14 houses

But analyzing housing sizes by chronological periods is complicated because it fails to consider other factors. One of these factors is architectural type. Table 8.3, also formed from Hirschfeld's data, shows this complication.

Hirschfeld found four main housing types: The simple house, the most basic and common type, consisted of one main structure built onto an open courtyard. The complex house was simply an expansion of a simple-house type. The courtyard house was a courtyard surrounded on all four sides by dwelling structures. Finally, the peristyle house or atrium house was a Greco-Roman innovation. It consisted of an inner garden surrounded by columns and rooms.[12] As Table 8.3 shows, the complex house, by virtue of its architecture, usually occupied the most space. Yet would one maintain that the complex houses were more expensive or lavish than the courtyard houses or especially the peristyle houses? One can also note that the simple and courtyard houses were the most popular (at least according to Hirschfeld's data).

10. Based on Hirschfeld, *Palestinian Dwelling*, 21–101. Compare Hirschfeld's data with that collected by Richard Alston, who compared housing sizes in Roman Egypt. He found very little change in sizes from one (lower level) of excavation of the village of Karanis to a later level. The mean area went from 73 m² to 75 m². See Alston, "Houses and Households in Roman Egypt," 25–39, esp. 28.

11. Hirschfeld usually includes the courtyard in the measurement of the house size.

12. Hirschfeld, *Palestinian Dwelling*, 21–22, 85.

Table 8.3: Hirschfeld's Architectural Typology[13]

House type	Average size	Sample size	Houses by chronological period
Simple houses	130 m²	19 houses	2 ER, 2 MR, 5 LR, 7 Byz, 3 other
Complex houses	1010 m²	8 houses	3 ER, 1 MR, 2 Byz, 2 other
Courtyard houses	569 m²	21 houses	4 Hell, 5 ER, 7 MR, 4 Byz, 1 other
Peristyle houses	793 m²	8 houses	1 Hell, 3 ER, 1 MR, 1 LR, 2 Byz

Another complicating factor was the location. One needs to ask where the houses were built: in a city, town, village, or on an isolated farm? Table 8.4 indicates that the largest houses tended to be built in the towns and on the isolated farms. Was this because the cities and villages tended to squeeze the houses together and thus leave less ground space for building? According to this table, the cities had house sizes similar to the villages. At any rate, just estimating standard of living based on house sizes can be quite deceptive.

Table 8.4: Average Size of Palestinian Houses Arranged by Location[14]

City	299 m²
Town	607 m²
Village	298 m²
Farmhouse	867 m²
Villa	961 m²

Is Domestic Space a Reliable Predictor of Standard of Living?

Was the standard of living rising, falling, or remaining the same in the Palestine of the Hellenistic Period through the Byzantine period? First, let us define standard of living. Standard of living may be defined not only as the acquisition of possessions but also as nutrition levels and

13. Ibid., 100–101.
14. Ibid.

longevity.[15] It is a law of modern economics that standard of living is tied to productivity.[16] Only when a society produces more goods and services does standard of living go up. But how does one find data in archaeological remains to inform us about productivity? The best we can do is to look for indirect evidence of standard of living. This conclusion brings us back to the four questions I asked above.

QUESTION 1: ONLY SQUARE METERS?

So, is domestic space a reliable predictor of standard of living? It may be an indication but the economic picture was much more complicated. First, what about the way the domicile was constructed? Were the stones hewn, hammered (i.e., partially hewn), or simply fieldstones picked up off the ground? What were the furnishings of the house? Were there frescoed walls or marble floors? Is there evidence of the use of a professional builder or architect? A well-constructed, luxuriously furnished house of modest dimensions could indicate quite a high standard of living.

It seems to me that those arguing for a prosperous Galilee in the late Second Temple period focus, as Morris does, mostly on constructions, especially houses, and secondarily, on market opportunities. I know of no studies like Ian Morris's with respect to Galilee, but it is common to cite the nice houses in Gamla, Khirbet Qana, and Yodefat as evidence that the villagers were not poverty-stricken, but that, on the contrary, the economy was booming. Some of the houses were well constructed and did not seem to have deteriorated because of inability to maintain them.[17] One or two of them were even rather elaborate, with frescoed walls. The conclusion is usually, then, that the economy was on the rise, and that people were in general doing rather well for themselves in Lower Galilee leading up to the Jewish War of 66–73 CE. This evidence is more nuanced than Morris's mere measurement of space and therefore, in my judgment, more reliable.

---

15. Mankiw, *Principles of Macroeconomics*, 11–12. See also Hitchener, "Advantages of Wealth and Luxury," who notes that economic growth should be defined by rise in real income per capita and also in population.

16. Mankiw, *Principles of Macroeconomics*, 11–12; Colander ibid., 177.

17. Richardson, *Building Jewish*, 57–71.

QUESTION 2: WHAT DO THE SKELETAL REMAINS INDICATE?

Do they harmonize with the architecture? One reason to ask for human pathological data in Palestine, as Ian Morris has done in general, is because of data from the Meiron excavation report. Although some of the houses were nice (one elaborate one was dubbed the "Patrician House"[18]), there were interesting results in the examination of the skeletal remains. First, there was a high rate of child mortality.[19] Second, a pathological examination of the children's skulls revealed that most had protein and iron deficiencies. The examiners concluded that these deficiencies were caused either by disease or "socioeconomic conditions" (i.e., poverty). In other words, the children may have been malnourished.[20] So the presence of nice houses does not necessarily indicate how equitable the economy was and thus may not reveal the overall standard of living. This case is intriguing since Meiron was a village in Galilee, but also ambiguous since this village tomb was used from the first century BCE until the fourth century CE.[21]

Some recent skeletal examinations have been done by M. Aviam in his excavations of Yodefat. At the SBL meeting in Boston in 2008 he reported on an examination of around twenty-five skeletons out of the 2,500 found at the site. He reported that they all "looked healthy."[22] This report is enormously helpful. But we need to enlarge the sample size to feel comfortable about any statistical results since Aviam's examination only equals 1 percent of the total.

---

18. Meyers et al., *Ancient Meiron*, 50–72.

19. See Hachlili and Smith, "Genealogy," 67–71, esp. 69. The children from 0–19 years of age in the Meiron tombs represented 47 percent of the total. This is roughly the same as the average percentage of children of that age in Greek tombs (49 percent) but much higher than for the tombs of Jericho (39 percent, a first-century-CE tomb) and two tombs in Jerusalem (43 percent, also from the first century).

20. Smith et al., "Skeletal Remains," 110–20. There were 197 individuals in this tomb. Ninety-five of them were under age 18. Seventy percent of the 95 persons were younger than five years.

21. One must be cautious even in assessing the nutritional evidence from human remains. Cereal-based economies in general could result in deficiencies even though there might be enough food to eat. See MacDonald, *What Did the Ancient Israelites Eat?*, 80–87.

22. Aviam, "Economy and Social Structure in First-Century Galilee."

QUESTION 3: WHAT ABOUT CULTURAL ISSUES?

Cultural pressures may have kept some houses smaller than the residents could afford, and made others look larger. In the first place, one needs to consider how far "belief systems" influenced house sizes rather than purely economic standing. Morris also ponders this question. He asks, how did people want to dwell? Did some prefer being closely clustered together even if they could afford a more spacious living arrangement? Were smaller dwellings based on poverty or on an ideal of "commitment to restraint and community homogeneity"? He concludes that housing designs may tell more about the ideology than economics.[23] Works written by contemporary residents of traditional villages in the Middle East express such an ideology. For example, the description of the typical "one roomed peasant home" in Palestine (obviously in a traditional village) is of a 35 m^2 dwelling with three major "areas" (not rooms): the living space and the storage space on the upper level and the lower level (underground) for livestock.[24] The authors of this monograph indicate that the building materials are plentiful and (evidently) free.[25] So why not build a larger dwelling? Or more appropriately, why *would* one? Why would one need anything larger?

Another issue in considering size of domestic space as an indicator of standard of living is the question of multiple households using the same structure. Richard Alston has warned of this error in logic in his study of houses in ancient Egypt. He advises against "simply correlating the area of ground plan to social status," because some of the large houses in his survey undoubtedly held multiple families. He concludes, "Since multiple-roomed houses could easily be divided between different domestic units, it is possible that those residing in a small house may have had a greater area per person than those residing in a large house."[26] Thus, house size alone may not indicate an increased standard of living but actually may show a decreased standard of living.

23. Morris, "Archaeology," 114–15.

24. See Amiry and Tamari, *Palestinian Village Home,* 27.

25. Ibid., 25.

26. Alston, "Houses and Households in Roman Egypt," 28–29.

Question 4: What about Do-It-Yourself Houses?

Finally, we asked above about houses built by the family from materials gathered free of charge in the neighborhood. Hirschfeld narrates how this was done by contemporaneous traditional villagers in Israel and compares his observations with the comments from the rabbinic literature. The process seems largely unchanged. The family gathered stones, earth for mortar, sticks, and lime. There may or may not have been a village master builder to supervise the construction (based on a house plan kept in his head). One is free to build as large a house as one has the energy to build it. The houses tended to be pretty similar. Thus, it is not simply the size but the luxury items and construction features that would be more definitive in determining the wealth of the occupants.

Housing construction alone is not sufficient—though it may be one clue—as the determiner of standard of living. But I propose that there could be a kind of construction more helpful in determining standard of living. Again—if we are to live by the principles of modern economists— standard of living rises only if productivity rises. Thus finding some large houses does not alone settle for us the efficiency of the economy (i.e., the size of the pie) or the equity of the economy (i.e., the size of the slice of pie the average family received).[27] But there may be a type of construction that would be more relevant. If we could show that family grain silos were increasing in size in the first century CE, it might go a long way toward settling this issue. This line of evidence is like that proposed by Hitchener and alluded to earlier. This type of argument and evidence seem to me much more helpful and convincing than arguing from house sizes.

So, where does all of this leave us? Did the standard of living increase in the late Second Temple Period and on into the Late Roman/Byzantine periods? Perhaps the answer given this question by Richard Saller[28] is the best. Saller answers yes and no. Saller cautions that in looking at increases of olive-oil production in one region or of cereal production in another, one must distinguish between per-capita growth and aggregate growth. There may be astounding growth in one region but not throughout the empire. The total economic production may increase but only because the population (and thus the number of workers) increased. Second, Saller warns that "scale of growth over time" is critical.[29] Saller concedes

---

27. Mankiw, *Principles of Macroeconomics*, 5, 11.

28. Saller, "Framing the Debate," 223–38.

29. See his tables in Saller, "Framing the Debate," 229–30.

that there was economic growth and growth in standard of living in the ancient economy starting around 100 BCE and peaking at the turn of the era until around 100 CE, whereupon it began to drop off again. But the rise in growth in GDP per capita was very slight.[30] He asks if the ancient people felt it and concludes that maybe they did but only marginally. To the modern economist this rise would hardly be noticeable. Was it noticeable to the ancients? Perhaps so, opines Saller. But he surmises that life did not change much for the ancients. Life expectancy remained low, and this should be factored in any estimation of standard of living. Thus Saller's cautious conclusion that we should imagine not significant growth but "gentle growth" seems to me wisest.

Conclusion

First, the methodology of Ian Morris, although a good starting point, must not be taken as a sound indicator of economic standard of living. Morris did not factor housing types and housing locations. We saw that certain styles tended to be larger, and that the houses of the countryside and the towns also tended to be larger. Second, there are other factors that complicate the picture. One is the excellence of construction. A rather small house constructed with the oversight of a professional architect, built with hewn stones, and furnished with the marks of wealth evidences a higher standard of living than a large domestic area constructed of fieldstones by the family. Finally, we reiterate Morris's call for more evidence of a pathological examination of skeletal remains. The human remains should harmonize with the architecture. Malnourished villagers would not live in fine houses. Their remains may indicate housing that has not survived.

30. GDP per capita refers to the total economic output (all goods and services produced in a year) divided by the number of persons. For modern data on GDP per capita for comparison, see Nation Master, "Economy Statistics." See also *Wikipedia*, "List of Countries by GDP." The *Wikipedia* essay's figures I give here are based on the International Monetary Fund's data. For example the lowest GDP per capita was the Democratic Republic of Congo in 2011 at $348. The highest was Qatar at an amazing $102,943 (in the year 2011). The United States GDP per capita was $48,387 in 2011.

PART THREE

The Early Church

9

Poverty and Wealth in the Jerusalem Church

"The believers were so close to one another and so united no one considered any of his possessions to belong to himself. Rather they considered all things to be owned in common. The apostles gave powerful testimony that Jesus the Lord had risen from the dead and great grace was on all of them. No one among them was needy because those who possessed lands or houses would sell them, and bringing the proceeds from the sale, would lay them at the apostles' feet who would distribute them to each one as there was a need." (Acts 4:32–34, author's translation)

WITH THESE WORDS THE author of Acts summarizes for us the remarkable experience of the Jerusalem church in the early stages of its existence. The church in this period of time demonstrated a unity of purpose and a sense of love and community that stand as models for the modern church. That period was one of exceptional self-sacrifice and sharing on the part of many of the wealthier disciples in order to care for the needy. Everyone so focused on the risen Christ that material possessions seemed unimportant. What was important was maintaining the life of the community of believers so that the testimony about the risen Christ could continue unimpeded. This was an ideal period in the history of the church, an experience that has only rarely been repeated. Even if the author has idealized the era, there is no good reason to doubt that some believers divested themselves of property.

What this text in Acts (and related ones) should mean precisely for the life of the church, however, has not found general agreement either in ancient or modern times. Some in the ancient church wanted every Christian to sell their possessions upon conversion and live as a pauper. Others believed that that way of life was only for those in a monastic order, while the ordinary Christian might still own property.[1] The reformers for the most part, except for the Anabaptists, saw this as a singular act for a particular time, which was the result of the leading of the Holy Spirit. In the nineteenth century some who dreamed of creating a utopia on earth referred to this period in the church as early Christian communism and sought to imitate the practice.[2]

The text remains a point of confusion. Most modern Christians in the Western world find the passage an embarrassment since for them capitalism and property ownership seem as natural and right as Christianity itself. Indeed, some even preach that God wants a Christian to become wealthy.

We want to address anew, therefore, what this text means. First, we shall ask, what was the problem? Then, what did the Jerusalem church do and why did they do it? Finally, what timeless lesson abides for the modern church?

The Problem

The problem to which this text in Acts alludes has been variously explained as follows:

1. This is an emergency situation brought about by the conversion of so many Jewish pilgrims who had been present for the feast of Pentecost (Acts 2:1, 9–11). Around three thousand people were baptized during the feast (Acts 2:41), and it is likely that many of these were not natives of Jerusalem or even Palestine. These pilgrim converts have remained in Jerusalem to continue as members of the community of believers but have no means of financial support.[3]

---

1. See Newhauser, *Early History of Greed*; Pesch, *Apostelgeschichte*, 189–92; Fiensy, *Jesus the Galilean*, 129–31.

2. Pesch, *Die Aostelgeschichte*, 189–92

3. Boles, *Acts*, 76.

2. Many elderly people came to Jerusalem to wait for their death, thinking it more righteous to die in the holy city (Luke 2:25, 36). These people were usually poor.[4]

3. Most of Jesus's disciples, who became the core of the Jerusalem church, were from Galilee. But many of these Galileans had sold everything in order to follow Jesus (Matt 10:28–30). Thus the Galileans were now impoverished.[5]

The first explanation probably has some validity. Converted Jewish pilgrims no doubt did contribute to the financial burden of the church. But the extent of this problem is questionable even if we accept literally the number three thousand (Acts 2:41). We should not assume that most converted pilgrims remained very long in Jerusalem, nor should we assume they were paupers. That they should make the trip to Jerusalem from Asia Minor, Greece, Egypt, Italy, or elsewhere indicates they must have possessed some means.

The second explanation is problematic because this phenomenon is not well attested in the sources. We cannot know if such people were numerous.[6] Again, however, this social group may have contributed somewhat to the financial burden of the church.

The third explanation has difficulties also. Peter is not quoted as saying in Mark 10:28 that the Galileans have in every case *sold* their possessions and have followed Jesus, but that a few of them have *left* everything (αφηκαμεν παντα). Some archaeologists believe, as a matter of fact, that they have found Peter's house in Capernaum, which remained in his possession and became a house church in the first century CE.[7] Further, were all of the 120 initially gathered persons (Acts 1:15) Galileans? That is hardly likely since the Galilean disciples seem to have followed Jesus in his itinerant ministry. That 120 people followed Jesus around, being fed by contributions from people whom Jesus encountered seems improbable. Thus how many Galileans would there have been in the Jerusalem church?

4. Batey, *Jesus and the Poor,* 36.

5. Jacquier, *Actes,* 147; Haenchen, *Die Apostelgeschichte,* 196.

6. There is one attested case known to me of bringing back the bones of a deceased person to be buried in Jerusalem (see Naveh, "New Tomb Inscription," 73) but this is not the same as returning to Jerusalem to die.

7. Corbo, *House of St. Peter,* 35–52; Strange and Shanks, "House Where Jesus Stayed," 26–37.

4. The best way to understand the problem that the Jerusalem church solved by its generosity is to view the situation in terms of its broad social and economic context. We see no reason to appeal to special circumstances or an emergency as is usually done. The situation is quite understandable in light of the ongoing problem of poverty in Jerusalem.

The broad picture of the economic, social, and political structure (the three were inextricably intertwined) of Palestine in the first century could be painted principally with two colors: the elite and the poor. The elite were almost always large landowners who lived in the cities as absentee landlords. Beginning in the Hellenistic period and accelerating in the Early Roman, a movement toward concentrating more and more land into the hands of fewer and fewer people brought two results: The first result was a circle of extremely wealthy elites who lived sumptuously in the cities off the profits of their lands. The second result was that more and more peasants in the countryside (especially Judea) began losing their land to the wealthy land entrepreneurs.[8]

The wealthy in Jerusalem were composed, first, of the four main high-priestly families (Boethus, Hanan, Kathros, and Phiabi); that is, those powerful and extraordinarily rich families that controlled the high-priesthood almost exclusively in the first century CE.[9] To this circle of the powerful wealthy also belonged certain lay aristocrats sometimes called "notables," "elders," "powerful ones," or "first men" (*War* 2.410, 411; *Life* 9; Mark 15:1).

The wealthy elites lived for the most part in large mansions in the western part of Jerusalem on the mountain overlooking the Tyropean Valley. There the air was fresher and cooler, far removed from the stinking hovels in the valley. Not only do the ancient literary sources indicate this place of residence, but archaeologists have recently excavated several large houses belonging obviously to wealthy people. One of these houses even contained an inscription that indicated the house belonged to a member of the high-priestly family called Kathros.[10]

---

8. Hengel, *Poverty and Riches*, 15–16; Applebaum, "Economic Life in Palestine," 631–700; MacMullen, *Roman Social Relations*, 38; Fiensy, *Social History*, 77–79.

9. Stern, "Aspects of Jewish Society," 605–9; Smallwood, "High Priests," 14–34.

10. Avigad, *Discovering Jerusalem*, 83–134; Avigad, "Burnt House," 66–72; Jeremias, *Jerusalem*, 224; Finkelstein, *Pharisees*, 1:12.

The elite of Jerusalem lived in an almost completely different world from the urban poor. The social and economic distance between the two classes was so great that we have difficulty now appreciating it.[11] The wealth of many in the elite class was legendary. Stories abound of luxury, wanton spending, and ostentatious displays of wealth.[12]

Another result of the movement toward large estates was that many peasants became landless. Some of them certainly remained in the rural areas to work as tenant farmers or agricultural day laborers. But many must have been forced into the cities where they formed an urban proletariat of day laborers. The laborers in Jerusalem who worked on the construction of the temple received a comfortable wage. The tomb of a family of such workers from the first century CE has been excavated at Givat Ha-Mivtar, just north of Jerusalem. Indications are that although this family worked at hard physical labor, they were not poor.[13] Others who lived in a sort of middle class, between the wealthy elite and the poor proletariat, were the small merchants and shop owners.

But for many others—perhaps most others—in Jerusalem life was an endless series of hard jobs and inadequate wages. One might work at any of numerous tasks as a bathhouse attendant, a cook, a messenger, a scribe, a manure gatherer, a thorn gatherer, a watchman over children or over the sick, or a burden bearer.[14]

The wages paid for such work could vary considerably. The common assertion that the days wage was usually one denarius (Matt 20:2) must be accepted cautiously. That wage was perhaps only average. In general, a skilled laborer, such as those working on the temple, received several denarii per day. An unskilled burden bearer would receive less. Hillel the scholar (first century BCE), for instance, received one-half denarius a day for carrying wood. Another poor man who lived in Jerusalem in the first century CE caught birds to sell and received on average one-half denarius. There are, however, examples of workers being paid only 1/24 denarius a day (*m. Sheb.* 8:4).[15]

---

11. Lenski, *Power and Privilege*, 284–85.

12. Finkelstein, *Pharisees*, 1:12–14; Jeremias, *Jerusalem*, 96.

13. Haas, "Anthropological Observations," 38–59; Naveh, "Ossuary Inscriptions," 33–37.

14. Krauss, *Talmudische Archäologie*, 2:106.

15. Finkelstein, *Pharisees*, 1:15–16; Jeremias, *Jerusalem*, 26; Sperber, "Costs of Living," 250–51.

The impossibility of a family subsisting on such meager wages has been demonstrated by A. Ben-David. An average family, which Ben-David maintains consisted of six to nine people, needed from 182 denarii to 273 denarii per year just to supply the barest minimum of daily caloric intake (400 grams of bread). Yet if an unskilled worker only earned one-half denarius a day, then the most he could make (excluding Sabbaths) would have been 150 denarii. That is too meager to supply the simplest diet, not to mention to provide clothing and shelter. Further, we should expect that these day laborers found work only sporadically.[16]

Not only were poor day laborers in Jerusalem, but many were reduced to begging, either out of physical disability or mere poverty. One social historian, G. Lenski, in a work on agrarian societies in antiquity and in the Middle Ages, observed that such societies almost always produce a group of people that are socially and economically alienated. This group, Lenski terms "expendables." Lenski writes: "Agrarian societies usually produced more people than the dominant classes found it profitable to employ."[17]

Palestine was a typical agrarian society in this regard in that it too had a population of beggars (Mark 10:46; Luke 14:24; t. Pe'ah 4:8; b. BB 9a).[18] Jerusalem was, according to J. Jeremias, a center for begging. Numerous beggars stationed themselves at holy places in the city, especially at the temple's gates (John 9:8; Acts 3:2; m. Shabb. 6:8). Beggars seem to have had their own habitual place of begging at which they sat daily to ask for alms. So numerous were the beggars around the temple that the Septuagint translation of 2 Sam 5:8 contains a prohibition against beggars entering the temple area.[19]

It would be surprising if the Jerusalem church—which allegedly boasted five thousand members at this time (Acts 4:4)—should not have contained a large group of both poor day laborers and beggars. Thus the church's ministry to the poor does not require us to speculate about an emergency caused by dallying pilgrims or the like. The church would naturally want to take care of the daily needs of its members, many of whom must have been extremely poor.

---

16. Ben-David, *Talmudische Ökonomie*, 45, 136; cf. Finkelstein, *Pharisees,* 1:16; Drexhage, "Wirtschaft und Handel," 8–16.

17. Lenski, *Power and Privilege,* 281–83.

18. Strack and Billerbeck, *Kommentar,* 2:533, 646

19. Jeremias, *Jerusalem,* 116–17.

The Jerusalem Church: Response

Precisely how the church met this problem has also been debated, with the sides drawn mainly between the communistic and noncommunistic explanations. E. Troeltsch[20] in 1911 popularized the communistic explanation when he termed the church's activity in Acts 4:32–34 "communism of love." This view has received a revival of support since the discovery of the Qumran scrolls. The Essenes both according to the Scrolls (1QS 1:12; 6:16–20) and Josephus (*War* 2.122–123) practiced a form of communism in which the novice retained possession of his private property until his final vows, at which he turned over everything he owned to the community.[21] Some scholars maintain, then, that the Jerusalem church practiced an Essene-type of communism or mandatory communism.[22]

Others maintain that the church practiced voluntary communism. Not all people, but only the truly spiritual ones, held all things in common. Barnabas's action (Acts 4:36–37) was then unusual.[23]

Still others maintain that, whether the example of Barnabas was typical or atypical, the right to own private property was always present in the Jerusalem church and was exercised both by spiritual and non-spiritual alike.[24]

Some would rather see the model of the church's actions in caring for the poor not so much in Essenism as in the ordinary Jewish charity called the *quppah* (קופה) or "basket" and the *tamhui* (תמחוי) or "tray."[25] The former was a weekly collection for the poor, the latter a daily collection. Two collectors for the first charity went from house to house and to the marketplace to solicit contributions for the poor, either in money or in produce. The poor who belonged to the village received most of the dole, but provision was also made for poor strangers and transients. The second charity was a daily collection of food to be given to those who had a special need for the next day.[26]

---

20. Troeltsch, *Social Teaching*, 1:63.

21. Rabin, *Qumran Studies*, 22–36.

22. Johnson, "Dead Sea Manual," 108; Williams, *Acts*, 87; Capper, "Interpretation of Acts 5:4," 117–31.

23. Albright and Mann, *Acts*, 39.

24. Marshall, *Acts*, 108; Boles, *Acts*, 75; Batey, *Jesus and the Poor*, 34; Haenchen, *Die Apostelgeschichte*, 165; Hengel, *Poverty and Riches*, 31–34.

25. Lake, "Communism," 148–49.

26. Strack and Billerbeck, *Kommentar*, 2:643–647; Moore, *Judaism*, 2:174–76.

We should probably not make too much of either the practice of the Essenes or the Jewish village charity. In the first case, communism was clearly mandatory for membership while in the case of the Jerusalem church it was not. The imperfect tenses of so many Greek verbs in our text indicates that the selling of houses was done sporadically and continuously, evidently when the need arose, and not as a condition of membership. Further, Acts 5:4, Peter's words to Ananias and Sapphira, indicates that the contribution of one's property was entirely voluntary. Third, Acts 12:12 indicates that some Christians who owned houses did not sell them. Fourth, we see no evidence that other churches practiced communism. The Antioch church, for example (Acts 11:27–30), took up a collection for the poor, which implies private property ownership.[27] Thus private property was possible for a Christian in the Jerusalem church.[28]

The practice of village charity also seems an unlikely model for the Jerusalem church. Not only are the sources that describe this practice late (after the first century CE), but they indicate that residents contributed occasionally a small quantity of grain or a few coins, but not that they ever sold or were urged to sell their possessions to give the proceeds to the poor. Such practice seems excessive and out of harmony with the rabbinic description of *quppah* (*t. Pe'ah* 4:9–18; *t. Demai* 3:16). The sources do refer to people on their deathbeds, however, ordering a portion of their estate or crops be given to the poor (*t. BQ* 11:3).

These two models, then, cannot adequately explain what happened in the Jerusalem church. The obvious place to search for the background to the early church's practice is the Old Testament, especially as it was interpreted by Jesus. Christianity was not merely imitative but creative.

A passage in Leviticus (25:23) is basic for our understanding of the Jerusalem church:

"The land shall not be sold in perpetuity, for the land is mine, for you are strangers and sojourners with me." This verse is embedded in a nexus of paragraphs in Leviticus 25 that present the laws concerning the Jubilee. The Jubilee, which occurred every fifty years (or forty-nine?) was a time of restitution of land to those who through poverty had lost it, and a time for liberating slaves who had sold themselves into slavery because of debt. In addition to the Jubilee, the law provided for the cancellation of debts every seventh year or Sabbatical Year (Lev 25:2–7; Deut

27. Johnson, *Sharing Possessions*, 22.

28. Hengel, *Property and Riches*, 31–34; Batey, *Jesus and the Poor*, 33–34.

15:1–8). Both of these closely related laws deal with the land, since one often lost one's land through indebtedness.[29] Second, both of these laws are based on the theological premise that the land of Israel is God's, and that the Israelites are his tenants.[30] Since the land is really God's, no one can sell or buy another's inherited ground in perpetuity. Land cannot be a commodity to be bought and sold at will. Land is God's gracious gift to his people, and, thus, no one has the right to impoverish someone else. One's land must be returned at least by the time of the Jubilee, and one's indebtedness must be forgiven in the Sabbatical Year. Thus care for the poor is based ultimately on God's ownership of the land.[31]

In Isa 61:1–2 the Jubilee is again emphasized. Here the one who receives the anointing of God's spirit is sent forth:

> To bring good tidings to the afflicted…to bind up the broken hearted, to proclaim liberty (דרור *deror*) to the captives to… proclaim the year of the Lord's favor . . . (Cf. Lev 25:10).

The Hebrew word *deror* in this text leaves no doubt that Isaiah is referring to the Jubilee. What is important is the close association between the Jubilee that this person announces and his ministry to the poor and afflicted.

We have no evidence that the Jubilee was observed in the postexilic period. Certainly it was not observed in the first century BCE and CE. In the first place, the rabbinic sources claim the Jubilee ceased after the exile (*y. Sheb* 10.4; *b. 'Arak.* 32b–33a; Sifra, *Behar Sinai* 7.1). Second, a text from Wadi Murabaat in the Judean desert (Mur 26:9–11), a document of sale dating from the time of Bar Cochba (132–135 CE), indicates that the piece of ground being sold was sold in perpetuity, evidently a clear rejection of Lev 25:23.[32] Third, the Qumran text known as 11Q Melchizedek looks forward to the restoration of the Jubilee when the heavenly redeemer figure, Melchizedek, comes at the end-time to judge Belial and his condemned angels. This document has been dated from the late second century BCE[33] to the early first century CE[34] and attests

---

29. Goodman, *Ruling Class,* 56–57; Oakman, *Economic Questions,* 72–77.

30. De Vaux, *Ancient Israel,* 165.

31. Davies, *Gospel and the Land,* 24–33; de Vaux, *Ancient Israel,* 165; von Rad, *Theologie,* 298.

32. Kippenberg, *Religion und Klassenbildung,* 145.

33. Puech, "11Q Melkisedeq," 483–513.

34. Van der Woude, "Melchizedek," 354–73.

that sometime within this period there was hope that in the end-time the social ideal of the Old Testament would be realized. Finally, the action of the Jewish rebels during the war of 66–74 CE may indicate both that the Jubilee was not being practiced and that there was a general longing for it. Simon bar Giora, one of the leaders of the revolt, attempted, apparently, to bring about a new social order of egalitarianism.[35] He not only attacked the wealthy Jews (*War* 2.652) but freed all slaves (*War* 4.508; cf. Lev 25:39–42). The sicarii or "dagger carriers" probably were invoking the Sabbatical Year legislation when they burned down the building in Jerusalem where the debt records were kept (*War* 2.427). Since the time of the formulation of the law known as *prosbul* (*m. Sheb.* 10:3) by the great Hillel (first century BCE), the cancellation of debts during the Sabbatical Year (Deut 15:2) had been abrogated.[36]

The above evidence leads to the conclusion that the Jubilee or Sabbatical Year social legislation was largely neglected by the first century CE. Instead, the Hellenistic monarchs and later the Romans had installed an exploitative economic policy that resulted in many peasants' losing their land and moving to new and growing urban centers.[37] This new economic situation may partly lie behind the Jewish War of 66–74 CE.

Jesus explained the kingdom of God partly in terms of the Jubilee. In his sermon delivered at Nazareth he quoted Isa 61:1–2 and then said "Today this scripture has been fulfilled in your hearing" (Luke 4:21). Jesus declared, then, that Isaiah was referring to him in this prophecy, and that he would "preach good news to the poor . . . proclaim release to the captives and recovering of sight to the blind . . . set at liberty those who are oppressed . . . proclaim the acceptable year of the Lord" (Luke 4:18–19). This was Jesus's ministry, in part: to bring about the Jubilee with the kingdom of God.[38]

This conclusion is not only based on Jesus's sermon at Nazareth and other allusions to Isa 61:1 (e.g., Matt 11:2–6) but on Jesus's teaching in general about wealth and poverty. To the rich Jesus warned, first of all, of the disharmony between wealth and the kingdom of God:

---

35. Applebaum, "Zealots," 155–70

36. Horsley and Hanson, *Bandits*, 211–12; Applebaum, "Zealots," 155–70.

37. Hengel, *Property and Riches*, 19, 35; Jones, "Urbanization," 78–85.

38. Ringe, "Jubilee Proclamation," 149–52; Yoder, *Politics of Jesus*, 34–77. Ringe argues for the authenticity of this pericope in the life of the historical Jesus.

> No one can serve two masters: for either he will hate the one
> and love the other, or he will be devoted to the one and despise
> the other. You cannot serve God and mammon. (Matt 6:24 and
> parallels; *Gos. Thom.* 47)

> And Jesus looked around and said to his disciples, "How hard it
> will be for those who have riches to enter the kingdom of God!"
> (Mark 10:23 and parallels; *Gos. Naz.;* Shepherd of Hermas, *Si-
> militudes* 9:20:1–4)

> Woe to you that are rich, for you have received your consolation.
> (Luke 6:24)[39]

Wealth and the kingdom of God do not harmonize with each other
because of the inherent power of wealth to corrupt (Mark 4:19), and
because most wealthy people in the ancient agrarian societies were dishonest, exploitative, and greedy (Luke 12:16–20, 16:19–25; cf. Jas 5:1–6).

Jesus's message to the wealthy, then, was essentially as follows:

> Do not lay up for yourselves treasures on earth, where moth and
> rust consume and where thieves break in and steal, but lay up
> for yourselves treasures in heaven, where neither moth nor rust
> consumes and where thieves do not break in and steal. (Matt
> 6:19–20 and parallel; *Gos. Thom.* 76)

How this message translated into life seems to have varied. Usually
this principle meant that one was to give alms generously to the poor
(Matt 6:2–4; 25:31–46; Mark 12:41–44; Luke 19:8). But Jesus also advised
a potential disciple on one occasion to sell all his possessions and give the
proceeds to the poor (Mark 10:17–25 and parallels; *Gos. Naz.*).

In Luke 14:33 Jesus is reported to have said, "So therefore, whoever
of you does not renounce all that he has cannot be my disciple." This
saying shows that the church believed that one might have to sell his or
her property to be a disciple. Jesus does not here explicitly say this meant
selling one's property and giving it to the poor but it could be interpreted
that way. At least this saying was urging a radical rejection of "serving
mammon." Jesus further narrated two parables in which he told about
a man who sold all that he had to acquire both the treasure in the field
and the pearl of great price (Matt 13:44–46 and par.). Since he said that
these treasures represented the kingdom of God, one could easily get the
impression that one might have to sell everything to enter the kingdom.

---

39. Cf. Mealand, *Poverty and Expectation,* 44–60.

The most interesting passage for our purpose is Luke 12:33: "Sell your possessions (πωλησατε τα υπαρχοντα) and give alms." Here again this saying does not necessarily command to sell all one's possessions but that giving alms to the poor was so important one must sometimes sell at least part of one's property. Thus the early church believed that Jesus wanted them to commit radically to helping the poor. The reason this verse is so interesting is that Acts 4:32 and 34 seem to echo the words attributed to Jesus here. Thus, in Luke and Acts there is a strain of divestiture of property in order to be a disciple of Jesus.

So Jesus's message to the rich was that wealth normally made one unfit for the kingdom. The remedy for this condition is to lay up treasures in heaven by giving away at least part of one's wealth in alms. On one occasion, at least, and perhaps others as well, Jesus admonished someone to give away *all* his wealth.

Yet Jesus did not always or even usually tell disciples to give away all their possessions. Zaccheus the tax collector was said to have given away only a portion of his possessions (Luke 19:8) although much of his wealth was obviously dishonestly acquired. Other wealthy friends of Jesus seem to have kept their possessions (houses) also (Luke 10:38–42; 14:1). Thus there was not just one appropriate response to the message of the kingdom as far as the handling of one's possessions were concerned, but several.[40]

Giving alms to the needy is not for Jesus merely charity, however. This action is not just to help needy people any more than Jesus's miracles were performed merely because people were sick (though both of these actions certainly were done in part for those reasons). Both actions are signs that the kingdom of God is breaking into history. When John the Baptist asked if Jesus was really the Messiah, Jesus responded by saying,

> Go and tell John what you have seen and heard: the blind receive
> their sight, the lame walk, lepers are cleansed, and the deaf hear,
> the dead are raised up, the poor have good news preached to
> them. (Luke 7:22–23)

These references to the poor and blind are probably an allusion to the Jubilee prediction of Isa 61:1–2.[41] Neither the miracles nor Jesus's ministry to the poor is just a sign of the kingdom, but part of the kingdom process. The kingdom of God has begun under Jesus to overthrow Satan.

40. Johnson, *Sharing Possessions*, 16–20; Fiensy, *Jesus the Galilean*, 145.
41. Ringe, "Jubilee Proclamation," 149–52.

This is explicitly said about miracles and implied about the ministry to the poor. The kingdom of God brings about Satan's downfall and with it his power to inflict sickness and the injustice of poverty. Thus Jesus's ministry "binds the strong man" (Satan) so that Jesus may plunder the strong man's house (Matt 12:29). Jesus can also say, "But if it is by the Spirit of God (Matt; "finger of God" Luke) that I cast out demons, then the kingdom of God has come upon you" (Matt 12:28).

Jesus and the Gospel writers indicate the same concept implicitly for the ministry to the poor by allusions to the overthrow of the rich and powerful. There is coming in the kingdom of God a reversal of fortunes. Thus Jesus said,

> Blessed are you poor . . . you that hunger...you that weep...
> (Luke 6:20–21) but woe to you that are rich . . . you that are full
> now . . . that laugh now . . . (Luke 6:24–25)

Jesus told the parable of a poor beggar and a wantonly wealthy man whose roles and fortunes in the next life are exactly reversed (Luke 16:19–25). He also narrated the parable of the banquet, in which the wealthy and powerful, because of their insolence, were excluded, but "the poor and maimed and blind and lame" attend (Luke 14:15–21). The latter parable is an obvious reference to the end-time when the wealthy will be excluded from God's grace but the poor and afflicted will be included. The kingdom of God brings a reversal in which the wealthy and powerful are "put down from their thrones" and the poor are "exalted" (Luke 1:52).

We must here emphasize that Jesus was not making poverty in itself virtuous and wealth in itself a vice. In this society wealth was usually acquired by depriving someone else of his patrimony. Wealth is land, and wealthy people are almost always large-landowners. Thus wealth and exploitation or greed seem to have gone hand in hand.

The ministry to the poor, then, is the beginning of what will ultimately be a complete reversal at the end-time and the overthrow of Satan and his minions, both human and nonhuman.

The ministry to the poor is just that: a ministry. It is not a social or political revolution. Jesus never tried to bring down the wealthy by force or demand that his followers do so. He preached his message of the kingdom to the wealthy and poor alike and waited for God to bring about the end-time judgment and reversal (Matt 13:47–50). The ministry to the poor was not a program, then, that had as its goal the creation of a utopian society, but the affirmation of belief in and solidarity with the kingdom of God and God's ultimate overthrow of injustice. As Troeltsch wrote, "It is rather the summons to prepare for the coming of the Kingdom of God."[42]

The Jerusalem church, then believed it was living out the kingdom of God as Jesus defined it. They believed that Jesus had said to "sell your possessions (ὑπάρχοντα) and give alms" (Luke 12:33); thus the believers did not consider any of their possessions (τι των υπαρχοντων) to belong to themselves (Acts 4:32). Jesus proclaimed that the Jubilee prophecy (Isa 61:1–2) was fulfilled in himself (Luke 4:21), and thus we read (Acts 4:34) that "no one among [the believers] was needy," a direct allusion to Deut 15:4.[43] This text regulates a Sabbatical Year release of debts so that "there will be (in the future) no needy among you." The Sabbatical Year or Jubilee is ultimately fulfilled only in the kingdom of God. The end-time brings the fulfillment of God's ideal for his people as expressed in the Old Testament. The overthrow of Satan and his minions also comes with the kingdom of God, as we saw from Jesus's teaching. Not only has Jesus broken the power of death by his resurrection (Acts 4:33), but now the power of kings and rulers is being thwarted in the midst of the believing community (Acts 4:25–31).

How did the community of believers, practically speaking, live consistently with their belief in the risen Christ who was conquering the "kings and rulers" (Acts 4:26)? First of all, they rejected the standards of this age. Wealth carries with it not only the advantage of affording one all one can eat, enough clothing, and comfortable living quarters. One's wealth or lack of wealth makes a statement also about power, prestige, and personal value. The symbolic function of wealth is probably just as important to most people as the provision for the basic human needs.[44] When some of the believers sold all or part of their lands to give alms to the poor, they were giving up the political power and prestige that wealth also provided them. This was a radical rejection, then, of the standards and values of the world.

Second, they put their possessions in the service of God. For some, that meant selling their lands or houses (Acts 4:34, 37); for others it meant using their houses as meeting places for the church (Acts 9:36;

42. Troeltsch, *Social Teaching*, 1:61.

43. Pesch, *Die Apostelgeschichte*, 184; Schille, *Die Apostelgeschichte*, 145; Johnson, *Sharing Possessions*, 128.

44. Johnson, *Sharing Possessions*, 37–43; Lenski, *Power and Privilege*.

10:2; 11:27–30). Selling all one's property was entirely voluntary (Acts 5:4). Not only did some Jerusalem Christians not do that (Acts 12:12), but apparently few if any at Antioch did (Acts 11:27–30), since they were able to take up a collection for the needs in Jerusalem. As L. T. Johnson notes, this account shows that the disciples in Antioch still had not only "private possessions but differences in wealth (Acts: 11:2)" since each gave alms as he had the ability.[45]

Thus there was not simply one right way to put into practice the new attitude toward wealth, but several. What was essential, however, was the rejection of non-Christian standards. From that point each believer was free to handle the possessions God had given, as God gave light to decide.

The Church Today

The answer to our final question, what timeless lesson abides for the modern church?, is now obvious. The modern church must also fight the temptation to view wealth from a worldly perspective. The essential problem is to change one's attitude. As Christians, we must recognize that none of our possessions really belongs to us (Acts 4:32). They are God's. That means not necessarily that we sell everything or give it away, but at least that we use all of our possessions for God. Such an attitude means that we live consistently with the end-time yearning for the overthrow of injustice and of those who exploit and impoverish others. Thus we give alms to alleviate the suffering of the poor and also because we live consistently with Jesus's teaching of the end-time Jubilee or reversal, in which the wicked and exploitative wealthy will be brought low and God's people who hunger and mourn now will be fed and laugh (Luke 6:21).

---

45. Johnson, *Sharing Possessions*, 22.

10

The Composition of
the Jerusalem Church

STUDIES ON THE THEOLOGY and practice of the Jerusalem church are legion.[1] These studies usually point out that early Christianity was closely tied to Judaism, practiced some kind of voluntary communism, had the Twelve Apostles and later the Seven as leaders and, of course, proclaimed Jesus as the Messiah.

This undertaking will examine the composition of the primitive Christian community. What sort of people were these, sociologically and culturally? Did the Christian movement, the "Way," attract only the poor, or other classes as well? Were these people culturally diverse?

We shall maintain below that although the early Jerusalem church was entirely Jewish, it was nonetheless socially and culturally pluralistic. Indeed, the primitive church reflected to a great extent the rich diversity of Jerusalem itself, the "most illustrious city in the east."[2] A city of sixty thousand or more inhabitants,[3] Jerusalem in the early Roman period contained the fabulously rich as well as the unbearably poor. Further,

1. See, e.g., Foakes-Jackson and Lake, *Beginnings*, 1:300–420; Cerfaux, "La première communauté"; Blevins, "The Early Church."

2. Pliny, *HN* 5.70.

3. This figure is in line with the estimates of Wilkinson, "Ancient Jerusalem"; Broshi, "Estimating the Population"; King, "Jerusalem"; Mazar, *Mountain of the Lord*, 210; Geva, "Jerusalem," 717–57, esp 721; and Reinhardt, "Population Size of Jerusalem," 263. Wilkinson estimates that at the time of Herod the Great there were 36,280 residents, and in the time of Agrippa II there were 76,130. Broshi estimates 40,000 residents for Herod's time and 80,000 just before the war.

most of the inhabitants were probably Palestinian natives, but the city also had a sizeable minority of Jews from the Diaspora (and of course some Gentiles as well).

Jerusalem is described by Josephus as mainly consisting of two parts: the Lower City and the Upper City. The Lower City, also called the Acra (*War* 5.253), consisted of the Ophel, the City of David, and the Tyropoeon Valley. The Upper City was on the hill now called Mount Zion (*War* 2.422). Josephus also writes of an area just north of the Lower and Upper Cities that he calls New Town (*War* 2.530; 5.331). By the time of the war in 66 CE, this last area was encompassed by the third north wall. But within most of our time frame (30–66 CE) only a small part of that suburb was enclosed—by the second north wall.[4] Finally, the temple mount formed one of the significant districts of ancient Jerusalem.

The Social Groups in Jerusalem

L. Finkelstein[5] has sketched the social situation in Jerusalem, which when informed by the sociologically sensitive work of G. Sjoberg,[6] can serve as a model for us.

The upper class lived mainly in the Upper City and consisted of the temple nobility and the lay nobility. Most of these, even the wealthy priests, were probably large-estate owners, though some may have been wealthy merchants.

Literary and archaeological sources[7] have identified many medium to large estates[8] in Judea and even around Jerusalem itself. Since large landowners tended in antiquity to live in the city as absentee landlords and to leave the administration of their estates to bailiffs, these land holdings may well have belonged to the members of the Jerusalem upper class.

The sources certainly testify that wealthy families lived in Jerusalem before the first Jewish war. The rabbinic sources tell of three wealthy men,

---

4. See the maps in, e.g., Wilkinson, *Jerusalem*, 62, 64; and Geva, "Jerusalem," 718.

5. Finkelstein, *Pharisees*, 1:4.

6. Sjoberg, *Preindustrial City*, 118–33.

7. See Applebaum, "Problem of the Roman Villa," 1–5; Applebaum, "Roman Villa in Judaea," in Applebaum, *Judaea in Hellenistic and Roman Times*; Applebaum, "Judaea as a Roman Province," 355–96; Fiensy, *Social History*, 21–73.

8. See Dohr, "Die italischen Guthöfe"; and White, *Roman Farming*, 385–87, for the categories of small, medium, and large estates in antiquity.

Naqdimon ben Gorion, Ben Kalba Shabua, and Ben Tzitzit, who lived in Jerusalem before and during the first Jewish war. They were allegedly capable of supplying Jerusalem for twenty-one years. One of them could supply wheat and barley, one oil and wine, and the third wood. These men were either large-estate owners whose estates produced these crops, or merchants. Even allowing for obvious exaggerations, the three must have possessed great wealth.[9]

The rabbinic sources also allude to other wealthy landowners who resided in or near Jerusalem during this time. Hyrcanus, father of Eleazar the famous student of Yohanan ben Zakkai, was a wealthy man who owned lands near Jerusalem.[10] Elisha ben Abuya was descended from a wealthy landowner who lived in Jerusalem before 66 CE.[11] Rabbi Dosa ben Harkinas was an elderly and wealthy scholar during the time of the school of Jamnia (70–125 CE). A. Büchler argued that he must have, therefore, lived in Jerusalem before the war, and that he had been able to maintain his wealth even in the aftermath of the destruction of Jerusalem.[12]

Probably the most significant class of wealthy landowners was the group of aristocratic priests, especially the high-priestly families. M. Stern[13] suggests that the statement of Hecataeus (*Diod.* 40.3.7) that Moses gave the priests a larger share of land than other Israelites reflects the social situation in Palestine in the Second Temple period. Certainly Hecataeus did not base this observation on the Old Testament since, according to the Law (Num 18:24; Deut 10:9, 12:12, 18:1), the priests and Levites did not own land. As Stern also notes, it is doubtful that the priests could have become wealthy from the tithes alone since the Mishnah indicates that many peasants did not always pay them (see *m. Demai*).

At any rate, a number of priestly families were quite wealthy. The most obvious example is the family of Josephus. He states that he has

9. *B. Git.* 56a and *Lam. Rab.* I.31. The latter source gives the names of four men. See Applebaum, "Economic Life in Palestine," 659. See Jeremias, *Jerusalem,* 95–96, 226. See also *'Abot R. Nat.* Rec A 6, Rec B 13; *Eccl. Rab.* 7.12 and *Gen. Rab.* 42.1 for the same three men called here the "great ones in Israel." Compare also Kreissig, "Die Landwirtschaftliche Situation," 234.

10. *'Abot R. Nat.* Rec A 6; *Gen. Rab.* 42.1; *Pirqe R. El.* I; Mendelsohn, "Eliezer ben Hyrcanus"; and Büchler, *Economic Conditions,* 40.

11. *Y. Hag.* 2.1.; *Eccl. Rab.* 7.18. See Büchler, *Economic Conditions,* 14; and Jeremias, *Jerusalem,* 92.

12. *B. Yebam.* 16a for R. Dosa and Büchler, *Economic Conditions,* 40.

13. Stern, "Aspects of Jewish Society," 586–87.

come from a wealthy and influential priestly family of the Hasmonaean line (*Life* 1–2; *Ant.* 16.187) and that he owned lands near Jerusalem (probably just west of the city) before the war (*Life* 422). Since, according to his autobiography, he is never seen residing on his farm, we can assume that he had a bailiff to oversee his tenants or slaves, and that he lived for the most part in Jerusalem.

Other priests, especially the high priests, were also wealthy. Ananias son of Nebedaeus (high priest in 48 CE) was wealthy enough to pay bribes to Albinus the Procurator and to the then-high priest, Jesus son of Damascus, so that he could continue a campaign of extortion against both the peasants and poorer priests (*Ant.* 20.205 7) to extract forcibly the tithes for himself and his servants.[14]

Wealth was especially prominent in the main high-priestly families, that is, the houses of Boethus, Hanan, Phiabi, and Kathros (Kadros).[15] The Talmud represents these families as powerful and ruthless:

> Woe is me because of the house of Boethus, woe is me because of their staves!
>
> Woe is me because of the house of Hanin, woe is me because of their whisperings!
>
> Woe is me because of the house of Kathros, woe is me because of their pens!
>
> Woe is me because of the house of Ishmail the son of Phabi, woe is me because of their fists.
>
> For they are High Priests and their sons are (Temple) treasurers and their sons-in-law are trustees and their servants beat the people with staves.[16]

That these priestly houses were wealthy can hardly be doubted. The wealth of the house of Boethus, for example, was legendary (*b. Git.* 56a;

14. See Stern, "Aspects of Jewish Society," 586–87; and Smallwood, "High Priests," 27.

15. See ibid., 605–9; Smallwood, "High Priests," 14–34. Stern wants to add the house of Kimchi to these other four families. Jeremias, *Jerusalem*, 194 maintained that the fourth great high priestly house was Kamaith instead of Kathros and that Kathros was a branch of Boethus.

16. *B. Pesah.* 57a. Translation in Epstein, *Babylonian Talmud*. See the notes on this passage also in Epstein. The whisperings represent secret meetings to devise oppressive measures. The pens write evil decrees. See the list in Appendix A of Smallwood, "High Priests," 31–32, of the high priests in the Herodian period and the families to which they belonged. This same lament appears in t. Menah. 13.21.

b. Yebam. 61a), as was that of the house of Phabi (*b. Yoma* 35b). Annas and Caiaphas of the house of Hanan apparently owned large mansions.[17] Some of their riches may have been acquired by extortion and violence, but such practices could not produce sustained wealth. They must have owned lands in Judea and perhaps elsewhere that brought them such large fortunes.[18]

The rabbinic sources also refer to several priests who lived between the two Jewish rebellions who were wealthy. That priests should have maintained their wealth even after the war is not surprising. As Büchler maintained, Josephus indicates that many priests quickly capitulated to the Romans and so were allowed to keep their lands (*War* 6.115).[19] The most celebrated of these wealthy priests was Eleazar ben Harsom, who allegedly owned one thousand villages.[20] Mentioned alongside ben Harsom is Eleazar ben Azariah, also of priestly descent, who possessed extraordinary wealth.[21] Also to be included in this list is Rabbi Tarfon, a wealthy sage who as a young man had participated as a priest in the temple ritual. R. Tarfon owned an estate in Galilee and may also have owned land near Joppa.[22]

Thus the literary evidence indicates that a wealthy, aristocratic class lived in Jerusalem in the first century CE, many of whom, but not all, belonged to influential priestly families. In this context we must add the testimony of Josephus. He writes of a significant group of wealthy citizens living in the Upper City of Jerusalem at the outbreak of the war who became the targets of the Sicarii ("dagger carriers") and other revolutionary factions (*War* 2.428, 652; 4.140–41.). Here Herod had built a palace, and Agrippa II and several chief priests had mansions there (*War* 1.402;

17. Jeremias, *Jerusalem*, 96. See John 18:15, 18; Mark. 14:53.

18. See Jeremias, *Jerusalem*, 108; and Stern, "Aspects of Jewish Society," 586–87. Goodman, *State and Society*, 33, also doubts that priests could have grown wealthy on even unearned tithes.

19. Büchler, "Die Schauplätze," 191.

20. See *b. Yoma* 35b; *b. Qidd.* 49b; *b. Betsa* 23a.

21. See *b. Yoma* 35b; *b. Qidd.* 49b; *b. Betsa* 23a. He traced his lineage back to Ezra, *b. Ber.* 27b and *y. Yebam.* 1.3. See Mendelsohn, "Eleazar ben Azariah."

22. *Y. Shebu.* 4.2; *b. Ned.* 62a; *Eccl. Rab.* 3.11; *b. Qidd.* 71a; *y. Yoma* 3.7; *t. Hag.* 3.36. See Oscher, "Tarfon"; and Finkelstein, "The Pharisees," 190. For lands near Joppa, see the tomb inscription of Tarfon's son in Frey, *CIJ* 2, no. 892.

2.422, 426, 428). In this district is also the traditional location of Caiaphas's house.[23]

The archaeological excavations of the Jewish quarter of Jerusalem confirm the impression we get from the literary sources that a significant wealthy class resided in Jerusalem before the war. The excavation team of N. Avigad[24] discovered in the Upper City large mansions owned obviously by very rich people. The "Herodian house" from the first century CE, and the "Burnt House"[25] from the first century CE are architectural testimony of this class. But just as interesting for our purposes are not only the huge mansions but the rows of slightly more modest houses that still, according to Avigad, "belonged to upper class families."[26] These houses are distinguished from other houses of the same period not only by their size but by their furnishings and decorations. The costly pottery, the wine imported from Italy, the elaborate frescoes and floor mosaics and the many water installations, among other items, point to the wealth of the occupants. That these people were Jewish is evident from the *mikvaot* found in many of the houses. This evidence, then, fits hand in glove with the literary evidence.

The lower classes consisted of the poorer priests and Levites, the small merchants, the craftsmen, and the unskilled laborers.[27] The lower-class priests, divided into twenty-four weekly courses (*Ant.* 7.365), lived in villages throughout Judea and Galilee.[28] But many priests resided in Jerusalem. The priests in Jerusalem at the time of Nehemiah numbered 1,192 (Neh 11:10-14; but cf. 1 Chr 9:13).[29] E. P. Sanders surmises reason-

---

23. See Broshi, "Excavations in the House of Caiaphas," 57–58; Wilkinson, *Jerusalem*, 133–36, 166, for Caiaphas's house. For Herod's palace see Bahat and Broshi, "Excavations in the Armenian Garden," 55.

24. Avigad, *Discovering Jerusalem*, 83–137; and Avigad, "How the Wealthy Lived."

25. The Burnt House apparently, from an inscription found in it, belonged to a member of the house of Kathros, the priestly family listed above. See Avigad, "Burnt House."

26. Avigad, *Discovering Jerusalem*, 95.

27. Cf. Finkelstein, *Pharisees*, 1:4; and Sjoberg, *Preindustrial City*, 121–25. Finkelstein actually lists both a middle class and a lower class, but most sociologists would be reluctant to identify a true middle class until the industrial age.

28. See Hachlili and Smith, "Genealogy" (on a priestly family in Jericho); *b. Ber.* 44a; *b. Ta'an.* 27a; *t. Yebam.* 1.10; Luke 1:39; *t. Sota* 13.8; *Ant.* 17.66; and Stern, "Aspects of Jewish Society," 584.

29. See Stern, "Aspects of Jewish Society," 595, who notes that Hecataeus writes of 1,500 priests, evidently referring to priests of Jerusalem (*C. Ap.* 1.188).

ably from this figure in Nehemiah's time that by the first century CE there were probably "a few thousand priests and Levites" in Jerusalem.[30]

The poorest priests worked at a trade such as stone cutting, the sale of oil, or in agriculture.[31] Sanders's contention that many priests were scribes, teachers of the law, and judges has some support also (Sir 45.17; *Life* 9.196–8; *C. Ap.* 2.187).[32]

Priests also received tithes, at least theoretically, but it is difficult to know how much income they actually received from them.[33] Not all peasants paid tithes (*m. Demai*; Philo, *Spec. Laws* 1.153–5). Further, the more powerful and wealthier priests on occasion seem to have robbed the poorer ones of their dues. In the time of Agrippa II, the high-priestly families sent their slaves to claim forcibly the tithes while the poorer priests went hungry (*Ant.* 20.179–81; cf. *b. Pesah.* 57a). This text from Josephus may hint at ongoing class animosity between the wealthier and poorer priests.

Likewise Levites formed a subgroup in the lower class. They were considered beneath the ordinary priests in station. In the main, they must have been of rather modest means. Stern remarked on the relative lack of references to Levites in the Second Temple sources.[34] Neh 11:18 gives the number of Levites as 460 in his day, less than half his figure for priests. We may assume that the same proportion existed in the first century CE.

Jeremias conjectured that the Levites' two subgroups, the singers and the servants or doorkeepers, were of unequal rank (*b. 'Arak.* 11b; *Ant.* 20.216–8). The singers were, he maintained, considered to be higher in social standing. Each desired in the time of Agrippa II to be given greater honors.[35] This is an interesting suggestion, although the evidence is slight.

30. Sanders, *Judaism,* 170. Jeremias, *Jerusalem,* 200, estimated that the total number of priests in Palestine was 7,200 and the total number of Levites was 9,600. Sanders (78) accepts that Josephus's (*c. Ap.* 2.108) total figure of 20,000 for the priests and Levites in Palestine is probably close to correct. See Frey, *CIJ* 2, nos. 1221, 1317, and 1400 and Naveh, "New Tomb Inscription," 73 for inscriptions in Jerusalem referring to priests.

31. See Stern, "Aspects of Jewish Society," 586–87, who cites t. Yoma 1:6; t. Betsa 3:8 and Hecataeus (Diod. 40.3.7).

32. Sanders, *Judaism,* 170–72. Jeremias also pointed out these roles for priests. See *Jerusalem,* 207, 234.

33. Stern, "Aspects of Jewish Society," 585–86.

34. Ibid., 597.

35. Jeremias, *Jerusalem,* 212–13. But see the note in Feldman, *Josephus,* 10:117,

Apparently Levites, like priests, found employment as scribes or craftsmen. One of the temple singers, Joshua ben Hananiah, for example, was a nailsmith.[36]

The lower class also included craftsmen and small merchants. One of the main sources of income was the temple, which required bakers, weavers, goldsmiths, washers, merchants of ointments, and money changers.[37] Further, the temple was still in the process of being built. This labor force included a large number of carpenters and stonemasons. Josephus reported that when the temple was completed in the procuratorship of Albinus (62–64 CE), it put eighteen thousand workers out of a job (*Ant.* 20.219). Thus the temple required a large force of craftsmen throughout most of the first century CE.

But in addition there were markets both in the Upper and Lower Cities where wares were sold (*War* 2.305, 315). Jerusalem was famous for jewelry, spinning, weaving, dyeing, tailoring, shoemaking, perfume, and incense, but also produced oil, pottery, ossuaries, stoneware and woodwork.[38] In the Lower City was the Tyropoeon Valley, with a main street running through it lined by shops on both sides. The name Tyropoeon Valley suggests that a cheese market stood there,[39] but we should expect that other goods were found there as well. Archaeologists have found remains of the street, its large drain, and some shops from Robinson's Arch next to the temple all the way south along Tyropoeon Street.[40]

There was also a market center in the New Town district, north of the first wall. The Mishnah refers to a weavers' and wool-dealers' market in Jerusalem (*m. 'Erub.* 10:9; *m. 'Ed.* 1:3). Josephus writes that metal workers, tailors, fullers, wool dealers, and timber merchants had a market in the New Town district (*War* 2.530; 5.147, 331; cf. *Lam. Rab.* 1.1).

---

who maintains that the doorkeepers were the upper rank of Levites. The Levites were, like the priests, divided into 24 weekly courses and thus served in the temple about twice a year (*Ant.* 7.366–67).

36. See Jeremias, *Jerusalem*, 234.

37. See Avi-Yonah, *Holy Land,* 194 and his references. The tomb of an artisan family that worked on the Temple has been found. See Naveh, "Ossuary Inscriptions," 33–37.

38. See Mazar, *Mountain of the Lord,* 210; Jeremias, *Jerusalem,* 4–9 and their citations.

39. Its name in Greek means "Valley of the cheese makers," but Avi-Yonah suggests it is a corruption of some unrecognizable Hebrew term. See *Holy Land,* 193.

40. Bliss and Dickie, *Excavations,* 133; Mazar, *Mountain of the Lord,* 205–6; Ben-Dov, *In the Shadow of the Temple,* 114.

Also in the lower class were the unskilled day laborers. Laborers could work in the fields or olive groves around Jerusalem plowing, weeding, harvesting, threshing, picking fruit, and doing other seasonal jobs.[41] Most often the laborer worked as a burden bearer who carried wood or reeds or other kinds of burdens, or who harvested crops. Some burden bearers even carried around other people.[42] Many unskilled laborers were watchmen. They were paid to watch over animals, fields of crops, children, the sick, corpses, and the city gates.[43] But laborers also performed the tasks as bathhouse attendants, messengers, manure gatherers, and thorn gatherers.[44]

The unskilled worker was apparently paid on average one denarius per day.[45] But many were certainly paid less. Hillel worked as a wood cutter in Jerusalem, earning one half denarius a day (b. Yoma 35b). Another poor man of Jerusalem made a living by trapping doves and lived on about one-fourth a denarius a day (Lev. Rab. 1.17).

We should expect that most of the craftsmen and small merchants lived near the Tyropoeon market and thus in the Lower City or in the less populated New Town. Archaeologists have discovered the ruins of some houses in the Lower City. M. Ben-Dov describes the area in the lower City known as the City of David as "slums" and terms it "run-down."[46]

The City of David (the southern part of the Ophel spur) was of course the oldest inhabited area in Jerusalem. Even in the Hellenistic period the evidence is that most residents lived there. Only in the first century BCE did people begin moving up the slope towards the Upper City.[47] Thus most of the lower class lived in the older district of the city. As we shall see below, however, Jews from the Diaspora and proselytes were also drawn to this area.

At the very bottom of the social and economic scale was the "submerged" class or the class of "outcasts." This class included slaves, beggars,

---

41. T. Ma'as. 2.13, 15; t. BM 7.5–6; m. BM 7:5, 7:4, 7:7, 6:1, 8:8; m. Pe'ah 5:5. See Krauss, Talmudische Archäologie, 2:105; and Goodman, State and Society, 39.

42. T. BM 7.4; m. BM 6:1; and Krauss, Talmudische Archäologie, 2:105.

43. See m. BM 7:8–9; m. BQ 8:1; m. Shebu. 8:1; and Krauss, Talmudische Archäologie, 2:106.

44. See Krauss, Talmudische Archäologie, 2:106.

45. See Matt 20:2, 9, 13; Tob 5:14; y. Sheb. 8:4; b. BB 87a; b. Abod. Zar. 62a; and Ben-David, Talmudische Ökonomie, 66; and Sperber, "Costs of Living."

46. Ben-Dov, In the Shadow of the Temple, 155. Cf. Finkelstein, Pharisees, 1:14.

47. Shiloh, Excavations, 30.

those from unapproved occupations, the diseased, and those from questionable births.[48]

According to the Talmud, the occupations that were scorned included prostitute, dung collector, donkey driver, gambler, sailor, tanner, peddler, herder, and usurer.[49]

Those groups inferior to the common people due to heredity would have included mainly those born illegitimately. *M. Qidd.* 4:1 lists a hierarchy of births ranging from priests to the lowly four: bastards, Gibeonites, those that must be silent when reproached about their origins, and foundlings.[50] Bastards were those born of an incestuous union (as defined by Leviticus 18 and 20). A bastard could not "enter the congregation of the Lord" (Deut 23:3). That is, he could not marry an Israelite.[51] The Gibeonite was supposedly a descendant of the Gibeonites whom Joshua made to become temple slaves (Josh 9:27), and they were also excluded from the Israelite community as far as intermarriage was concerned (*b. Yebam.* 78b).[52] Those that must be silent when reproached about their origins were those that did not know who their father was (*m. Qidd.* 4:2).[53] The foundling is a child taken up from the street whose father and mother are unknown (*m. Qidd.* 4:2).[54]

With regard to the diseased we should think especially of the lepers, who seem to have abounded in Palestine.[55] Such people were declared unclean by a priest (Lev 13:11, 25) and had to remain apart from everyone else, crying out from a distance "Unclean!" (Lev 13:45–46). Lepers lived then a life of social ostracism.

Beggars also appeared frequently in first-century Palestine. They were lame (Matt 21:14; Mark 10:46; Luke 16:20; John 5:3; Acts 3:2; *m. Shabb.* 6:8) or blind (John 9:1) and sat along the roadside in the country

---

48. Finkelstein, *Pharisees*, 1:4 used the term "submerged," and Sjoberg, *Preindustrial City*, 133 used the designation "outcasts." See also Fiensy, *Social History*, 164–67.

49. Luke. 7:37–39, Matt 21:31; *m. Qidd.* 4:14; *m. Ketub.* 7:10; *m. Sanh.* 3:3; *b. Qidd.* 82a; *b. Sanh.* 25b; and Jeremias, *Jerusalem*, 303–12.

50. The translation of these terms is by Danby, *Mishnah*. Cf. also *m. Hor.* 3:7–8.

51. See Dembitz, "Bastard."

52. See Jastrow, *Dictionary.*

53. See ibid.

54. See ibid. The Talmud (*b. BM* 87a) says a man should not marry a foundling.

55. Mark 1:40; 14:3, Luke 17:12; *m. Meg.* 1:7; *m. Mo'ed Qat.* 3:1; *m. Sota* 1:5; *m. Zebah.* 14:3; *L.A.B.* 13:3; Apocryphal Syriac Psalm 155. The word seems to have been generally used for infectious skin diseases. See Leviticus 13.

(Mark 10:46) or along the streets and alleys in the city (Luke 14:21). Jeremias suggests that beggars were especially numerous in the temple precincts.[56]

Slaves in Jerusalem were mostly domestics of the wealthy. A Jew could become a slave as punishment for stealing, out of poverty or from indebtedness. The Hebrew slaves would presumably be liberated in the Sabbatical Year. Gentile slaves or "Canaanites" were slaves for life. Jeremias and Krauss note that slaves were sold on a special platform in Jerusalem.[57]

The royal courts of the Herodian family had many domestic slaves (*War* 1.511, 673; *Ant.* 17.199). The high priests also had numerous slaves (Mark 14:4–7; John 18:18, 26; *Ant.* 20.181, 206–207). Thus the wealthy elites could own scores or even hundreds of slaves who served as household servants, bodyguards, eunuchs in the harem (*War* 1.511; *m. Yebam.* 8:4) and met other purposes. But other well-to-do residents could also own a few slaves (cf. *m. Ed.* 5:6), such as the physician of Jerusalem (*m. Rosh Hash.* 1:7) or Mary the mother of John Mark (Acts 12:13).

In the ancient cities the submerged class, especially the destitute, the beggars, and the terribly ill, usually lived on the outskirts of the city.[58] The farther one was from the center socially and economically, the farther one lived also from the center geographically. Thus the wealthy lived mainly in the Upper City, the lower class in the Lower City and the New Town, and the outcasts lived on the fringes of the city if indeed they had residences at all.

We must say a word about the role of women. Women for the most part shared the social status of their husbands. In one case, however, a rich woman bought the high-priesthood for her future husband (*m. Yebam.* 6:4; *b. Yebam.* 61a; *Ant.* 20.213). Thus sometimes the husband shared the social status of the wife.

By most accounts, women in the patriarchal Palestinian Jewish society lived according to strict rules of modesty and retirement.[59] Jeremias

---

56. Jeremias, *Jerusalem*, 116–17.

57. See Ben-David, *Talmudische Ökonomie*, 70; Jeremias, *Jerusalem*, 312, 36; Krauss, *Talmudische Archäologie*, 2:362.

58. See Sjoberg, "Preindustrial City," 15–24; MacMullen, *Roman Social Relations*, 48–87; and Rohrbaugh, "Pre-Industrial City in Luke-Acts," 125–49.

59. See Jeremias, *Jerusalem*, 359–62; Strack and Billerbeck, *Kommentar*, 3:427–36; Witherington, "Women, New Testament," 6:957–58; Stagg and Stagg, *Women*, 15–54; Swidler, *Women*, 114–25, 167–73.

could write: "Eastern women take no part in *public life*." It is true that they were sensitive about being veiled in public or at least about having their hair tied up on top of the head (Sus 32; *m. Shabb.* 6.5; *m. Ketub.* 2:1; *m. Sota* 1:5; *m. BQ* 8:6). Men were admonished in the Talmud not to talk much with women (*m. 'Abot* 1:5; cf. *m. Qidd.* 4:12; *b. Ber.* 43b). Women of means apparently were kept in seclusion, seldom venturing into public (Philo, *Spec. Laws* 3.169; Philo, *Flaccus* 89; 4 Macc 18:7). Women were for the most part under the power of either a father or a husband (*C. Ap.* 2.201; *m. Ketub.* 4:4). And of course one can certainly find misogynist statements in the literature (*War* 2.121; Philo, *Hypoth.* 11.14; *L.A.E.* 18.1).

Yet some caution is in order in interpreting this evidence. In the first place, there was a Hasmonaean queen, Alexandra (*Ant.* 13.405–431), who ruled from 76 to 67 BCE. She obviously had a public life and wielded power. Further, many of the Herodian women do not at all seem shy and retiring—for example, Herod's mother-in-law, also named Alexandra, and the infamous Salome (*Ant.* 15.42–45; Mark 6:22). The women of the high-priestly house of Boethus flaunted their wealth in public (*Lam. Rab.* 1.50; cf. *b. Git.* 56a). Women of wealth, then, could be quite the opposite of the stereotype we encounter in some of the sources.

But the women of the lower class probably did not usually fit the stereotype either. Common sense would indicate that they could not be cloistered away from the public but had to work beside their husbands producing and selling their wares (*m. Ketub.* 9:4).[60] Since most of them lived in one-room houses that doubled as workshops, the life of the retiring and pampered élites was impossible.

The Talmud (*b. Git.* 90a) quotes a saying from a Palestinian sage that illustrates this point. The sage, R. Meir, indicates there are three types of men. One keeps his wife locked away; one allows her to converse with male relatives; the third, a base fellow, allows his wife to go out with her hair down and spin in the streets. Thus, women often lived in tension with the stereotype.

The documents relating to a Jewish woman named Babatha (dating to the early second century CE) are informative. They are, it is true, from

---

60. Jeremias makes this point (*Jerusalem*, 362). See also the interesting work of Prost in *History of Private Life*, 9–16, who points out that craftsmen from antiquity to fairly recent times opened their homes to the public. These were usually only one-room residences. Thus women—who also helped produce the goods—could not have remained secluded. On the use of residences as workshops in ancient cities see also MacMullen, *Roman Social Relations*, 48–87.

a period later than our primary focus and do not pertain explicitly to Jerusalem but surely nonetheless provide insight into the role and status of women. The documents indicate that Babatha managed a considerable agricultural business yet needed a male representative in her contacts with authorities.[61]

Therefore we would conclude that although this society was very patriarchal, we should not read too literally the statements of the Talmud and other sources. The practical necessities of living demanded that women often exceed customary expectations in public life and independence.

Thus Jerusalem in our period of consideration (30–66 CE) was inhabited by a population varied in its socioeconomic composition. The wealthier class tended to live in the Upper City and the lower class in the Lower City or in the burgeoning New Town. Many in the submerged class were probably homeless and wandered the streets and alleys begging, or otherwise lived on the outskirts of the city.

The Socioeconomic Composition of the Jerusalem Church

The Jerusalem church was probably fairly representative of the city's population. There were well-to-do members, though one cannot say they were among the wealthy elite. Simon of Cyrene owned a farm in the vicinity of Jerusalem (Mark 15:21). Barnabas sold his lands (in Judaea or in Cyprus? See Acts 4:36–37.) and gave the proceeds to the poor. Ananias and Sapphira (Acts 5:1) also possessed lands. We cannot be certain that the "fields" referred to in these texts were medium-sized estates or larger, but the sale of the property in the cases of Barnabas and especially of Ananias (whose lands are called κτημα) seem to have involved a not inconsiderable sum of money. Therefore, we would suggest that the latter two landowners—Ananias and Barnabas—owned medium-sized estates.[62] In addition, Mary, mother of John Mark, owned a house large enough to serve as a place of assembly for the primitive church and owned at least

---

61. On the Babatha collection see Isaac, "Babatha Archive," 62–75; and Broshi, "Agriculture and Economy," 230–40.

62. Kreissig, "Die Landwirtschaftliche Situation," 223, argued that these men owned large estates. Appplebaum, "Economic Life in Palestine," 2:259, urges caution in assuming too much from these examples. Jeremias, *Jerusalem*, 96, maintained that Joseph of Arimathea (Mark 15:42) also was a large-estate owner.

one domestic slave (Acts 12:12–17). She, like her kinsman Barnabas (Col 4:10), was wealthy. Manaen, the foster-brother of Herod Antipas (Acts 13:1), became later a leader in the church at Antioch. He was obviously from Palestine and probably a sometime resident of Jerusalem. Finally, one of Jesus's close disciples may also have been wealthy. Levi the tax collector (Mark 2:13–17) may have been rich since he could give a banquet in which many people reclined at their meal. Such a banquet suggests a large house. Certainly tax collectors could become quite wealthy (see Luke 19:1–10; *War* 2,287).

The lower class was certainly represented as well in the Jerusalem church. The occupation of some of Jesus's twelve disciples is reported in the Gospels. James and John's father, Zebedee, was the owner of a somewhat prosperous fishing business in Galilee, which could employ day laborers. Whether James and John still lived *in absentia* by this income or were entirely supported by the gifts of others we cannot know.[63] Peter and Andrew had also been fishermen (Mark 1:16). Jesus's brother James one of the pillars of the Jerusalem church (Acts 15:13–21; 21:17–25; 1 Cor 15:7; Gal 1:19; 2:9; *Ant.* 20.200), was presumably a carpenter by trade like Jesus (Mark 6:3). We would reasonably expect that most of the members of the Jerusalem church were craftsmen or small merchants, but the sources do not clearly indicate this.

The text of Acts (6:7) does state, "A great number of the priests were obedient to the faith." These were not of course from the high-priestly family since the latter actively persecuted the church (Acts 4:1–21; 5:17–42). Some have alleged that these priests were Essene priests and thus not from those serving in the temple.[64] There were probably Essenes living in Jerusalem since one of the gates at the southwest of the city was called by Josephus the Essene Gate (*War* 5.145), and Josephus may even refer to the Essene latrines.[65] It is also true that one of the traditional locations of the Upper Room (Acts 1:13) is in the general vicinity of the Essene

---

63. See Mark 1:19–20. On fishing in Galilee see Wuellner, *Meaning of Fishers of Men*, 45–63; Hoehner, *Herod Antipas*, 67; Clark, "Sea of Galilee," 348–50; Freyne, "Sea of Galilee," 899–901.

64. See Cullmann, "The Significance of the Qumran Texts." See the rebuttal of this view in G. Schneider, *Die Apostelgeschichte*, 430; and Haenchen, *Acts*, 269.

65. See *War* 5.145 the "Bethso"; and 1QM 7:6–7; 11QT 46; and Yadin, "The Gate of the Essenes," 90–91. The Essene Gate would be south of where the present Zion Gate stands. Yadin maintained that the latrines were west of the Hippicus tower (the modern Jaffa Gate). Others affirm that the latrines were near the Jerusalem University College on the southwest point of Mt. Zion. See Mackowski, *Jerusalem*, 64.

Gate.[66] Yet we do not know for sure that the Jerusalem Essenes had priests like those at Qumran (e.g., see 1QS 1:18). The simplest conclusion is that some of the ordinary temple priests—who numbered in Jerusalem perhaps two thousand—became members of the Jerusalem church.

We have reference to at least one Levite among the Christian community: Joseph Barnabas (Acts 4:36), who was named above as possibly a wealthy member. Since Barnabas was a Levite, his kinsman, John Mark (Col 4:10), was evidently one as well. Mark's mother, Mary, was also a woman of some means, as we indicated above. Since Barnabas was a native of Cyprus, however, he may not have served in one of the twenty-four courses in the temple.

The submerged class was also a part of the Jerusalem church. One would assume that the beggars and diseased people healed by Jesus (John 5:1–14; 9:1–12) or by the apostles (Acts 3:1–10; 5:12–16) became members of the church. In addition to the impoverished widows (Acts 6:1), there must have been other destitute persons cared for by the church (Acts 2:44–47; 4:34). These texts, which admittedly tend to be utopian in style, give the impression that the church assisted a considerable proletariat. We read nothing in Acts about church members of unapproved occupations and questionable births, though we might expect that Jesus's overtures to such people were continued by his disciples (Mark 2:13–17; Luke 15:1–2). Likewise, only Rhoda (Acts 12:13) appears in our sources as a servile member of the church, but there must have been others.

Women played a significant role in the Jerusalem Christian community. They were of course a prominent part of Jesus's ministry.[67] In the Upper Room before Pentecost Mary the mother of Jesus and other unnamed women[68] were part of the praying community (Acts 1:14). Women were among the first converts (Acts 5:14), and they were persecuted by Saul of Tarsus (Acts 8:3; 9:1–2; 22:4–5.).[69] Sapphira, wife of Ananias, a wealthy member of the church, was condemned along with

---

66. See Mackowski, *Jerusalem*,143–44.; and Wilkinson, *Jerusalem*, 168–69. On the other hand, one of the traditional sites of the Upper Room is near the possible location of Caiaphas's house. Does this mean that the primitive Christians were Sadducees? To argue from geographical proximity seems very tenuous. See the map in Mackowski and in Bahat, *Illustrated Atlas*, 55.

67. See Witherington, *Women*, 88–112; Massey, *Women*, 7–27.

68. Lüdemann suggests these women were the apostles' wives. See *Early Christianity*, 44.

69. See Swidler, *Biblical Affirmations of Women*, 291–92.

her husband for lying about their donation (Acts 5:1–11). That she was named alongside her husband probably indicates that she was a woman of influence. Another wealthy woman, Mary, mother of John Mark (Acts 12:12), offered her house for the assembly of the believers. Thus in the church as well as in urban society in general, certain women of wealth and influence could play prominent roles.

What is striking about our main source for early Jerusalem Christianity—the book of Acts—is that so little is said about socioeconomic class distinctions. The wealthy are hardly noticed at all except in a few cases of their extraordinary generosity. We cannot document that any of the high-priestly family or any of the governing élites were members of the earliest church. The lower class had the fewest references in the ancient sources, although one could speculate that they had the largest representation. The submerged class enters the story only to indicate that the church is caring for them. The central figures are those that perform ministries of some kind, whether they come from the upper or lower class. One should stop short of concluding that class went unnoticed in this religious community, but the traditions we have certainly deemphasize it.

Second, we should note that all the classes were represented. Neither the wealthy nor the impoverished were excluded. Earliest Christianity was not a movement within one socioeconomic class, but from the beginning, was as pluralistic as the city of Jerusalem itself. The observation made by G. Theissen and others about the Pauline churches is also true for the Jerusalem church. Christianity was no proletarian movement. It appealed to a broad spectrum of classes.[70]

The Cultural Groups among Jerusalem's Jews

The predominantly Jewish city of Jerusalem was bicultural. Most of the residents spoke and understood only Aramaic; some were bilingual; still others could probably speak only Greek.

Certainly the mother tongue of most Palestinian Jews was Aramaic: "The prominence of Aramaic at every level as the main language of Palestinian Jewry is now solidly backed by evidence."[71] Even in Jerusalem

---

70. Thiessen, *Social Setting*, 69. See also Meeks, *First Urban Christians*, 73; and Malherbe, *Social Aspects*, 31.

71. Schürer, *History of the Jewish People*, 2:26. The same was true for most parts of

Aramaic was predominant. The ossuary inscriptions in Jerusalem are mostly in a Jewish script.[72] The native languages tended to remain strong even under the cultural assault of Greek in the eastern part of the empire and Latin in the west.

Yet many, especially the educated and merchants, did learn Greek out of either an interest in Greek literature or a desire to appear sophisticated or for business reasons. The incursion of the Greek language and culture into Jewish Palestinian society is quite evident on many fronts. Coins were minted in Palestine with Greek inscriptions; the Hebrew and the Aramaic languages adopted numerous Greek loanwords; many Palestinian Jews had Greek names; the architecture of the residences and the pottery show Greek influences; the government—as far back as Herod the Great—was Hellenized; there was a gymnasium; and numerous inscriptions, papyri, and ostraca in Greek have been found.[73] N. Avigad writes from his experience excavating the houses of the wealthy: "The pursuit of things Hellenistic was then not uncommon in Jerusalem, particularly among the Hellenistic nobility."[74] The same pursuit existed in most cities and towns in the eastern empire.[75] To be Greek to some extent was highly desired by the wealthy.

But others were Greek culturally because they grew up in Greek centers of the Diaspora. Even their tomb and ossuary inscriptions were chiseled in Greek. Hengel reports on an ongoing project of collecting all the known epitaphs from Jerusalem. So far, of all the ossuaries with inscriptions (many ossuaries are not inscribed), the Greek inscriptions make up 39 percent of the total. Most of the rest are in a Semitic language only, but some are bilingual. Hengel concludes that those people inscribed their ossuaries in Greek whose family used Greek as the vernacular. Thus he suggests (conservatively) that the Greek-speaking population of Jerusalem was 10 to 20 percent of the total population.[76]

---

the empire. Native languages persisted as dominant for centuries in North Africa, Britain, Gaul and Spain. See Rostovtzeff, *Roman Empire*, 193; Jones, *Greek City*, 291–92.; Brunt, *Social Conflicts*, 170–72.

72. See Frey, *CIJ* 2:244–339.

73. See Hengel, *Hellenization of Judaea*, 8,9, 12; Mussies, "Greek in Palestine and the Diaspora," I.2.1040–1064; Krauss, *Lehnwörter*; Jeremias, *Jerusalem*, 74; Avigad, *Discovering Jerusalem*, 83, 120; Fitzmyer, *Wandering Aramean*, 35.

74. Avigad, *Discovering Jerusalem*, 120.

75. See, e.g., Lewis, *Life in Egypt*, 39.

76. Hengel, *Hellenization of Judaea*, 10. L. Y. Rahmani is managing this project.

Based on our figure for the total population of Jerusalem (sixty thousand residents), Greek-speaking Jews numbered between six thousand and twelve thousand.

There is evidence that many if not most of these Jews grew up in the Diaspora. There are ossuary and epitaph inscriptions in Greek of a man called Africanus Furius; of Justus the Chalcidian; of Nicanor from Alexandria; of Maria, wife of Alexander from Capua; of Rabbi Samuel from Phrygia, of Anin from Scythopolis;[77] and possibly of a family from Cyrenaica.[78]

P. Thomsen maintained that at least some of these were brought to Jerusalem after their deaths to be buried in the holy city.[79] This suggestion is certainly possible. We know for sure of at least one case of this.[80] Yet we have plenty of literary evidence of Jerusalem residents from the Diaspora. Ananel the priest came from Babylonia (*Ant.* 15.22, 34, 39–51), and Boethus the priest came from Alexandria (*Ant.* 15.319–22; 17.78, 339; 18.3; 19.279–80). The New Testament refers to other Jerusalem residents who came from the Diaspora: Simon of Cyrene (Mark 15:21), Barnabas of Cyprus (Acts 4:36), Nicolas a proselyte from Antioch (Acts 6:5). One ossuary inscription seems to state clearly that a family has immigrated to Jerusalem: "The bones of those who immigrated . . . the house of Izates" (in Greek).[81]

There were also proselytes in Jerusalem, former non-Jews who had grown up in Greek culture. One of the Seven in Acts was Nicolas the proselyte from Antioch (Acts 6:5). The ossuaries tell of others: "Judas, son of Laganio, the proselyte" (in Greek).[82] In addition, the royal family of Adiabene, which had converted to Judaism, had palaces and tombs in Jerusalem. Queen Helena, her son Menobazus, and Grapte, another relative, had residences (*War* 4.567; 5.55, 119, 252–53; 6.355; *Ant.* 20.17–37,

---

77. See Frey, *CIJ* 2, nos. 1226, 1227, 1233, 1256, 1284, 1372, 1373, 1374, 1414.

78. See Avigad, "Depository of Inscribed Ossuaries"; Sevenster, *Do You Know Greek?*, 147; Hengel, *Between Jesus and Paul*, 17.

79. Thomsen, "Die lateinischen und griechischen Inschriften," 116. See Sevenster's discussion, *Do You Know Greek?*, 146–47.

80. See the Abba inscription in which the deceased boasts of bringing back the bones of Mattathiah to be buried in Jerusalem. Yet Abba also illustrates the other position. He was born in Jerusalem, had gone into exile in Babylonia, and had returned. See Naveh, "New Tomb Inscription," 73.

81. Frey, *CIJ* 2, no. 1230.

82. Frey, *CIJ* 2, no. 1385. But see also no. 1386: "Maria the fervent proselyte" (in Hebrew).

75–80). These palaces were located in the lower city, not far from the Siloam pool. B. Mazar believes that a large building excavated on the southeast edge of the Ophel was one of these palaces. He suggests that this area was the popular place of residence for the highly placed Jewish proselytes from abroad.[83]

Therefore we conclude that a considerable number of Diaspora Jews had immigrated to Jerusalem by the first century CE. As Hengel maintains, we have to assume an independent Jewish Hellenistic culture in Jerusalem. Jerusalem was the "most important center of the Greek language in Jewish Palestine."[84]

In addition to the residents of Jerusalem who spoke Greek, there were thousands from the Diaspora who came to the feasts. Estimates vary as to the number of pilgrims who came to Passover and the other feasts. J. Jeremias concluded that 125,000 pilgrims arrived on average at Passover. E. P. Sanders arrived at the figure of 300,000 to 500,000. Of these, tens of thousands were from the Diaspora and rest from Palestine.[85] If we assume that 30,000 of the pilgrims were from the Greek-speaking Diaspora, then we have at various times of the year an even larger number of Greek-speaking Jews in Jerusalem.

These pilgrims had to stay somewhere, and it appears that they stayed in community centers built especially for them. Archaeologists have discovered several buildings south of the temple mount with a large number of rooms, ritual baths, and many cisterns.[86] There was also an inscription found that indicated that one Paris, a Jew from Rhodes, had donated a pavement in the vicinity, evidently for a community center for pilgrims.[87]

The most significant inscription, the Theodotus Greek inscription, was found in the City of David. Theodotus, the ruler of the synagogue, donated a building for studying Torah and included guest rooms to house pilgrims, and ritual baths to prepare them to enter the temple.[88]

83. Mazar, "Herodian Jerusalem," 230–337; Mazar, *Mountain of the Lord*, 213; and Ben-Dov, *In the Shadow of the Temple*, 155.

84. Hengel, *"Hellenization" of Judaea*, 9, 11.

85. See Jeremias, *Jerusalem*, 83; Sanders, *Judaism*, 127–28.

86. Mazar, "Herodian Jerusalem," 236; Ben-Dov, *In the Shadow of the Temple*, 153–54.

87. Isaac, "Donation for Herod's Temple"; and Ben-Dov, *In the Shadow of the Temple*, 155.

88. The text is in Frey, *CIJ* 2, no. 1404; and Deissmann, *Light*, 439–40. A text and

Thus pilgrims were housed in the synagogue. This Theodotus, since he calls himself in the inscription the "son of Vettenus" (a Roman name), is believed by many to have been a freedman. He would have been freed and granted citizenship by the help of someone from the Roman *gens Vettena*. Thus there is a speculation that this synagogue is the "synagogue of the freedmen" alluded to in Acts 6:9.[89]

Acts 6:9 may be referring to no less than five synagogues: one for freedmen, one for the people from Cyrenaica, one for Alexandrians, one for those from Cilicia, and one for those from Asia. The synagogue of the Alexandrians is referred to in the rabbinic sources (*t. Meg.* 3.6; *y. Meg.* 3.73) and possibly a synagogue for people from Tarsus is named (*b. Meg.* 26a).[90] The Talmudic assertion that there were 390 synagogues in Jerusalem (*b. Ketub.* 105a) may be an exaggeration, but certainly one should assume that a great many of them existed before the war. A substantial percentage of these synagogues must have been for Greek-speaking Jews (cf. Acts 24:12).[91]

Thus the Lower City, especially the City of David and the Ophel, was the locus for Greek-speaking Jews. The noble proselytes had palaces there; evidence of hospices for pilgrims from the Diaspora was found there in two inscriptions; one of these hospices was connected to a synagogue for Greek-speaking Jews; archaeologists have uncovered what could be guest rooms.

---

translation are also found in Hengel, *Between Jesus and Paul*, 17, 148. See also Hengel, "Hellenization," 13.

89. See Hengel, *Between Jesus and Paul*, 18. But contrast Deissmann, *Light*, 441. Compare the Goliath family in Jericho. One of them was a freedman who returned to Palestine after many years. See Hachlili and Smith, "Genealogy," 33.

90. See Strack and Billerbeck, *Kommentar*, 2:663 and Jeremias, *Jerusalem*, 5, 66. Conzelmann, *Acts*, 47 maintains that there is only one synagogue in mind in Acts 6:9 as did Bruce, *Acts*, 133. On the other hand, Marshall, *Acts*; and Haenchen, *Acts*, 271, maintain that there are two synagogues in view.

91. Cf. *y. Meg.* 3.1, which gives 480 synagogues for Jerusalem. Shanks, *Judaism in Stone*, 20, is not so sure the Talmudic numbers are exaggerations. The example of Rome may be useful. At least eleven different synagogue communities can be identified, according to Hengel. The members of each were distinguished by nationality, profession, and the like (*Between Jesus and Paul*, 14–15). See also Lüdemann, *Early Christianity*, 83.

Cultural Diversity in the Jerusalem Church

The Jerusalem church was distinguished by its two groups: the Hebrews and the Hellenists (Acts 6:1). The traditional view since John Chrysostom was that these groups were differentiated by language. The former group spoke a Semitic language and the latter group spoke Greek (*Homilies* 11, 14, 21). Various other views have been advanced, mainly that the Hellenists were Gentile Christians,[92] that the Hellenists were related to the Qumran Essenes,[93] that the Hebrews were Essenes,[94] and other suggestions.[95]

Yet since C. F. D. Moule's important article,[96] a consensus has been building in favor of the traditional view of Chrysostom. This view has been strongly supported by Hengel, C. C. Hill, and others.[97] Moule concluded that the Hellenists were "Jews who spoke *only* Greek," and the Hebrews were those "who, while able to speak Greek, knew a Semitic language also."[98] As Hill remarks, the second part of this conclusion may be suspect—it is doubtful that most "Hebrews" could speak Greek, although surely some could—but Moule's language-based distinction between the two groups is surely correct.[99] Thus the Jerusalem church had two factions separated by language and culture.

The Hebrews were of Palestinian origin. Some of them had possibly been pilgrims for the feast of Pentecost and had remained after conversion, but we should expect that most of them were inhabitants of Jerusalem.

---

92. See Cadbury, "Hellenists," 5:59–74.

93. Cullmann, "Significance of Qumran," 29: "I do not assert that these Hellenists were former Essenes (which is not impossible) but that they came from a kind of Judaism close to this group." See Haenchen, *Acts*, 260–61 and Black, *Scrolls and Christian Origins*, 76–77, for a rebuttal of Cullmann.

94. Black, *Scrolls and Christian Origins*, 77.

95. Hengel lists twelve views (*Between Jesus and Paul*, 4–6). See also the bibliography given in Bruce, *New Testament History*, 219 n. 1.

96. Moule, "Once More," 100–102.

97. Hengel, *Between Jesus and Paul*, 8–11, and Hill, *Hellenists and Hebrews*, 22–24. In addition see Fitzmyer, *Wandering Aramean*, 123; Conzelmann, *Acts*, 45; Lietzmann, *History of the Early Church*, 70; Loisy, *Birth*, 113; Larsen, "Die Hellenisten und die Urgemeinde"; Schneider, *Die Apostlegeschite*, 406; Pesch, *Die Apostelgeschichte*, 227; Bruce, *Acts*, 128; Marshall, *Acts*, 125–26; Haenchen, *Acts*, 260.

98. Moule, "Once More," 100.

99. Hill, *Hebrews and Hellenists*, 23.

Likewise the Hellenists could have been in part pilgrims from the Diaspora. The simplest explanation, however, is that most of them came from the ranks of the Greek-speaking Jews of Jerusalem who lived and worshiped in the Lower City, especially in the City of David. This location contrasts with the traditional sites of the Upper Room, both of which are in the Upper City.

Thus we should see at least three locations for the activity of the Jerusalem church: the Upper Room in the Upper City, the Hellenistic synagogues in the Lower City, and of course the temple. The evidence indicates that sociologically and culturally the church was quite diverse.

The Jerusalem church, almost from the very beginning if not actually from Pentecost on, was culturally pluralistic. One cannot speak of an Aramaic stage followed by a Hellenistic Jewish stage.[100] The stages were always contemporaneous. The two subcultures within the early church—the Aramaic and the Greek—were two springs flowing from the same source and in turn nourishing together the subsequent Gentile Christianity.

Likewise one cannot determine that a portion of the New Testament (e.g., a pericope of the Gospels) originated outside Palestine because of "Hellenistic" influences.[101] To consider Palestine and earliest Christianity only in terms of the Aramaic culture is now quite impossible.

---

100. See, e.g., Schulz, *Spruchquelle*, 57–184, who posits these stages for the hypothetical source Q.

101. See, e.g., Bultmann, *History of the Synoptic Tradition*, 48, 299, who made decisions of provenance based on such considerations.

11

What Would You Do for a Living?

HISTORIANS HAVE LONG CONCERNED themselves with the questions of the theology of the early church. What was the Christology, ecclesiology, or pneumatology of these pioneers of Christianity? These questions, as important as they are, often give the impression that all Christians in the ancient world were theologians or clergypersons. This chapter seeks to understand the common church members by reflecting on the kinds of jobs they held. We soon understand that these folk were not only involved with understanding their faith but also with the mundane task of making a living in a largely non-Christian pagan society.

First, we must define some terms. By early Christianity we mean the pre-Constantinian era. Second, we will not distinguish between orthodox Christianity and the other types such as Gnostic Christianity, Montanism, the Ebionites, and so forth. People who considered themselves Christian believers were classed together. We will first examine the occupations that Christians considered unworthy of their new faith. Next we will discuss the occupations actually engaged in by the members of the early church as these occupations are witnessed to by the writings of the New Testament, the church fathers, the martyrologies, the apocryphal literature, non-Christian pagan literature, papyri, and inscriptions.

What Would Christians Not Do for a Living?

Occupation and confession were interlinked in early Christianity. We are accustomed in modern Western society to compartmentalizing our jobs, political views, and family relationships from our religious beliefs. The ancients did not do that. One's religion permeated one's political, economic, and kinship values even as one's kinship, politics, and economics permeated one's religious commitments.[1] For the early Christians, some occupations were compatible with the new faith and some were not. Even those that were compatible in theory might not be compatible if engaged in improperly.

The Christian prohibition of certain occupations was based on three principles: (1) Occupations that infringed on the moral teachings of the faith were condemned. These included prostitution and all connected with it. (2) Occupations that devalued human life were forbidden. These included the military, gladiatorial contests, and even competitions such as chariot racing, where the participants might have to kill or injure someone (though Christians seemed to be in the stands when their fellow Christians were being martyred). In addition, civil magistrates in the church were usually disapproved of because they might have to sentence someone to death. (3) Occupations that participated in idolatry in any way were forbidden. Obviously, then, one could not be a pagan priest, but some Christians even warned against incense selling, sculpting, masonry, painting, and the like in the service of a pagan temple.

Already in the New Testament there is reference to the occupations based on vice. Paul found it necessary to instruct the Corinthian church members that certain occupations or lifestyles had become unacceptable for the new believers: "Neither sexually immoral persons, idolaters, adulterers, male prostitutes, pederasts, thieves, greedy people, drunken people, verbally abusive people, nor robbers will inherit the kingdom of God and some of you were doing these things" (1 Cor 6.9–10). Thus, the recent converts had to be instructed regarding the relationship of confession to occupation.

Over a century later we again find a listing of unapproved occupations. The two most detailed lists—those of Tertullian of Carthage and Hippolytus of Rome, both around 200 CE (see Table 11.1)—explicitly refer to prostitutes and all those connected to prostitution. Tertullian says no prostitutes, pimps (*lenones*), panders (*perductores*), attendants of prostitutes (*aquarioli*), or brothel keepers can be accepted because they are connected with immorality (*Idol.* II; *Apol.* 43)[2]. Hippolytus's *Apostol-*

---

1. Hanson and Oakman, *Palestine in the Time of Jesus.*
2. See Glover, *Tertullian,* 192

ic Tradition lists prostitutes, panders (πορνοβοσκος), and sodomites[3] or licentious men.[4]

Table 11.1: Forbidden and Restricted Occupations according to Tertullian (*Idol.* 11, *Apol.* 43) and Hippolytus (*Trad. Ap.*)

TERTULLIAN	HIPPOLYTUS
Forbidden Occupations	Forbidden Occupations
Prostitute	Prostitute
Pimp	Pimp
Pander	
Brother Keeper	
Attendant of Prostitutes	
	Sodomite
	Actor
	Charioteer
Soldier (but if one at conversion may continue)	Soldier (but if one at conversion may continue; must be taught not to execute people or to take the military oath)
Gladiator	Gladiator
Trainer of Gladiators	Trainer of Gladiators
	Huntsman in the arena
	One doing wild animal shows
	Public official concerned with gladiatorial shows
Frankincense seller (probably; must not sell to pagan temples)	
	Priest of idols
	Keeper of idols
	Magistrate of a city
	Military governor
	Teacher of children (but if no other way to make a living may continue)
Magician	Magician
Sorcerer	Charmer

3. So Dix, *Apostolic Tradition*, 27.

4. So Easton, *Apostolic Tradition*, 42. The *Apostolic Tradition* of Hippolytus is extant mostly in the Coptic versions (Sahidic and Boharic). Dix, *Apostolic Tradition*, gives the Greek words that were transliterated into the Coptic.

TERTULLIAN	HIPPOLYTUS
Astrologer	Astrologer
Soothsayer	Interpreter of Dreams
	Maker of amulets
	Seller of quack medicines
Occupations with Restrictions	Occupations with Restrictions
Plasterer (must not work on pagan temples)	
Painter (must not work on pagan temples)	Painter (must not make idols)
	Sculptor (must not make idols)
Stonecutter (must not work on pagan temples)	
Bronze worker (must not work on pagan temples)	
Engraver (must not work on pagan temples)	

The *Apostolic Tradition* also prohibits Christians from being actors or those who make shows in the theater. We know from other writers that the theater was sternly condemned in the early church. Theophilus of Antioch (160 CE) wrote that Christians were forbidden to go to the theater (*Auto.* 3.15). Tertullian maintained that the theater was connected with idolatry (*Spect.* 10). Minucius Felix (Rome, 210 CE) condemned all shows, mimes, actors, and the theater in general (*Oct.* 37). Cyprian of Carthage (250 CE) condemned mimes because they encouraged adultery and produced effeminate men (*Ep.* 1.8). A Christian may not, according to Cyprian, remain an actor, nor may a Christian teach the art of acting to anyone. If the Christian is a new convert and has no other way to make a living than teaching acting, he must rely on Christian charity (*Ep.* 60.1–2). Novatian (Rome, 250 CE) condemned all public shows and Greek contests in poetry, music, and athletics (he specifically mentioned the shot put contest). Although idolatry was the mother of all public amusements, and they should be avoided because of that connection, he was also offended that the Greek athletic competitions were in the nude (*Spectacles* 1–8). Thus, the Christian opposition to sexual immorality led not only to prohibiting occupations that explicitly depended on that vice (prostitution) but also to prohibiting occupations that could encourage adultery (thus acting/miming and even athletic contests).

The Christian attitude toward military service was usually negative, though at times it could be ambivalent. Condemnations of making war are numerous and found over a wide geographical area. Both Justin Martyr (155 CE, Rome; *1 Apology* 39; *Dial.* 110) and Irenaeus (180 CE, Gaul; *Haer.* 4.34.4) applied the prophecy of turning swords into plowshares (Isa 2:3–4) to the Christian movement and affirmed that Christians were not to make war. Tatian (160 CE, Rome and Syria; *Oratio ad Graecos* II) announced that he declined any interest in military command, and Clement of Alexandria (200 CE, *Paed.* 1.12) wrote that Christians are not trained for war but for peace. Cyprian of Carthage challenged his congregation by affirming that the hand that holds the Eucharist must not be corrupted by sword and blood (*De Bono Patientiae*). Origen (230 CE; Alexandria and Caesarea) responded to the pagan Celsus's observation (late second century) that Christians were not fulfilling their duty to the emperor by refraining from the military service. Origen argued that Christians did more good for the emperor and his armies by praying for them than others did by fighting under them (*Cels.* 8.68–69, 73). Arnobius (300 CE, North Africa; *Adversus Nationes* 1.6) maintained that Christians were completely pacifist, preferring to have their own blood shed than to shed the blood of another. Lactantius (300 CE; Asia Minor; *Inst.* 6.20) wrote that Christians cannot kill at all, neither in war nor even by accusing someone of a capital crime in a court of law.

Tertullian addressed this issue at length twice. He maintained that to take the military oath of allegiance to the emperor was completely unacceptable for Christians, and that violence contradicted the Christian way of life. When Jesus disarmed Peter in the Garden of Gethsemane, he disarmed every soldier. Since Jesus declared that anyone who lives by the sword will die by the sword, how can any Christian carry one? When Jesus would not even take someone to court to sue him, how can a Christian take part in battle (*Idol.* 19; *Cor.* 11)? Yet, surprisingly, having written these things, Tertullian conceded that if one were already a soldier and converted to Christianity, he might continue, though he must be aware that it would cause great difficulty. The best course of action, according to Tertullian, would be to quit the military (*Cor.* 11).

Clement of Alexandria too seems to have allowed one to remain a soldier if he converted while serving in the military. In the *Protrepticus* 10 he advised that if a person was a farmer when he became a Christian he should continue being a farmer but now one that meditated on God while tilling the fields. If one had been a sailor at his acceptance of the new faith, he could continue sailing the seas, but now he should rely on the heavenly captain. And if one had been a soldier when knowledge had taken hold of him, he should listen to the just commander. Thus, it appears that in all three cases, the farmer, sailor, and soldier, the new convert is allowed to continue his occupation but now with a Christian emphasis. The *Apostolic Tradition* of Hippolytus, however, agreed with Tertullian and Clement. A military leader who converts must resign his commission. An ordinary soldier who does so may remain a soldier but must be taught not to execute people and must not take an oath. One already a Christian who wishes to become a soldier must be cast out of the church.

The arrangement given in Hippolytus may record accurately the Christian relationship to the military: Christians converted while in the military could remain if they did not fight in a war. R. H. Bainton suggests that Christian soldiers would serve in a police function: guarding the emperor, keeping the peace, aiding governors in provinces, guarding prisoners, caring for the mail, doing secretarial duties, and aiding in fire protection.[5] In these functions Christian soldiers would not be called upon to kill anyone, but if a war began, they would have to refuse to fight.

After the accession of Constantine in 324 CE the Christian attitude toward war began to change.[6] Now Christians began to see the military service more in terms of just war. If the war is just, so the argument goes, it is possible for a Christian to participate. This idea was developed fully by Augustine in the fifth century, especially in response to the barbarian invasions (*Civ. Dei* 1.21, 26).

In spite of the condemnations of military service, we know of several examples of Christian soldiers. Whether they were all serving in the capacity described by Bainton is unknown and questionable. In the New Testament there are four notable cases of encounters with believing soldiers. John the Baptist encounters some soldiers who ask his ethical advice. John replies that soldiers should not extort or falsely accuse people, and that they should be content with their wages (Luke 3:14). Thus there is no instruction to either quit the army or to refrain from battle. Second, Jesus encountered a centurion whose son/servant he healed (Matt 8:5–13; Luke 7:1–10; John 4:46–54) and was impressed with the centurion's faith.

---

5. Bainton, *Christian Attitudes*, 79.

6. Hornus, *It Is Not Lawful*, 168; Bainton , *Christian Attitudes*, 66

Third, Acts 10 narrates the conversion of the first Gentile to the faith, Cornelius, a centurion in Caesarea. Upon his conversion, there is nothing indicated about instructions to refrain from warfare. Finally, there is a narrative of a jailer, presumably a soldier, in Philippi who was baptized in the night by Paul and Silas (Acts 16:25–34), again with no information about pacifist teaching.

Cadoux[7] maintains that there is no reliable example of a Christian soldier after the stories of the Acts of the Apostles (late first century CE) until the time of Emperor Marcus Aurelius (160–180 CE). The oft-re-ported incident of the *Legio XII Fulminata* or Thundering Legion, which took place around 173 CE, is the first literary reference to Christian sol-diers after the New Testament period. This legion, which contained many Christians recruited in Armenia, was campaigning in Germany when the heat and lack of water threatened their safety. The Christians in this legion prayed for rain and were answered immediately (Dio Cassius 72; Eusebius, *H.E.* 5.5; Tertullian, *Apol.* 5). Thus, this narrative, which may have legendary elements, indicates a large number of Christians in the military in the later half of the second century.

Tertullian himself noted the presence of Christians in the military, even though he opposed their service. He wrote that Christians had by his time filled every place among the pagans, even the military camp (*Apol.* 37). His treatise on a Christian soldier's refusal to wear a laurel wreath refers to many other Christian soldiers who condemned this behavior (*Cor.* I). The references to soldiers in the *Apostolic Tradition* of Hippoly-tus also demonstrate that there were numerous Christian soldiers, since Hippolytus found it necessary to handle this problem in some detail. Thus, one gets the impression that by the close of the second century in North Africa and in Rome many Christians served in the military to the displeasure of the Christian leaders.

Eusebius gives us the same impression a century later. He notes that by the end of the third century there were numerous Christians in the imperial palaces, governing provinces, and serving in the military (*H.E.* 8.1). But in the year 303 CE Galerius sought to rid the armies of Christians by forcing them to either renounce their faith or be stripped of their rank (*H.E.* 8.4). Eusebius reports that many of them (one would think not all, however) left the army at that time. Thus there were enough

---

7. Cadoux, *Early Church*, 276; cf. Bainton, *Christian Attitudes*, 67–69; Hornus, *It Is Not Lawful*, 122

Christians in the armies to get the attention of Diocletian's lieutenant, Galerius.

Also of importance among the literary sources are the martyr narratives. The earliest recorded execution of a Christian soldier was Basileides in 205 CE, who was executed for refusing to take an oath. Marinus was likewise beheaded in 260 CE, and Marcellus of North Africa was executed in 298 CE. On the other hand, Maximilian (295 CE), who was being forced into military service, refused to serve. The proconsul tried in vain to convince him to serve by noting that there were already many Christians in the armies. After Maximilian's continued refusal, he was executed by the sword. Three other soldier martyrdoms take place in the early fourth century, before the reign of Constantine: The forty martyrs of Sebaste in Armenia (308 CE), Julius the Veteran (Moesia Inferior, 304 CE), and Dasius (Moesia Inferior, 304 CE). The last account is important because it too refers to "many foolish men who call themselves Christians." In other words they did not behave as uprightly as Dasius (see *Christ. Mart.*, xxvi–xlix, 133–279).

In addition to the literary references to Christian soldiers there are several tomb inscriptions. Hornus[8] has identified seven inscriptions that are certainly Christian and four that are probably so. He lists among the seven three from Rome, one undated, and two from the third century; three from Phrygia in Asia Minor, two from the third century, and one from the early fourth; and one from Thrace. In the four other cases soldiers in grave inscriptions tell of deceased Christian family members. Were the soldiers also Christians, or only their family members? Hornus allows that they probably were Christians as well. These are from Dalmatia (late third century), Asia Minor, and Rome. To these inscriptions we should add the papyrus letters described by Judge and Pickering from 297 CE in Egypt, which refer to a soldier of "at least moderate means" who was probably a Christian.[9]

Thus there is evidence for Christian soldiers spread throughout the empire. Bainton surmised, however, that the strongest opposition to Christian military service was in the churches in the East. He believes that North Africa was divided on the issue, and that Rome was less opposed to Christians in the military (because of the three military epitaphs

---

8. Hornus, *It is Not Lawful*, 119–21.

9. Judge and Pickering, "Papyrus Documentation," 52.

in Christian cemeteries). The eastern frontier, however, had the most extensive Christian participation in the army.[10]

Could Christians serve in the army? Probably most Christians frowned on it before the time of Constantine. Nevertheless, the church had the problem of what to do with soldiers who converted. Must they leave the service, or could they continue? The church for the most part seems to have settled on the arrangement noted above: stay in the army, but do not kill anyone. But even that decision would probably not have been acceptable to every Christian. There were undoubtedly some who fought and killed.

Christians were also concerned about other violent occupations. The gladiatorial contests and even the chariot races concerned them. Theophilus of Antioch (*Auto.* 3.15), Athenagoras (177 CE, Athens; *Leg.* 35), Minucius Felix of Rome (*Oct.* 37), Tertullian of Carthage (*Spect.*11, 19) and Cyprian of Carthage (*Ep.* 1.7) wrote that Christians were forbidden to witness gladiatorial contests. Tatian condemned both gladiators and boxers (*Oratio ad Graecos* 23); while Clement of Alexandria classed gladiators with parasites, flies, and weasels (*Paed.* 2.1). The *Apostolic Tradition* of Hippolytus forbids receiving anyone into the church who is a gladiator (μονομαχος), a trainer of gladiators, a huntsman in the arena (κυνηγος), or a public official concerned with the gladiatorial shows. Thus no one connected in any way with the gladiatorial contests could, according to Hippolytus, be accepted as a Christian.

There were probably two reasons for this strong denunciation of the gladiatorial contests. First of all the contests involved the taking of human life and feeding the crowd's hunger for watching dying people.[11] Second, the amphitheater was used to reinforce loyalty to the emperor cult and other local pagan deities.[12] Thus the gladiatorial contests were permeated with religious significance. The same reasons lay behind the disgust for chariot races on the part of Christians. Again the *Apostolic Tradition* refuses to admit into the church anyone who is a charioteer (ηνιοχος). This prohibition is consistent with the condemnation of the chariot games in general found in Tertullian (*Spect.* 9), Minucius Felix (*Oct.* 37), Athenagoras (*Leg.* 35), and Novatian (*Spectacles* 5). According

---

10. Bainton, *Christian Attitudes*, 71–72.

11. Auguet, *Cruelty*, 46–53.

12. Futrell , *Blood in the Arena*, 93.

to Roland Auguet,[13] the chariot games even more than the gladiatorial contests had the imprint of pagan religion on them. Further, chariot racing often became violent when opponents tried to overturn others' chariots, to the delight of the crowd.

Finally, in this second category of occupations prohibited because of the devaluing of human life is that of civil magistrate (despite the case of Erastus, which will be discussed below). Hippolytus (*Trad. Ap.*) declares that no magistrate (αρχων) of a city who wears the purple may be received for baptism. Tatian had declared that he did not wish to rule (*Oration ad Graecos* II) while in the *Letter to Diognetus* 10:5 (second century) the desire to dominate others or rule others is condemned. Celsus, the critic of Christianity in the second century, complained that Christians declined public office, neglecting their duty (Origen, *Cels.* 8.75). Minucius Felix wrote, "Nor do we consist of the lowest plebians even if we do refuse your honors and your purple" (*Oct.* 31). Canon 56 of the Council of Elvira (Spain in 306 CE) forbade a Christian to hold the office of the *duovir* or city magistrate.[14]

Cadoux suggests five reasons why Christians refrained from seeking or perhaps even accepting public office in the city.[15] (1) Such positions were associated with idolatry, and their holders would be expected to participate in pagan rituals. (2) The social standing of most Christians made them unable to seek public office. (3) Christians did not value the worldly glory, and thus the glory of their society. (4) Christianity taught forgiveness and nonresistance, and punishing wrongdoers would contradicted this teaching. (5) Christian repudiation of retaliation was so great that they would not endure even watching someone being put to death. Tertullian gives most of these reasons in his treatment of Christians and idols. He declares that Christians could hold public office only if they would have nothing to do with sacrifices, giving public shows, taking oaths, passing judgments on people, or giving penalties (*Idol.* 17). Tertullian's point was that it is not possible to hold a public office and avoid these things.

Yet, we again detect that there were Christian public officials, for Tertullian refers to a dispute in the churches over this matter. Those who argued in favor of Christians holding public office pointed to Joseph and

13. Auguet, *Cruelty*, 124, 131.

14. Kyrtatas, *Social Structure*, 101.

15. Cadoux, *Early Church*, 225–26.

Daniel in the Hebrew Bible, men who were loyal to God but still held important posts in pagan governments (*Idol.* 17). Thus Tertullian's view was evidently not the only one in the ancient church. Furthermore, Tertullian himself seems to witness the Christian involvement in both the army and the magistracy in a passage admittedly full of rhetorical exaggeration: "We have filled every place: cities, insulae, fortresses, towns, markets, even army camps, tribes, town councils,[16] the palace, the senate, the forum" (*Apol.* 32). Harnack was perhaps overreaching, but not by much, when he suggested that by the end of the third century "the court, the civil service, and the army were full of Christians."[17] City magistrates who were converted to Christianity, like soldiers, had a difficult decision to make. Undoubtedly, some did give up their positions, but one should not imagine that this was the inevitable choice.

The third and final category of prohibited occupations in the early church was that with a connection to idolatry. Tertullian and Hippolytus condemned any kind of work that had direct association with idolatry, and were critical of any that had indirect connection with it. Hippolytus (*Trad. Ap.*) excludes from consideration for church membership any priest of idols or keeper of idols. Further, he counsels that Christian sculptors and painters must be taught not to make idols. Thus the occupation was acceptable if it was not used for idolatry. Tertullian verbally thrashed Christian artisans who made idols and attempted to justify their lucrative business by appealing to the Apostle Paul's admonition to work with one's hands (*Idol.* 4–5, 7). To his horror, Tertullian could even point to idol makers who had been chosen for ecclesiastical office (*Idol.* 7). He will allow no associations with paganism at all. Thus stucco workers, painters, stonemasons, bronze workers, and engravers must not work on pagan temples (*Idol.* 8). He even has serious doubts about incense sellers since one never knows how the incense will be used (possibly in a pagan ritual, *Idol.* 11). Once again, the necessity of condemning such practices indicates that many Christian artisans did work for pagan temples and even fashioned idols for a living.

Also included under this category would be the occupations associated with the magical arts. Hippolytus forbids the occupations of magician (μαγος), charmer, astrologer (αστρολογος), interpreter of dreams, seller of quack remedies, and amulet maker. Tertullian also condemns Christians

---

16. Town councils: *decuriae*; see Glover, *Tertullian*, 168.

17. Von Harnack, *Mission and Expansion*, 311.

who practice astrology for a living and even mentions one in particular who challenged him on this issue (*Idol.* 9). Thus, some Christians were trying to continue telling people's fortunes by the stars. Elsewhere, Tertullian maintains that there were among Christians no magicians (*magi*), soothsayers (*aruspices*), diviners (*arioli*), and astrologers (*mathematici*). Allowing for the rhetoric, we would conclude that these occupations would have been rare among Christians since the idolatrous connections would have repulsed most.

Finally, both Hippolytus and Tertullian have reservations about a Christian working as a teacher. Hippolytus argues that if someone teaches children worldly knowledge, it would be better for him to quit teaching altogether. If, however, that person has no other skill (τεχνη) by which to make a living, let him have forgiveness. Tertullian is much less generous about this occupation. He maintained that a Christian should not be a schoolmaster because he would have to teach children pagan literature as well as perform certain customary pagan rites (*Idol.* 10).

The profession of faith on the part of the members of the new religion often resulted in difficult decisions regarding their occupations. Some Christians evidently continued their old lifestyles in about the same way as before conversion, incurring the harsh critique of the ecclesiastical writers.[18] Others must have made sweeping changes such as quitting a military or magisterial post, abandoning a trade or craft, or renouncing any contact with magical practices and the like. Perhaps we should imagine that most Christians, however, stood in the middle of these two extremes, ambivalent and even conflicted over the practical application of their newly found faith.

What Christians Did for a Living

Historians point out that Christian thought brought dignity to manual labor.[19] The classical authors often referred to craftsmen as inferior beings whose bodies were deformed by hard work and whose minds were like those of slaves (Cicero, *Off.* 1.42, Aristotle, *Pol.* 1.5.10; Dio Chrysostom, *Or.* 7.110; Lucian of Samosata, *Fug.* 12–14).[20] But Pauline references (1

18. See ibid.

19. Agrell, *Work,* 150–51; Richardson, *Biblical Doctrine,* 43; Latourette, *History of Christianity,* 246; Munier, "Labour," 469.

20. Burford, *Craftsmen,* 29; MacMullen, *Roman Social Relations,* 115–17.

Cor 9:1–27; Eph 4:28; 1 Thess 4:9–12; 2 Thess 3:6–15) indicate that work was thought of in the Pauline communities as "divinely commissioned for man."[21] Thus Christianity, like Judaism, did not share the disdain for working with the hands that we find so frequently in the Greco-Roman literature. Further, early Christianity was primarily an urban movement. Not many peasants or country folk were involved in the movement until the late third or early fourth century.[22] The occupations that we would expect to be most often mentioned in the literary sources, therefore, should be urban occupations: skilled crafts and unskilled manual labor. Paul instructed the Thessalonian believers "to work with your own hands" in quietness (1 Thess 4:11). From this and similar texts Best and Meeks conclude that most of the Thessalonian Christians were "manual workers, whether skilled or unskilled."[23] Meeks argues further that this instruction was what Paul in all likelihood typically gave to new converts and that we should therefore conclude that most early Christians throughout the empire were handworkers. This is confirmed by Eph 4:28, writes Meeks, where the Deutero-Pauline author again urges the reader to labor with his hands.[24]

Such information as we have for first-century Christianity would seem to agree with Meeks's thesis. We read in the New Testament of a metalworker (2 Tim 4:14); tentmakers (Acts 18:3); a general handworker (1 Cor 9:6); Tertius, a scribe (Rom 16:22), a purple dealer (Acts 16:14–15, evidently financially well off); and day laborers (Jas 5:4). But the New Testament also gives witness to other occupations: lawyer (Titus 3:13), city manager (Rom 16:23, see below on Erastus), physician (Col 4:14), merchants (Jas 4:13), and soldiers (Luke 3:14, 7:1–10 and Acts 10:1–49, well-to-do centurions; Acts 16:25–34, a jailer). There are also several slaves listed in the New Testament, which we will discuss later.

The literary sources for the second century also indicate that most Christians were handworkers. The *Didache* (100 to 140 CE in Syria) admonishes its readers to put guests of the congregation to work: If the guest is a craftsman (τεχνιτης), let him work and then let him eat, but if he is not a craftsman, use your own judgment about whether to feed

---

21. Agrell, *Work*, 151.

22. Meeks, *First Urban Christians*, 9–50; Frend, *Rise of Christianity*, 132, 421–22, 572.

23. Best, *Thessalonians*, 176; cf. Meeks, *First Urban Christians*, 64.

24. Meeks, *First Urban Christians*, 65.

him (12.3–4). Athenagoras of Athens affirms that among Christians one could find uneducated persons, craftsmen, and old women (*Leg.* 11). Celsus, the pagan detractor of Christianity, charged that the Christian movement consisted of leather cutters, fullers, and woolworkers (Origen, *Cels.* 3.55–56, 58). Eusebius refers to Theodotus the shoemaker, a second-century Christian heretic (*H.E.* 5.28). Thus, the impression one forms is that most second-century Christians were hand laborers.

Yet there are also references to occupations above mere manual labor. A Christian physician in Gaul was martyred in 180 CE (*Christ. Mart.*, 77). Callistus, bishop of Rome, was originally a banker and an imperial slave (Hippolytus, *Heresies* 9.7). A second Theodotus, also considered a heretic and a disciple of Theodotus the shoemaker, was a banker (Eusebius, *H.E.* 5.28). Christians may have been heavily involved in the banking business at some point[25] since Pliny (*Epistles* 10) mentions in his second-century letter to Trajan that Christians took an oath not to deny a deposit to anyone who asked for it back.

The sources for the third century mention similar Christian occupations. Tertullian referred to sculptors, painters, stucco workers, stonecutters, soldiers, and artisans in general (*Idol.* 4–5, 8; *Cor.* 1). Hippolytus (*Trad. Ap.*) listed painters, sculptors, and soldiers. Tertullian complained that at least one Christian persisted in practicing astrology for a living (*Idol.* 9). Three of the celebrated soldier martyrdoms happened in the third century: the forty martyrs of Armenia (Sozomen , *Ecclesiastical History,* 9.2), Marcellus of Tingis in Mauretania (*Christ. Mart.,* xxxvii 251–59), and Basileides (*Christ. Mart.,* xxvii, 133–35). For the brief period of the fourth century before the accession of Constantine we have only reference to two soldiers: both Julius the Veteran and Dasius were martyred in Moesia Inferior (*Christ. Mart.,* xxxix, 261; xli, 273–79).

We have postponed until now any discussion of Christian slaves and freedmen. First, we will survey the evidence for Christian slaves/freedmen in general. Next, we will discuss specifically imperial slaves/freedmen.

The New Testament gives us evidence to the presence of large numbers of slaves in the early congregations. Paul's long list of greetings to Roman Christians (Romans 16) surely included several slaves and former slaves. Peter Lampe concluded that of the twenty-six persons listed in that text we can identify the origins of fourteen of them. Of these, ten

---

25. Kyrtatas, *Social Structure,* 124; Horsley, *New Documents,* 5:139.

PART THREE—THE EARLY CHURCH

were probably of servile origin. Thus over two-thirds of the names on this list (whose origins can be identified) were slaves or freed persons.[26] We have good reason to conclude that the Corinthian church also had a large percentage of slaves and former slaves. Paul's references to the "household of Stephanus" (1 Cor 1:16) and Chloe's people (1 Cor 1:11) indicate large houses with significant numbers of slaves, evidently many of them believers. The much-discussed Erastus, the οικονομος or city manager/treasurer of Corinth, was probably a freedman.[27] Paul even devoted a small letter to the issue of slavery (Philemon). Admonitions to Christian slaves to obey their masters as an act of Christian service also testify to the importance of slaves in the early Christian community (Col 3:22–25; Eph 6:5–9; 1 Tim 6:1–2; 1 Pet 2:18–21). Finally, the Acts of the Apostles refers to two slaves who were believers in the Way: Rhoda (12:13) and the Ethiopian eunuch (8:26–40).

Pliny the Younger, in a letter to Emperor Trajan (*Epistles* 10) written from Asia Minor in 110 CE, described two female slaves among the sect of Christians. Ignatius, also in 110 CE, greeted fellow believers in the "house of Tavia" in his *Letter to the Smyrnaeans* 13.2 (in Asia Minor). Evidently this house was a large household with several Christian slaves. In addition, Ignatius admonished slaves of Philippi (Macedonia) to endure their slavery to the glory of God (*Polycarp* 4). Also in the second century was the martyrdom of Blandina, a slave of Gaul, who was tortured to death (Eusebius, *H.E.* 5.1). Third-century sources also mention slaves. The martyrdoms of Revocatus and Felicitas, Christian slaves, took place in 201 CE in Carthage (*Christ. Mart.*, xxvii, 108–9). Tertullian wrote that Christians collected charitable donations on a regular basis, part of which went toward caring for aging slaves (*Apol.* 39).

Of special interest are the imperial slaves and freedmen. The career of a slave in the imperial service could be one of upward mobility and increasing wealth. Often sons of slaves would be sent to special schools and then as young men would begin to work their way up through the bureaucratic system.[28] Thus a Christian of lowly origin could in the course of a lifetime of imperial service acquire great wealth and power. Already in the New Testament we find reference to imperial slaves/freedmen. Paul refers in Philippians to Caesar's household and to the *praetorium*

26. Lampe, "Roman Christians," 228.

27. Bartchy, *First-Century Slavery*, 59–60.

28. Finn, "Social Mobility," 31–37.

(πραιτωριον; 4:22 and 1:13) where he is imprisoned, probably meaning the slaves in the imperial service.[29]

Toward the end of the first century Clement of Rome wrote his letter to the Corinthian church and sent it by three men named Claudius, Valerius, and Fortunatus. The first two persons bear names suggestive of imperial freedmen, affirms Dimitris Kyrtatas.[30] Lightfoot, followed by others,[31] postulated that Clement of Rome himself was an imperial freedman of the household of Titus Flavius Clemens, the cousin of Emperor Domitian, who reigned from 81 to 96 CE.[32] (See the epistle of 1 Clement.)

In the second century, the companion of Justin the Martyr (died 165 CE) was one Euelpistus, one of Emperor Marcus Aurelius's slaves (*Christ. Mart.*, 51). Irenaeus indicated that there were believers in the royal court of imperial freedmen, Carpophorus and Callistus, and a Christian imperial concubine, Marcia, in the reign of Commodus (176–192 CE; *Haer.* 9.7).

The third century witnessed an increased presence of Christians in the imperial service. Eusebius narrated that the royal house of Emperor Alexander Severus (reigned 222–235 CE) consisted mostly of believers (*H.E.* 6.28). Likewise Emperor Valerian (253–260 CE) was said to have filled his palace with godly people and to have had a veritable church of God in his house until he became alarmed at the growing numbers of Christian bureaucrats and sought to strip them of their power and possessions (Eusebius, *H.E.* 7.10; Cyprian, *Ep.* 81). By the time of Diocletian (284–305 CE) Eusebius could write that in the imperial palaces emperors had been for some time allowing their wives, children, and slaves to adopt Christianity (*H.E.* 8.1). Under Diocletian, however, many Christian soldiers and imperial slaves were either stripped of their honors or put to death (*H.E.* 8.1, 8.6). Eusebius narrates especially the martyrdom of Dorotheus and Gorgonius, who along with many other imperial slaves were martyred under Diocletian. Thus by the end of the third century,

29. Ibid., 33; Kyrtatas, *Social Structure*, 79.

30. Kyrtatas, *Social Structure*, 79.

31. Lightfoot, *Apostolic Fathers*, 1.1.25–61; Finn, "Social Mobility," 33; Kyrtatas, *Social Structure*, 80. For a survey of views on the social standing of early Christians, see Malherbe, *Social Aspects*, 29–32.

32. The dates for Roman emperors are taken from Keppie, *Understanding Roman Inscriptions*, 136–37.

there seems to have been a growing body of Christian bureaucrats in the imperial system.[33] Many of these must have acquired great wealth.

The grave inscriptions in Christian cemeteries and catacombs also refer to slaves, although the references are relatively rare.[34] Orazio Marucchi lists seven such inscriptions from Italy.[35] Cadoux cites two inscriptions from the second century that name imperial freedmen.[36] Kaufmann gives the inscriptions from the tombs of three Christian freedmen.[37] Of special interest are quotations of epitaphs of Christian imperial slaves. There are Publius Aelius Rufinus, probably a freedman of Emperor Hadrian (117–138 CE) and Marcus Aurelius Januarius, freedman of Marcus Aurelius (161–180 CE). One inscription, from the catacomb of Domitilla, may even connect us with the above-mentioned list of names in the Epistle to the Romans 16: "Julia, (freedwoman or slave of) Augusta Agrippina. Narcissus (slave of) Augustus Trajan. Agrippinianus put (this here)."[38] Kaufmann suggested that Narcissus and Julia (both mentioned in Rom 16:11, 15) were husband and wife and former slaves of Nero's mother who were still serving the imperial household in the time of Emperor Trajan (98–117 CE). Thus the two listed by Paul were imperial slaves who continued to serve the palace into the second century. Kaufmann affirmed, probably too uncautiously, "The identification of this Narcissus with the one named by the apostle seems to me as good as certain."[39]

One is therefore struck by the frequent mention of Christian slaves both generally and especially with reference to imperial slaves. It is tempting to conclude that a large percentage of the Christian population in the first three centuries was of servile origin. Kyrtatas has argued strongly against this conclusion, maintaining that there was only a "small number" of slaves in the early church.[40] He correctly notes that relatively few Christian sepulchral inscriptions indicate servile origins.[41] But his own evidence would seem to contradict his conclusions. We have as much

33. Kyrtatas, *Social Structure*, 81–82.

34. Marucchi, *Christian Epigraphy*, 223; Kajanto, *Onomastic Studies*, 8.

35. Marucchi, *Christian Epigraphy*, numbers 224–27 for slaves and 243 for an imperial freedman.

36. Cadoux, *Early Church*, 392.

37. Kaufmann, *Handbuch*, 102.

38. Translation from ibid., 98.

39. Ibid., 99.

40. Kyrtatas, *Social Structure*, 45.

41. Ibid., 48; cf. Kajanto, "Onomastic Studies," 8 and Marucchi, *Christian Epigraphy*, 223.

literary evidence for Christian slaves as for any occupation. The relative lack of sepulchral references to servile origin may have been because of the Christian disregard for social ranking (Gal 3:28; Lactanius, *Inst.* 5.14–15).[42] Rather, the literary sources would suggest strongly that from the beginning up through the third century there were undoubtedly many slaves and freed persons in the church. Table 11.2 summarizes our results so far.

Table 11.2: Christian Occupations in the First Four Centuries Based on Literary Evidence

FIRST CENTURY	SECOND CENTURY
*Lawyer; #City Manager; *Physician; ^Metal worker#Tentmaker; #Scribe; *Merchants; *Bankers; ~Day Laborers; #Craftsmen; +Craftsmen; +Purple dealers; ~Soldier (3); *Imperial slaves; *^#Slaves; Scribe	Physician (Gaul); *Imperial slaves; #~Artisans; ^+Slaves (Gaul); ~Woolworkers; ~Leatherworkers; ~Fullers
THIRD CENTURY	**FOURTH CENTURY**
*Imperial slaves; @Astrologer; @Sculptors; @Painters; @Stonecutters; @Stucco workers; @Artisans; *@^~Soldiers (also in Mauretania)	Soldiers (Moesia Inferior; Armenia)

*Rome/Italy #Achaia @Carthage +Macedonia

^Asia Minor &Egypt =Dalmatia ~Syria

The inscriptions are also very helpful in discovering what occupations early Christians pursued. We will discuss below the occupations noted on Christian epitaphs or in the few papyri that are clearly Christian. Those inscriptions and papyri identified as Christian[43] may paint for us a landscape of the types of occupations Christians pursued. After we have surveyed the evidence, Table 11.3 will summarize our results.

By far the most controversial of the inscriptions comes from first-century Corinth. It reads in Latin: *Erastus pro aed sp stravit.* The epigrapher of the Corinthian materials, John Harvey Kent, understood the inscription as follows: *[praenomen nomen] Erastus pro aedili[ta]te s(ua) p(ecunia) stravit*—"Erastus in return for his aedileship laid (the pavement)

42. Kajanto, *Onomastic Studies*, 15; Marucchi, *Christian Epigraphy*, 223.

43. See Keppie, *Understanding Roman Inscriptions*, 121–24.

at his own expense."[44] In other words, the Erastus of the inscription paid for a pavement to be laid in return for his being appointed to the office of *aedile* (commissioner of public buildings). Kent identified this Erastus with the Erastus of Rom 16:23 (see also 2 Tim 4:20; Acts 19:21–22) based on the following three reasons: (1) This inscription dates around the middle of the first century, about the same time as the Epistle to the Romans. (2) The name Erastus was not a common name.[45] Thus one would suspect that any other reference to an Erastus might be the same person. (3) Paul's description of Erastus in Rom 16:23 (the οικονομος or manager of the city) is near enough to an *aedilis* to be the same function. Kent concluded that the Erastus of Romans and the Erastus of the inscription were the same person, that he was probably a freedman, and that he had acquired considerable wealth.[46]

Meggitt (following Cadbury[47]) recently challenged all three of Kent's arguments. The inscription's date is not clearly the mid-first century, maintains Meggitt; it could be the latter part of the century. The two titles (οικονομος and *aedilis*) could mean the same thing but they are not a perfect fit. Finally, Erastus was not such an uncommon name. Meggit has found fifty-five examples of the name in Latin and twenty-three in Greek.[48]

We would suggest that the date of the inscription is not as crucial as it might seem. Why should we suppose that the date of the inscription has to be the same as the date of the Epistle to the Romans? One can easily imagine that a person such as Erastus would have continued to serve the city of Corinth for many years in the first century. Second, Mason has established without question that the Greek term οικονομος can be used for the Latin *aedilis*.[49] His investigation into the Greek translations of Latin institutions has made it more historically sound to accept that the terms could be referring to the same office.[50] Finally, that the name Erastus is found frequently in antiquity is significant but not conclusive.

44. Kent, *Corinth*, 99.

45. Kent had also affirmed that this was the only occurrence of the name Erastus among the inscriptions of Corinth. This has proven incorrect. Another Erastus has been found from the second century. See Clarke, *Secular and Christian Leadership*, 55.

46. Kent, *Corinth*, 99–100.

47. Cadbury, "Erastus," 42–58.

48. Meggitt, "Social Status," 218–23.

49. Mason, *Greek Terms*, 71.

50. Clarke, *Secular and Christian Leadership*, 50; Winter, *Welfare of the City*, 185–92.

We must ask what are the chances of there being two Erasti in Corinth from approximately the same period of time who held important city offices? A host of historians and commentators have accepted Kent's identification of the two persons.[51] Although one cannot be certain, on the whole it seems better to conclude that these two Erasti were the same person. Thus, one of the earliest inscriptions refers to a wealthy Christian who held a high-ranking office in the city of Corinth.

The third-century inscriptions and papyrus texts attest to the following occupations: From Italy are a shorthand writer or amanuensis (*notarius*), a woolworker,[52] a wagon driver,[53] a record keeper, and (surprisingly) the treasurer of the gladiatorial games and of the wine.[54] From Nicomedia in Asia Minor is an inscription of a Christian woodcarver.[55] The sources from Egypt attest to two bankers,[56] a well-to-do gymnasiarch or director of the gymnasium, three wealthy merchants, and a worker in the central tax administration.[57]

From fourth-century Rome and Italy we have inscriptional evidence for Christians as wagon drivers,[58] dealers in huts or cottages, a female chamber servant, physicians, a stonecutter or mason, an artisan (*artefex*), and a lawyer.[59] From Achaia in the fourth century have come epitaphs of a Christian clothing merchant, innkeeper, teamster, and a pickler who also trapped lobsters and fish.[60] The inscriptions from Asia Minor indicate that there were butchers and a (female) physician among the Christians.[61] In Egypt a papyrus text was found from the fourth century that refers to a Christian sailor who was reprimanded for being drunk.[62] Two inscriptions, one from Carthage and one from Macedonia, name the

---

51. Theissen, *Social Setting*, 75–79; Meeks, *First Urban Christians*, 58–59; Harrison, *Paulines*, 100–105; Clark, *Secular and Christian Leadership*, 50–56; Winter, *Welfare of the City*, 185–92; Fitzmyer, *Romans*, 750.

52. Diehl, *Inscriptiones*, 1:134, 124.

53. Kaufmann, *Handbuch*, 111.

54. Carletti, *Iscrizioni*, 30–32.

55. Horsley, *New Documents*, 5:127.

56. Ibid., 5:139.

57. Judge and Pickering, "Papyrus Documentation," 50–51, 69, 70.

58. Kaufmann, *Handbuch*, 112.

59. Diehl, *Inscriptiones*, 1:117, 118, 120, 127, 140.

60. Kent, *Corinth*, 173–79.

61. Horsley, *New Documents*, 1:136–37; 2:16.

62. Ibid., 2:173.

Christians in certain tombs as procurators or managers of large landed estates. Fortunatus of Carthage was the *procurator* of the estate (*fundus*) of Benbenesis.[63] Flavius Callistus was the επιτροπος (steward) of imperial lands (χωριων δεσποτικων) near Thessalonica.[64] These were two very important managerial positions, perhaps carried out by wealthy freedmen, sometime in the early to mid-fourth century.[65] Even more surprising is the identification of Ovinius Gallicanus as a Christian consul, reported by T. D. Barnes.[66] Gallicanus, one of the consuls of Rome in 317 CE, a position only open to those of senatorial rank, made a large donation to a Christian church in Ostia. Thus he appears to have been a Christian and would be the earliest known Christian of such a high rank.

We now summarize the results of our survey of the inscriptions and papyri. To get a sense of both the sweep of the history of Christian occupations and the ancient world in general Table 3 includes inscriptions/papyri up to the sixth century. It does not list government occupations or military positions after the time of Constantine since the holders of those offices may not have been typical for Christians in the pre-Constantinian age. It does, however, give the inscriptional evidence for soldiers prior to Constantine discussed above under prohibited occupations. The occupations are listed by century with those inscriptions undated placed last. Most of these undated inscriptions would be presumably from somewhere between the fourth and sixth centuries. The vast majority of the Christian inscriptions, however, do not indicate any occupation for the deceased.[67]

63. Ennabli, *Inscriptions,* 336.

64. Feissel, *Recueil des inscriptions,* 118.

65. Ignatius, *Polycarp* 8:2 referred to another επιτροπος around the year 110 CE He greeted the wife of the επιτροπος and her household in Smyrna in Asia Minor. That he did not greet the procurator himself probably means that the latter was not a Christian.

66. Barnes, "Statistics and the Conversion," 142.

67. The largest collection of inscriptions having to do with Christian occupations is found in Diehl, *Inscriptiones,* 1:116–45, with over 170 Latin inscriptions from tombs in Italy, North Africa, Gaul, Sardinia, and Dalmatia, but sometimes lacking dates. Those occupations from Asia Minor, Syria, and Egypt in the fifth and sixth centuries and the undated ones from those regions were given in Horsley, *New Documents* volumes 1 and 2. Those occupations cited from Achaia during his time period were given in Kent, *Corinth.*

Table 11.3: Christian Occupations in the First Six Centuries Based on Inscriptions and Papyri

FIRST CENTURY	SECOND CENTURY
#Aedile (Erastus)	*Imperial slaves; *Record keeper

THIRD CENTURY	FOURTH CENTURY
*Woolworker; *Shorthand taker; *Record keeper *Treasurer of the gladiatorial games; *Wagon driver; *Wood-carver; &Banker (2); &Gymnasiarch; &Merchant(3); &Tax office administrator (2); *Soldier (3); ^Soldier (3); ^Soldier (2); &Soldier; Soldier; @Imperial slave	*Dealer in huts; *Female chamber servant; *Stonecutter; *Artisan; *Physician (2); *Banker; *Lawyer; *Wagon driver; @Chief physician; @Manager of a large landed estate; #Merchant; #Innkeeper; #Teamster, #Pickler; +Manager of an Imperial estate; &Sailor; ^Butcher, ^Soldier; *Consul

FIFTH CENTURY	SIXTH CENTURY
*Chamber servant; *Bread baker; *Stone cutter; *Merchant;*Banker; *Minter; *Lawyer (3); #Poultryman; ^Banker; =Lawyer	*Chief physician; *Goldsmith; *Merchant; *Linen merchant; *Hay seller; *Goat seller; *Pig seller; *Banker (4); *Secretary; *Teacher

UNDATED	
*Dealer in huts; *Shepherd; *Weeder; *Butler; *Slave who carried the child's satchel; *Barber (3); *Miller (2); *Cook; *Pickler; *Tanner; *Pastry maker (2); *Physician (7); *Bread baker; *Butcher; *Carpenter; *Goldsmith; *Ironsmith (2); *Linen maker; *Cobbler (4); *Stonecutter; *Sculptor (2); *Artisan (2); *Builder; *Dice maker; *Mirror maker; *Painter (4); *Merchant (4); Papyrus seller; *Elephant handler (?); *Linen seller (2); *Fruit dealer; *Bottle maker; *Oil seller; *Pig seller; *Fish seller (2); *Banker (2); *Minter (2); *Shorthand writer (3); *Teacher (3); *Lawyer (5); #Captain of the guard; #Bath attendant; #Guardsman; #Grainman; #Pheasant breeder; #Goatherd; #Banker (2); ^Architect; &Chief physician; &Scribe; @Merchant; =Sculptor; =Cobbler; Fish seller (Sardinia); Physician (Gaul); Purple worker (Syria)	

*Rome/Italy #Achaia @Carthage +Macedonia ^Asia Minor &Egypt =Dalmatia

What did the early church look like? There are certainly references to poor people among the early believers. Paul wrote that there were not many wise, powerful, or noble Christians at Corinth (1 Cor 1:26–28). Minucius Felix in the second century admitted that many Christians were poor (*Oct.* 36). Celsus wrote in his attack on Christianity:

> The following are the rules laid down by (Christians). Let no one come to us who has been instructed, or who is wise or prudent . . . but if there be any ignorant, or unintelligent, or uninstructed, or foolish persons, let them come with confidence . . . they desire and are able to gain over only the silly, and the mean, and the stupid, with women and children. (Origen, *Cels.* 3.44[68])

Based on such texts some historians concluded that most early Christians were poor people and slaves.[69] Our survey above, however, does not offer support for this thesis. The overwhelming majority of Christians were not poor, if by poor we mean destitute, starving, and anxious about finances. We found evidence of skilled craftsmen and bureaucrats who would have made at least an acceptable living. I therefore maintain[70] that most Christians were laborers, either skilled craftsmen or unskilled workers. Tables 11.2 and 11.3 support such a conclusion. Further, we have maintained (*pace* Kyrtatas[71]) that a significant minority of Christians were slaves/freed persons as again the evidence in the tables suggests.

Scholars are even beginning to notice clues that indicate that quite a number (a significant minority) of the early Christians were well off. The evidence would require a separate article adequately to cover this issue. In summary, however, the New Testament,[72] the second- and third-century Christian authors,[73] and the papyri and inscriptions from the second and third centuries[74] refer to Christians of wealth and even a few of significant social standing. Rodney Stark too argues that the Christian faith attracted

68. Translation from Crombie, *Works of Origen*, 481–82.

69. For a survey of views on the social standing of early Christians see Malherbe, *Social Aspects*, 29–32.

70. With Meeks, *First Urban Christians*, 64–65.

71. Kyrtatas, *Social Structure*, 45.

72. Judge, *Social Patterns*, 52–58; Malherbe, *Social Aspects*, 41–57; Winter, "Public Honoring," 87–103.

73. Cadoux, *Early Church*, 393; Kyrtatas, *Social Structure*, 101–6; Frend, *Rise of Christianity*, 132.

74. Judge and Pickering, "Papyrus Documentation," 47–71; Kaufmann, *Handbuch*, 101–2; Marucchi, *Christian Epigraphy*, 244–47.

more interest among the wealthy than had been supposed.[75] Our survey found references to several wealthy Christians as well.

We should, to be sure, distinguish between wealth and social standing. That there were few Christians of senatorial or equestrian rank before Constantine is a safe conclusion.[76] But that there were many successful, wealthy, and upwardly mobile persons in the Christian movement seems also undeniable. Christianity was a religion of "fairly well-off artisans and tradespeople."[77]

Conclusion

As the Christian movement spread in the first three centuries, it had to decide on the appropriate ethical conduct of its members. New people were coming from every occupation imaginable to seek teaching and baptism. Could converts be allowed to continue in the same line of work as before they came to faith? Increasingly the church leaders said no. Certain principles—sexual immorality, the devaluing of human life, and idolatry—eliminated some occupations and curtailed others. Religious confession had to have an effect on occupation.

Of course, not every church member was compliant with these rules, and it is even probable that not every congregation or locality accepted and enforced the rules of Tertullian and Hippolytus. No group is able to achieve total conformity with its rules. The nonconformists are even hinted at in the very sources that construct the ethical structure concerning Christian labor. We can imagine some Christians quite shameless in their refusal to listen to the church leaders on such ethical questions. On the other end of the spectrum were probably ethical rigorists who would not practice any trade except those narrowly defined as acceptable to the new faith. But common sense would dictate to us that most Christians

---

75. Stark, *Rise of Christianity,* 29–47.

76. Barnes, "Statistics and the Conversion," 136, identifies only ten Christians of senatorial rank between 180 and 312 CE. For references to Christian senators see Acts of Peter 4; Eusebius, *H.E.* 6.21 (?), 7.16. Cf. Tertullian, *Apol.* 37 and Cyprian, *Ep.* 81. Were Titus Flavius Clemens, cousin of Emperor Domitian, his wife Domitilla, and Anicius Glabrio Christians in 95 CE? Se Dio Cassius 67.14, Suetonius, *Domitian* 15, and Eusebius, *H.E.* 3.18. Frend, *Martyrdom,* 214–16 and Cross, *Oxford Dictionary,* 499, 679 doubt it.

77. Meeks, *First Urban Christians,* 65.

struggled between conscience and pocketbook to earn a living and remain Christian in an overwhelmingly pagan society.

What would a typical Christian congregation have looked like in the first three hundred years? If you had attended a worship service what sort of people would you have seen?

A representative survey of Tables 11.2 and 11.3 present the following results:

- **Artisans:** tentmakers, metalworkers, woolworkers, leatherworkers, sculptors, painters, stonecutters.

- **Educated artisans**: lawyers, physicians, record keepers/shorthand takers, scribes

- **Merchants**: purple sellers, bankers

- **Bureaucrats**: city manager, tax office administrator, imperial slaves/freedmen, managers of large estates, treasurer of gladiatorial games

- **Soldiers**

- **Slaves**

You could have seen people from just about every walk of life. There would have been a few abysmally poor, a significant minority of slaves (in the Roman church several imperial slaves/freedmen), a few soldiers and bureaucrats, almost no people of senatorial or equestrian rank, and a large number of artisans and merchants. We can find no evidence that Christianity appealed to only one social level. If most Christians were artisans and merchants, most urban people in general were from these groups. If very few people of senatorial rank were Christians before Constantine, there were also relatively very few senators in the empire. But virtually every social level is represented in the early church at some point.

The artisans and merchants ranged from the financially secure to the well-to-do. They had little status, but they nonetheless had their craft or business to make a living and contribute to the needs of the church. The majority of Christians were in the large urban group between the miserably poor and the upper classes of senators, equestrians, and decurions.[78]

---

78. Gager, *Kingdom and Community*, 96–106.

Bibliography

Abel, F. M. *Geographie de la Palestine.* 2 vols. Etudes bibliques. Paris: Gabalda, 1967.

Adan-Bayewitz, David. *Common Pottery in Roman Galilee.* Bar-Ilan Studies in Near Eastern Languages and Culture. Ramat-Gan, Israel: Bar-Ilan University Press, 1993.

———. "Kefar Hananya, 1986." *IEJ* 37 (1987) 178–79.

Adan-Bayewitz, David, et al. "Preferential Distribution of Lamps from the Jerusalem Area in the Late Second Temple Period (Late First Century BCE—70 CE)." *BASOR* 350 (2008) 37–85.

Adan-Bayewitz, David, and Mordechai Aviam. "Jotapata, Josephus, and the Siege of 67." *JRA* 10 (1997) 131–65.

Adan-Bayewitz, David, and I. Perlman. "The Local Trade of Sepphoris in the Roman Period." *IEJ* 40 (1990) 153–72.

Agrell, Göran. *Work, Toil and Sustenance: An Examination of the View of Work in the New Testament, Taking into Consideration Views Found in Old Testament, Intertestamental, and Early Rabbinic writings.* Translated by Stephen Westerholm. Stockholm: Verburm, 1976.

Ahlström, Gösta W. "Wine Presses and Cup-Marks of the Jenin-Megiddo Survey." *BASOR* 231 (1978) 19–49.

Albright, W. F., and C. S. Mann. *The Acts of the Apostles.* AB 31. New York: Garden City, 1967.

Alföldy, Géza. *Die römische Gesellschaft: Ausgewählte Beiträge.* Heidelberger althistorische Beiträge und epigraphische Studien 1. Stuttgart: Steiner, 1986.

———. *Römische Sozialgeschichte.* Wissenschaftliche Paperbacks: Sozial-und Wirtschaftsgeschichte 8. Wiesbaden: Steiner, 1975.

Alston, Richard. "Houses and Households in Roman Egypt." In *Domestic Space in the Roman World: Pompeii and Beyond,* edited by R. Laurence and Andrew Wallace-Hadrill, 25–39. Journal of Roman Archaeology Supplementary Series 22. Portsmouth, RI: JRA, 1997.

Alt, Albrecht. *Kleine Schriften zur Geschichte des Volkes Israel.* Vol. 3. Edited by Martin Noth. Munich: Beck, 1959.

Amiry, Suad, and Vera Tamari. *The Palestinian Village Home.* London: British Museum, 1989.

Andreau, Jean. "Twenty Years after Moses I. Finley's *Ancient Economy.*" In *The Ancient Economy,* edited by Walter Scheidel and Sitta von Reden, 33–49. New York: Routledge, 2002.

———. "Wages: Classical Antiquity." In *Brill's New Pauly: Encyclopedia of the Ancient World: Antiquity*, edited by H. Cancik and Helmuth Schneider, 15:542–44. 16 vols. Leiden: Brill, 2010.

Angela, Alberto. *A Day in the Life of Ancient Rome.* Translated by Gregory Conti. New York: Europa, 2009.

Applebaum, S. "Economic Life in Palestine." In *The Jewish People in the First Century: Historical Geography, Political History, Social, Cultural and Religious Life and Institutions*, edited by S. Safrai and M. Stern, 2:631–700. 2 vols. CRINT I/2. Assen: Van Gorcum, 1976.

———. "Judea as a Roman Province: The Countryside as a Political and Economic Factor." *ANRW* II.8 (1978) 355–96.

———. *Judaea in Hellenistic and Roman Times.* SJLA 40. Leiden: Brill, 1989.

———. "The Problem of the Roman Villa in Eretz Israel." *Eretz Israel* 19 (1987) 1–5.

———. "The Zealots: The Case for Reevaluation." *JRS* 61 (1971) 155–70.

Arav, Rami. *Bethsaida: A City by the North Shore of the Sea of Galilee.* Bethsaida Excavation Project. Reports & Contextual Studies 4. Kirksville, MO: Truman State University Press, 2009.

Arlandson, James Malcolm. *Women, Class, and Society in Early Christianity: Models from Luke-Acts.* Peabody, MA: Hendrickson, 1997.

Arnal, William E. *Jesus and the Village Scribes: Galilean Conflicts and the Setting of Q.* Minneapolis: Fortress, 2000.

Auguet, Roland. *Cruelty and Civilization: The Roman Games.* London: Routledge, 1994.

Aviam, Mordechai. "Economy and Social Structure in First-Century Galilee: Evidence from the Ground-Yodefat and Gamla." Paper presented at the annual meeting of the Society of Biblical Literature, Boston, MA, November 2008.

———. "Galilee: The Hellenistic to Byzantine Periods." In *NEAEHL* 2:453–58.

———. *Jews, Pagans and Christians in the Galilee: 25 Years of Archaeological Excavations and Surveys: Hellenistic to Byzantine Periods.* Land of Galilee 1. Rochester, NY: University of Rochester, 2004.

———. "Yodefa." *Hadashot Arkhelogiyot* 112 (2000) 18–19.

———. "Yodefat/Jotapata." In *The First Jewish Revolt: Archaeology, History, and Ideology*, edited by A. M. Berlin and J. Andrew Overman, 121–33. London: Routledge, 2002.

Avigad, Nahman. "The Burnt House Captures a Moment in Time." *BAR* 9 (1983) 66–72.

———. "A Depository of Inscribed Ossuaries in the Kidron Valley." *IEJ* 12 (1962) 1–12.

———. *Discovering Jerusalem.* Oxford: Blackwell, 1980.

———. "How the Wealthy Lived in Herodian Jerusalem." *BAR* 2 (1976) 22–35.

Avi-Yonah, Michael. *The Holy Land.* Rev. ed. Grand Rapids: Baker, 1977.

———. "Shihin or Asochis" *EncJud* 14:1398.

Badian, E. "Triclinium." In *Oxford Classical Dictionary*, edited by N. G. L. Hammond and H. H. Scullard, 1093–94. Oxford: Clarendon, 1970.

Bagati, B. "Nazareth, Excavations." In *NEAEHL* 3:1103–5.

Bahat, Dan. *The Illustrated Atlas of Jerusalem.* New York: Simon & Schuster, 1990.

Bahat, Dan, and Magen Broshi. "Excavations in the Armenian Garden." In *Jerusalem Revealed: Archaeology in the Holy City*, edited by Y. Yadin and E. Stern, 55–56. Jerusalem: Israel Exploration Society, 1975.

Bainton, Roland H. *Christian Attitudes toward War and Peace.* New York: Abingdon, 1960.

Bammel, Ernst. "The Revolution Theory from Reimarus to Brandon." In *Jesus and the Politics of His Day*, edited by Ernst Bammel and C. F. D. Moule, 11–68. Cambridge: Cambridge University Press, 1984.

Baron, Salo Wittmayer. *A Social and Religious History of the Jews*. 2nd ed. 18 vols. New York: Columbia University Press, 1952.

Barnes, Timothy. "Statistics and the Conversion of the Roman Aristocracy." *JRS* 85 (1995) 135–47.

Barnett, P. W. "The Jewish Sign Prophets—AD 40–70: Their Intentions and Origin" *NTS* 27 (1981) 679–97

Bartchy, S. Scott. *First-Century Slavery and the Interpretation of 1 Corinthians 7:21*. SBLDS 11, 1973. Reprinted, Eugene, OR: Wipf & Stock, 2003

Batey, Richard A. "Is Not This the Carpenter?" *NTS* 30 (1984) 249–58.

———. *Jesus & the Forgotten City: New Light on Sepphoris and the Urban World of Jesus*. Grand Rapids: Baker, 1991.

———. *Jesus and the Poor*. New York: Harper & Row, 1972.

———. "Sepphoris: An Urban Portrait of Jesus." *BAR* 18 (1992) 50–62.

Beals, Ralph L., and Harry Hoijer. *An Introduction to Anthropology*. 3rd ed. New York: Macmillan, 1965.

Bedford, P. R. "The Economy of the Near East in the First Millennium BC." In *The Ancient Economy: Evidence and Models*, edited by J. G. Manning and Ian Morris, 58–83. Social Science History. Stanford: Stanford University Press, 2005.

Bell, H. Idris. *Egypt from Alexander the Great to the Arab Conquest*. Gregynog Lectures for 1946. Oxford: Clarendon, 1948.

Ben-David, Arye. *Talmudische Ökonomie*. Hildesheim: Olms, 1974.

Ben-Dov, Meir. *In the Shadow of the Temple: The Discovery of Ancient Jerusalem*. Translated by Ina Friedman. New York: Harper & Row, 1985.

Berlin, Andrea M. "Jewish Life before the Revolt: The Archaeological Evidence." *JSJ* 36 (2005) 417–70.

Best, Ernest. *A Commentary on the First and Second Epistles to the Thessalonians*. London: Adam & Charles Black, 1972.

Betlyon, John W. "Coinage." In *ABD* 1:1076–89.

Bietenhard, Hans. *Der Tosefta—Traktat Sota*. Judaica et Christiana 9. Berlin: Lang, 1986.

Black, Matthew. *The Scrolls and Christian Origins: Studies in the Jewish Background of the New Testament*. 1961. Reprinted, BJS 48. Chico: Scholars, 1983.

Blevins, William L. "The Early Church: Acts 1–5." *RevExp* 71 (1974) 463–74.

Bliss, Frederick Jones, and Archibald Campbell Dickie. *Excavations at Jerusalem*. London: Palestine Exploration Fund, 1878.

Blümner, Hugo. *Technologie und Terminologie der Gewerbe bei Griechen und Römern*. 4 vols. Hildesheim: Olms, 1969.

Boles, H. Leo. *A Commentary on Acts of the Apostles*. Nashville: Gospel Advocate, 1976.

Bowman, John Wick. *Jesus' Teaching in Its Environment*. Richmond: John Knox, 1963.

Branscomb, Harvie. *The Teachings of Jesus: A Textbook for College and Individual Use*. Nashville: Cokesbury, 1931.

Broshi, Magen. "Agriculture and Economy in Roman Palestine: Seven Notes on the Babatha Archive." *IEJ* 42 (1992) 230–40.

———. "Estimating the Population of Ancient Jerusalem." *BAR* 4/2 (1978) 10–15.

———. "Excavations in the House of Caiaphas, Mt. Zion." In *Jerusalem Revealed: Archaelology in the Holy City*, edited by Y. Yadin and E. Stern, 57–60. Translated and abridged by R. Grafman. Jerusalem: Israel Exploration Society, 1975.

Brown, Raymond E. *Gospel according to John.* 2 vols. AB 29, 29A. Garden City, NY: Doubleday, 1966.

Bruce, F. F. *Commentary on the Book of Acts.* NICNT. Grand Rapids: Eerdmans, 1954.

———. *The New Testament Documents.* 5th ed. Eerdmans Pocket Editions. Grand Rapids: Eerdmans, 1960.

———. *New Testament History.* New York: Doubleday, 1969.

Brunt, P. A. *Italian Manpower, 225 B.C.—A.D. 14.* Oxford: Clarendon, 1971.

———. *Social Conflicts in the Roman Republic.* Norton Library. Ancient Culture and Society. New York: Norton, 1971.

Buchanan, George Wesley. "Jesus and the Upper Class." *NovT* 7 (1964) 195–209.

Büchler, A. *Economic Conditions of Judea after the Destruction of the Second Temple.* London: Oxford University Press, 1912.

———. *The Political and Social Leaders of the Jewish Community of Sepphoris in the Second and Third Centuries.* London: Jews College, 1909.

———. "Die Schauplätze des Bar-Kochbakrieges." *JQR* 16 (1904) 143–205.

Bultmann, Rudolf. *History of the Synoptic Tradition.* Translated by John Marks. Oxford: Blackwell, 1963.

Burford, Alison. *Craftsmen in Greek and Roman Society.* New York: Cornell University, 1972.

———. "The Economics of Greek Temple Building." *Proceedings of the Cambridge Philological Society*, n.s. 11 191 (1965) 21–34.

Cadbury, Henry J. "Erastus of Corinth." *JBL* 50/2 (1931) 42–58.

———. "The Hellenists" In *The Beginnings of Christianity*, edited by F. J. Foakes-Jackson and K. Lake 5:59–74. 5 vols. Grand Rapids: Baker, 1979.

Cadoux, Cecil John. *The Early Church and the World: A History of the Christian Attitudes to Pagan Society and the State Down to the Time of Constantinus.* Edinburgh: T. & T. Clark, 1925.

Capper, B. J. "The Interpretation of Acts 5:4." *JSNT* 6 (1983) 117–31.

Carletti, Carlo. *Iscrizioni cristiane a Roma: testimonianze di vita cristiana.* Bologna: EDB, 2004.

Carney, Thomas F. *The Shape of the Past: Models and Antiquity.* Lawrence, KS: Coronado, 1975.

Cartledge, Paul. "The Economy (Economics) of Ancient Greece." In *The Ancient Economy*, edited by Walter Scheidel and Sitta von Reden, 12–32. New York: Routledge, 2002.

Cary, M. *A History of Rome.* 2nd ed. London: Macmillan, 1954.

Case, Shirley Jackson. *Jesus, A New Biography.* Chicago: University of Chicago Press, 1927.

Cerfaux, L. "La première communauté chrétienne a Jérusalem (Act., II, 41–V, 42)." *Ephemerides Theologicae Lovanienses* (1939) 5–31.

Chancey, Mark. "Disputed Issues in the Study of Galilee" Paper presented at the annual meeting of the Society of Biblical Literature, Boston, MA, November 2008.

Charlesworth, James H. *Jesus within Judaism.* ABRL. New York: Doubleday, 1988.

———, ed. *The Old Testament Pseudepigrapha.* 2 vols. New York: Doubleday, 1983–1985.

————. *The Old Testament Pseudepigrapha and the New Testament.* SNTSMS 54. Cambridge: Cambridge University Press, 1985.

Chesneaux, Jean. *Peasant Revolts in China, 1849–1949.* Translated by C. A. Curwen. New York: Norton, 1973.

Clarke, Andrew D. *Secular and Christian Leadership in Corinth: A Socio-Historical and Exegetical Study of 1 Corinthians 1–6.* AGJU 18. Leiden: Brill, 1993.

Clark, Kenneth W. "Galilee, Sea of." In *IDB* 2:348–50.

Colander, David C. *Macroeconomics.* 7th ed. Boston: McGraw-Hill, 2008.

Corbo, Virgilio C. *The House of St. Peter at Capernaum.* Translated by Sylvester Saller. Publications of the Studium Biblicum Franciscanum. Collectio minor 5. Jerusalem: Franciscan, 1972.

Cornfield, Gaalya, gen. ed. *Josephus: The Jewish War.* Grand Rapids: Zondervan, 1982.

Conzelmann, Hans. *Acts of the Apostles: A Commentary on the Acts of the Apostles.* Translated by James Limburg et al. Hermeneia. Philadelphia: Fortress, 1987.

Cranfield, C. E. B. *The Gospel according to Saint Mark.* CGTC. Cambridge: Cambridge University Press, 1963.

De Ste. Croix, G. E. M. *The Class Struggle in the Ancient Greek World.* Ithaca, NY: Cornell University Press, 1981.

Crombie, Frederick. *The Works of Origen.* In *The Ante-Nicene Fathers* 4. 1885. Reprinted, Peabody, MA: Hendrickson, 1994.

Cross, F. L., and E. A. Livingstone, eds. *The Oxford Dictionary of the Christian Church.* 3rd ed. Oxford: Oxford University Press, 1997.

Crossan, John Dominic. *The Birth of Christianity: Discovering What Happened in the Years Immediately after the Execution of Jesus.* San Francisco: HarperSanFrancisco, 1998.

————. *The Essential Jesus: Original Sayings and Earliest Images.* San Francisco: HarperCollins, 1994.

————. *The Historical Jesus: The Life of a Mediterranean Jewish Peasant.* San Francisco: Harper, 1991.

Crossan, John D., and Jonathan L. Reed. *Excavating Jesus.* San Francisco: Harper Collins, 2001.

Cullmann, Oscar. "The Significance of the Qumran Texts for Research into the Beginning of Christianity." *JBL* 74 (1955) 213–26. Reprinted in *The Scrolls and the New Testament,* edited by Krister Stendahl, 18–32. New York: Harper & Brothers, 1957.

Damaschke, A. *Bibel und Bodenreform.* Sociale Zeitfragen 28. Berlin: Mann, 1924.

Danby, Herbert, trans. *The Mishnah.* London: Oxford University Press, 1933.

Danker, Frederick W. *A Greek-English Lexicon of the New Testament and Other Early Christian Literature.* 3rd ed. Chicago: University of Chicago Press, 2000.

Dar, Shimon. *Landscape and Pattern: An Archaeological Survey of Samaria 800 B.C.E.—636 C.E.* With a historical commentary by Shimon Applebaum. BAR International Series 308. Oxford: BAR, 1986.

Davies, John K. "Hellenistic Economies." In *The Cambridge Companion to the Hellenistic World,* edited by Glenn R. Bugh, 73–92. Cambridge: Cambridge University Press, 2008.

————. "Linear and Nonlinear Flow Models for Ancient Economies." In *The Ancient Economy: Evidence and Models,* edited by J. G. Manning and Ian Morris, 127–56. Social Science History. Stanford: Stanford University Press, 2005.

Davies, W. D. *The Gospel and the Land: Early Christianity and Jewish Territorial Doc-trine*. Berkeley: University of California Press, 1974.

Davies, W. D., and Dale C. Allison Jr. *A Critical and Exegetical Commentary on the Gospel according to Saint Matthew*. Vol. 1, *Introduction and Commentary on Matthew 1–7*. 3 vols. ICC. Edinburgh: T. & T. Clark, 1988.

Day, John. "Agriculture in the Life of Pompeii." *YCS* 3 (1932) 167–208.

Deissmann, Adolf. *Light from the Ancient East: The New Testament Illustrated by Recently Discovered Texts of the Graeco-Roman World*. Translated by Lionel R. M. Strachan. Grand Rapids: Baker, 1965.

De Luca, Stefano. "Urban Development of the City of Magdala/Tarichaeae in the Light of the New Excavations: Remains, Problems and Perspectives." The Magdala Project. Website, http://www.magdalaproject.org/WP/?p=247&langswitch_lang=en/.

Dembitz, L. N. D. "Bastard." In *Jewish Encyclopedia*. Online: http://www.jewish encyclopedia.com/articles/2648-bastard/.

Derrett, J. D. M. "Fresh Light on the Parable of the Wicked Winedressers." *RIDA* 10 (1963) 11–41

De Ste. Croix, G. E. M. *The Class Struggle in the Ancient Greek World*. Ithaca: Cornell University Press, 1981.

Diehl, E., ed. *Inscriptiones Latinae Christianae Veteres*. 4 vols. Dublin: Weidmann, 1970–1985.

Dittenberger, Wilhelm. *Sylloge Inscriptionum Graecarum*. 4 vols. 3rd ed. Leipzig: Hirzelium, 1915–24.

Dix, Gregory. *The Treatise of the Apostolic Tradition of St. Hippolytus of Rome, Bishop and Martyr*. London: SPCK, 1937.

Dobson, Brian. "Legionary Centurion or Equestrian Officer? A Comparison of Pay and Prospects." *Ancient Society* 3 (1972) 193–207.

Dohr, Hans. "Die italischen Guthöfe nach den Schriften Catos und Varros." PhD diss., Köln, 1965.

Drexhage, Hans-Joachim. "Wirtschaft und Handel in den frühchristlichen Gemeinden." *RA* 76 (1981) 1–72.

Duling, Dennis C., and Norman Perrin. *The New Testament, Proclamation and Pare-nesis, Myth and History*. 3rd ed. Fort Worth: Harcourt, Brace, 1994.

Dyson, Stephen L. "Native Revolt Patterns in the Roman Empire." In *ANRW* II.3 (1975) 138–75.

Easton, Burton Scott. *The Apostolic Tradition of Hippolytus*. New York: Macmillan, 1934.

Edwards, Douglas R. "First-Century Urban/Rural Relations in Lower Galilee: Exploring the Archaeological and Literary Evidence." In *SBLSP* 27 (1988) 169–82.

———. "Khirbet Qana: From Jewish Village to Christian Pilgrim Site." *The Roman and Byzantine Near East* 3 (2002) 101–32.

———. "The Socio-Economic and Cultural Ethos of the Lower Galilee in the First Century: Implications for the Nascent Jesus Movement" In *The Galilee in Late Antiquity*, edited by L. I. Levine, 53–91. New York: Jewish Theological Seminary of America, 1992.

Eliade, Mircea. *The Sacred and the Profane: The Nature of Religion*. Translated by Wil-lard R. Trask. New York: Harcourt Brace, 1959.

Ennabli, Liliane. *Inscriptions funéraires chrétiennes de Carthage.* 3 vols. Collection de l'Ecole française de Rome, 25. Recherches d'archéologie africaine. Rome: École française de Rome, 1975–82.

Epstein, I., trans. *The Babylonian Talmud.* London: Soncino, 1948.

Feissel, Denis. *Recueil des inscriptions chrétiennes de Macedoine du IIIe au VIe siècles.* Bulletin de correspondance hellénique Supplément 8. Paris: Dépositaire, 1983.

Feldman, Louis H., ed. *Josephus.* Vols. 9–10. 10 vols. LCL. Cambridge: Harvard University Press, 1981.

Fiensy, David A. "Ancient Economy and the New Testament." In *Understanding the Social World of the New Testament,* edited by Dietmar Neufeld and Richard E. DeMaris, d. 194–206. London: Routledge, 2009.

———. "Did Large Estates Exist in Lower Galilee in the First Half of the First Century CE?" *JSHJ* 10 (2012) 1–22.

———. "Jesus' Socioeconomic Background." In *Hillel and Jesus: Comparative Studies of Two Major Religious Leaders,* edited by James H. Charlesworth and L. Johns, 225–55. Minneapolis: Fortress, 1997.

———. "Jesus and Debts: Did He Pray about Them?" *ResQ* 44 (2002) 233–39.

———. *Jesus the Galilean: Soundings in a First Century Life.* Piscataway, NJ: Gorgias, 2007.

———. *The Social History of Palestine in the Herodian Period.* Studies in the Bible and Early Christianity 20. Lewiston, NY: Mellen, 1991.

Finley, M. I. *The Ancient Economy.* 2nd ed. Sather Classical Lectures 43. Berkeley: University of California Press, 1985.

Finkelstein, Louis. *The Pharisees: The Sociological Background of Their Faith.* 2 vols. The Morris Loeb Series. Philadelphia: Jewish Publication Society of America, 1962.

———. "The Pharisees: Their Origin and their Philosophy." *HTR* 22 (1929) 185–261.

Finn, T. M. "Social Mobility, Imperial Civil Service and the Spread of Early Christianity." In *Studia Patristica* 17, edited by E. A. Livingstone, 31–37. Oxford: Pergamon, 1982.

Fitzmyer, Joseph A. *Romans.* AB 33. Garden City, NY: Doubleday, 1993.

———. *A Wandering Aramean: Collected Aramaic Essays.* SBLMS 25. Missoula, MT: Scholars, 1979.

Fitzmyer, Joseph A., and Daniel J. Harrington. *A Manual of Palestinian Aramaic Texts (Second Century B.C.—Second Century A.D.).* Biblica et orientalia 34. Rome: Biblical Institute Press, 1978.

Foakes-Jackson, F. J., and K. Lake. *The Beginnings of Christianity: The Acts of the Apostles.* The Beginnings of Christianity, part 1. 5 vols. Grand Rapids: Baker, 1979.

Foster, G. M. "What Is a Peasant?" In *Peasant Society: A Reader,* edited by J. M. Potter, et al., 2–14. The Little, Brown Series in Anthropology Boston: Little, Brown, 1967.

Frankel, Raphael. "Galilee." In *ABD* 2:879–95.

Frayne, Joan M. *Subsistence Farming in Roman Italy.* Fontwell, UK: Centaur, 1979.

Frend, W. H. C. *Martyrdom and Persecution in the Early Church: A Study of Conflict from the Maccabees to Donatus.* Oxford: Blackwell, 1965.

———. *The Rise of Christianity.* Philadelphia: Fortress; London: Darton, Longman & Todd, 1984.

Frey, Jean-Baptiste. *Corpus Inscriptionum Iudaicarum.* 2 vols. Rome: Pontificio Instituto di Arche-ologia Cristiana, 1952.

Freyne, Sean. "Archaeology and the Historical Jesus." In *Archaeology and Biblical Interpretation*, edited by J. R. Bartlett, 117–44. London: Routledge, 1997.

———. *Galilee, from Alexander to Hadrian*. Wilmington, DE: Glazier, 1980.

———. "The Geography, Politics, and Economics of Galilee and the Quest for the Historical Jesus." In *Studying the Historical Jesus: Evaluations of the State of Current Research*, edited by Bruce Chilton and Craig A. Evans, 75–121 . NTTS 19. Leiden: Brill, 1994.

———. "Herodian Economics in Galilee: Searching for a Suitable Model." In *Modeling Early Christianity: Social-Scientific Studies of the New Testament in Its Context*, edited by Philip F. Esler, 23–46. London: Routledge, 1995.

———. "Sea of Galilee." In *ABD* 2:899–901.

Funk, Robert W., and Roy W. Hoover, eds. *The Five Gospels*. New York: Macmillan, 1993.

Furfey, Paul H. "Christ as τεκτων." *CBQ* 17 (1955) 324–35.

Futrell, Alison. *Blood in the Arena: The Spectacle of Roman Power*. Austin: University of Texas Press, 1997.

Gager, John G. *Kingdom and Community: The Social World of Early Christianity*. Prentice-Hall Studies in Religion Series. Englewood Cliffs, NJ: Prentice-Hall, 1975.

Garnsey, P., ed. *Non-Slave Labour in the Greco-Roman World*. Rev. ed. Cambridge Philological Society Supplementary volume 6. Cambridge: Philological Society, 1980.

Geva, H. "Jerusalem." In *NEAEHL* 2:717–757.

Glotz, Gustave. *Ancient Greece at Work: An Economic History of Greece from the Homeric Period to the Roman Conquest*. The History of Civilization. Pre-history and Antiquity. New York: Routledge, 1926.

Glover, T. R., trans. *Tertullian, Apology, De Spectalulis*. LCL. Cambridge: Harvard University Press,, 1931.

Golomb, B., and Y. Kedar. "Ancient Agriculture in the Galilee Mountains." *IEJ* 21 (1971) 136–40.

Goodman, Martin. "The First Jewish Revolt: Social Conflict and the Problem of Debt." *JJS* 33 (1982) 414–27.

———. *The Ruling Class of Judaea: The Origins of the Jewish Revolt against Rome, A.D. 66–70*. Cambridge: Cambridge University Press,1987.

———. *State and Society in Roman Galilee*. Totowa, NJ: Rowman & Allanheld, 1983.

Grant, Michael. *A Social History of Greece and Rome*. New York: Scribner, 1992.

Groh, D. E. "The Clash between Literary and Archaeological Models of Provincial Palestine." In *Archaeology and the Galilee: Texts and Contexts in the Greco-Roman and Byzantine Periods*, edited by D. R. Edwards and C. Thomas McCollough, 29–37. South Florida Studies in the History of Judaism 143. Atlanta: Scholars, 1997.

Haas, N. "Anthropological Observations on the Skeletal Remains from Givat ha-Mivtar." *IEJ* 20 (1970) 38–59.

Hachlili, R., and P. Smith. "The Genealogy of the Goliath Family." *BASOR* 235 (1979) 67–71.

Haenchen, Ernst. *Die Apostelgeschichte*. KEKNT. Göttingen: Vandenhoeck & Ruprecht, 1957.

———. *The Acts of the Apostles*. Translated by Bernard Noble et al. Oxford: Blackwell, 1971.

Handelman, H.. *Struggle in the Andes.* Latin American Monographs 35. Austin: University of Texas Press, 1975.

Hanson, K. C., and Douglas E. Oakman. *Palestine in the Time of Jesus: Social Structures and Social Conflicts.* Minneapolis: Fortress, 1998. 2nd ed., 2008.

Harnack, Adolf von. *The Mission and Expansion of Christianity in the First Three Centuries.* London: Williams & Norgate, 1961.

Harrison, P. N. *Paulines and Pastorals.* London: Villiers, 1964.

Heberle, R. "Social Movements." In *International Encyclopedia of the Social Sciences,* edited by David L. Sills, 14:438–44. 19 vols. New York: Macmillan, 1968.

Heichelheim, F. M. "Roman Syria." In *Economic Survey of Ancient Rome,* edited by T. Frank, 4:121–257. Baltimore: Johns Hopkins University Press, 1938.

Heinemann, J. H. "The Status of the Laborer in Jewish Law and Society in the Tannaitic Period." *HUCA* 25 (1954) 163–325.

Hennecke, Edgar, et al. *Neutestamentliche Apokryphen in deutscher Übersetzung.* Edited by Wilhelm Schneemelcher. 2 vols. Tübingen: Mohr/Siebeck, 1959.

———. *The New Testament Apocrypha.* 2 vols. Philadelphia: Westminster, 1963–1965.

Hengel, Martin. *Between Jesus and Paul: Studies in the Earliest History of Christianity.* Translated by John Bowden. London: SCM, 1983.

———. *Crucifixion in the Ancient World and the Folly of the Message of the Cross.* Translated by John Bowden. Philadelphia: Fortress, 1977.

———. "Das Gleichnis von den Weingärtnern Mc 12:1–12 im Licht der Zenonpapyri und der rabbinischen Gleichnisse." *ZNW* 59 (1968) 1–39.

———. *The "Hellenization" of Judaea in First Century after Christ.* In collaboration with Christoph Markschies. Philadelphia: Trinity, 1989.

———. *Property and Riches in the Early Church: Aspects of a Social History of Early Christianity.* Translated by John Bowden. Philadelphia: Fortress, 1974.

———. *Die Zeloten: Untersuchungen zur jüdischen Freiheitsbewegung in der Zeit von Herodes I. bis 70 n. Chr.* AGJU 1. Leiden: Brill, 1961.

———. *The Zealots: Investigations into the Jewish Freedom Movement in the Period from Herod I until 70 A.D.* Translated by David Smith. Edinburgh: T. & T. Clark, 1989.

Herbert, Sharon C., and Andrea M. Berlin. "A New Administrative Center for Persian and Hellenistic Galilee: Preliminary Report of the University of Michigan, University of Minnesota Excavations at Kedesh." *BASOR* 329 (2003) 13–59.

Herrenbrück, Fritz. "Wer warren die 'Zöllner?'" *ZNW* 72 (1981) 178–94.

Herz, J. "Grossgrundbesitz in Palästina im Zeitalter Jesu." *Palästina Jahrbuch* 24 (1928) 98–113.

Hill, Craig C. *Hellenists and Hebrews: Reappraising Divisions within the Earliest Church.* Minneapolis: Fortress, 1992.

Hirschfeld, Yizhar. "The Early Roman Bath and Fortress at Ramat Hanadiv Near Caesarea." *The Roman and Byzantine Near East: Some Recent Archaeological Research. JRA* 14 (1995) 28–55.

———. *The Palestinian Dwelling in the Roman-Byzantine Period.* Jerusalem: Franciscan, 1995.

———. *Ramat Hanadiv Excavations.* Jerusalem: Israel Exploration Society, 2000.

Hirschfeld, Yizhar, and Miriam Feinberg-Vamosh. "A Country Gentleman's Estate: Unearthing the Splendors of Ramat Hanadiv." *BAR* 31/2 (2005) 18–31.

Hitchener, R. Bruce. "The Advantages of Wealth and Luxury." In *The Ancient Economy: Evidence and Models,* edited by J. G. Manning and Ian Morris, 207–22. Social Science History. Stanford: Stanford University, 2005.

———. "Olive Production and the Roman Economy: The Case for Intensive Growth in the Roman Empire." In *The Ancient Economy,* edited by Walter Scheidel and Sitta von Reden, 71–83. New York: Routledge, 2002.

Hixon, C., et al. "3-D Visualizations of a First-Century Galilean Town." In *Virtual Reality in Archaeology,* edited by J. A. Barceló et al., 195–204. BAR International Series 843. Oxford: BAR, 2000.

Hobsbawm, E. J. *Primitive Rebels.* Norton Library. New York: Norton, 1965

Hock, Ronald F. *The Social Context of St. Paul's Ministry: Tentmaking and Apostleship.* Minneapolis: Fortress. 1980.

Hoehner, Harold W. *Herod Antipas.* SNTSMS 17. Cambridge: Cambridge University Press, 1972.

Hollenbach, Paul. "Liberating Jesus for Social Involvement." *BTB* 15 (1985) 151–57.

Hopkins, Keith. "Rome, Taxes, Rents and Trade." In *The Ancient Economy,* edited by Walter Scheidel and Sitta von Reden, 191–230. New York: Routledge, 2002.

Hornus, Jean-Michel. *It Is Not Lawful for Me to Fight: Early Christian Attitudes toward War, Violence, and the State.* Scottdale, PA: Herald, 1980.

Horsley, G. H. R. *New Documents Illustrating Early Christianity,* Vols. 1–8. North Ryde, Australia: Macquarie University, 1981–1998.

Horsley, Richard A. *Archaeology, History, and Society in Galilee: The Social Context of Jesus and the Rabbis.* Valley Forge, PA: Trinity, 1996.

———. *Galilee: History, Politics, People.* Valley Forge, PA: Trinity, 1996.

———. "The Historical Jesus and Archaeology of the Galilee: Questions from Historical Jesus Research to Archaeologists." In *SBLSP* (1994) 91–135.

———"Jesus and Galilee: The Contingencies of a Renewal Movement." In *Galilee through the Centuries: Confluence of Cultures,* edited by E. M. Meyers, 57–74. Duke Judaic Studies 1. Winona Lake, IN: Eisenbrauns, 1999.

———. *Jesus and the Spiral of Violence: Jewish Resistance in Roman Palestine.* San Francisco: Harper & Row, 1987.

Horsely, Richard A., and J. S. Hanson. *Bandits, Prophets, and Messiahs.* Minneapolis: Winston, 1985.

Instone-Brewer, David. *Prayer and Agriculture.* Traditions of the Rabbis in the Era of the New Testament 1. Grand Rapids: Eerdmans, 2004.

Isaac, B. "The Babatha Archive: A Review Article." *IEJ* 42 (1992) 62–75.

———. "A Donation for Herod's Temple in Jerusalem." *IEJ* 33 (1983) 86–92.

Jacquier, E. *Le Actes des Apotres.* Paris: Libraire Victor Lecoffre, 1926.

Jacobs, J., and S. Ochser. "Sihin" *Jewish Encyclopedia,* http://www.jewishencyclopedia.com/search?utf8=%E2%9C%93&keywords=SIHIN&commit=search/.

Jastrow, Marcus. *A Dictionary of the Targumim, the Talmud Babli and Yerushalmi, and the Midrashic Literature.* 2 vols. in 1. New York: Judaica Press, 1975.

Jensen, Morton Hørning. "Rural Galilee and Rapid Changes: An Investigation of the Socio-Economic Dynamics and Developments in Roman Galilee." *Biblica* 93 (2012) 43–67.

Jeremias, Joachim. *Jerusalem in the Time of Jesus.* Translated by F. H. Cave and C. H. Cave. Philadelphia: Fortress, 1969.

———. *The Prayers of Jesus.* Philadelphia: Fortress, 1978.

Jevons, F. B. "Some Ancient Greek Pay-Bills." *The Economic Journal* 6/23 (1896) 470–75.

Johnson, Luke Timothy. *Sharing Possessions: Mandate and Symol of Faith*. OBT 9. Philadelphia: Fortress, 1981.

Johnson, Sherman E. "The Dead Sea Manual of Discipline and the Jerusalem Church of Acts." *ZAW* 66 (1954) 106–20.

Jones, A. H. M. *Cities of the Eastern Roman Provinces*. Revised by Michael Avi-Yonah. 2nd ed. Oxford: Clarendon, 1971.

———. "Colonus" In *Oxford Classical Dictionary*, edited by N. G. L. Hammond and H. H. Scullard, 266. Oxford: Clarendon, 1970.

———. *The Greek City from Alexander to Justinian*. Oxford: Clarendon, 1940.

———. "The Urbanization of Palestine." *JRS* 91 (1931) 78–85.

The Judaic Classics. Chicago: Davka, 1991–1995 (CD-ROM).

Judge, E. A. *The Social Pattern of the Christian Groups in the First Century: Some Prolegomena to the Study of New Testament*. London: Tyndale, 1960.

Judge, E. A., and S. R. Pickering. "Papyrus Documentation of Church and Community in Egypt to the Mid-Fourth Century." *JAC* 20 (1977) 47–71.

Kajanto, Iiro. *Onomastic Studies in the Early Christian Inscriptions of Rome and Carthage*. Acta Instituti Romani Finlandiae 2:1. Helsinki, 1963.

Kaufmann, Carl Maria. *Handbuch der altchristlichen Epigraphik*. Freiburg: Herder, 1917.

Kautsky, John H. *The Politics of Aristocratic Empires*. Chapel Hill: University of North Carolina Press, 1982.

Kent, J. H. *Corinth: Results of Excavations Conducted by the American School of Classical Studies at Athens*, vol. 8, part 3, *The Inscriptions 1926–1950*. Princeton: Harvard University Press, 1966.

Keppie, Lawrence. *Understanding Roman Inscriptions*. Baltimore: Johns Hopkins University Press, 1991.

King, Philip J. "Jerusalem." In *ABD* 3:753.

Kippenberg, Hans G. *Religion und Klassenbildung im antiken Judäa*. SUNT 14. Göttingen: Vanderhoeck & Ruprecht, 1978.

Klausner, Joseph. *Jesus of Nazareth: His Life, Times, and Teaching*. Translated by Herbert Danby. New York: Macmillan, 1925.

Klein, S. "Notes on Large Estates in the Land of Israel." *BJPES* 1/3 (1933) 3–9 (in Hebrew).

———. "Notes on Large Estates in the Land of Israel." *BJPES* 3/4 (1938) 109–16 (in Hebrew).

Kloppenborg, John S. "The Growth and Impact of Agricultural Tenancy in Jewish Palestine (III BCE—I CE)." *JESHO* 51 (2008) 31–66.

Krauss, Samuel. *Antoninus und Rabbi*. Vienna: Israelitisch-theologische Lehranstalt, 1910.

———. *Griechische und lateinische Lehnwörter im Talmud, Midrasch und Targum*. Hildesheim: Olms, 1964.

———. *Talmudische Archäologie*. 3 vols. Grundriss der Gesamtwissenschaft des Judentums. Hildesheim: Olms, 1966.

Kreissig, H. "Die Landwirtschaftliche Situation in Palästina vor dem Judäischen Krieg." *Acta Antiqua* 17 (1969) 223–54.

———. *Die sozialen Zusammenhänge des judäischen Krieges*. Schriften zur Geschichte und Kultur der Antike 1. Berlin: Akademie, 1970.

Kyrtatas, Dimitris J. *The Social Structure of the Early Christian Communities.* London: Verso, 1987.

Lake, Kirsopp. "The Communism of Acts II and IV–VI and the Appointment of the Seven." In *The Beginnings of Christianity*, edited by F. J. Foakes-Jackson and Kirsopp Lake, 5:140–150. 5 vols. London: Macmillan, 1933.

Lampe, Peter. "The Roman Christians of Romans 16." In *The Romans Debate*, edited by Karl P. Donfried, 216–30. Rev. and expanded ed. Edinburgh: T. & T. Clark, 1991.

Landau, Y. H. "A Greek Inscription Found Near Hefzibah." *IEJ* 16 (1966) 54–70.

Larsen, E. "Die Hellenisten und die Urgemeinde." *NTS* 33(1987) 205–25.

Latourette, Kenneth Scott. *A History of Christianity.* New York: Harper, 1953.

Lenski, Gerhard E. *Power and Privilege.* McGraw-Hill Series in Sociology. New York: McGraw-Hill, 1966.

Lenski, Gerhard, and Jean Lenski. *Human Societies: An Introduction to Macrosociology.* New York: McGraw-Hill, 1982.

Lewis, C. T. *Latin Dictionary.* New York: American, 1888.

Lewis, Naphtali. *Life in Egypt under Roman Rule.* Oxford: Clarendon, 1983.

Lietzmann, Hans. *A History of the Early Church.* 3rd, rev ed. . Cleveland: World, 1961.

Lightfoot, J. B. *The Apostolic Fathers.* 2 vols. London: Macmillan, 1890.

Loisy, A. F. *The Birth of the Christian Religion, and The Origins of the New Testament.* New Hyde Park, NY: University Books, 1962.

Lüdemann, Gerd. *Early Christianity according to the Traditions in Acts.* Translated by John Bowden. Minneapolis: Fortress, 1989.

Loffreda, S. "Capernaum." In *NEAEHL* 1:291–95.

McCown, C. C. "Ο ΤΕΚΤΩΝ." In *Studies in Early Christianity*, edited by Shirley Jackson Case, 173–89. New York: Century, 1928.

MacDonald, Nathan. *What Did the Ancient Israelites Eat? Diet in Biblical Times.* Grand Rapids: Eerdmans, 2008.

Mackowski, R. M. *Jerusalem, City of Jesus.* Grand Rapids: Eerdmans, 1980.

MacMullen, Ramsay. *Enemies of the Roman Order: Treason, Unrest, and Alienation in the Empire.* Cambridge: Harvard University Press, 1966.

———. *Roman Social Relations, 50 B.C. to A.D. 284.* New Haven: Yale University Press, 1974.

Magen, I. *The Stone Vessel Industry in the Second Temple Period.* Judea and Samaria Publications 1. Jerusalem: Israel Exploration Society, 2002.

Magness, Jodi. *Stone and Dung, Oil and Spit: Jewish Daily Life in the Time of Jesus.* Grand Rapids: Eerdmans, 2011.

Malherbe, Abraham J. *Social Aspects of Early Christianity.* 2nd ed. 1983. Eugene, OR: Wipf & Stock, 2003.

Malina, Bruce J. *The New Testament World: Insights from Cultural Anthropology.* Atlanta: John Knox, 1981. 2nd ed., 1993. 3rd ed., 2001.

———. "Rhetorical Criticism and Social-Scientific Criticism." In *The Social World of the New Testament*, edited by Jerome H. Neyrey and Eric C. Stewart, 5–21. Peabody, MA: Hendrickson, 2008.

Malina, Bruce J., and Jerome H. Neyrey. "Ancient Mediterranean Persons in Cultural Perspective: Portrait of Paul." in *The Social World of the New Testament*, edited by Jerome H. Neyrey and Eric C. Stewart, 255–76. Peabody, MA: Hendrickson, 2008.

Malina, Bruce J., and Richard L. Rohrbaugh. *Social Science Commentary on the Synoptic Gospels.* Minneapolis: Fortress, 1992.

Mankiw, N. Gregory. *Principles of Macroeconomics.* Mason, OH: Thomson/Southwestern, 2004.

Mann, Michael. *The Sources of Social Power.* 2 vols. Cambridge: Cambridge University Press, 1986–93.

Manning, J. G., and Ian Morris, eds. *The Ancient Economy: Evidence and Models.* Social Science History. Stanford: Stanford University Press, 2005.

———. "Introduction." In *The Ancient Economy: Evidence and Models,* edited by J. G. Manning and Ian Morris, 1–44. Social Science History. Stanford: Stanford University Press, 2005.

Manson, T. W. *The Gospel of Luke.* Moffatt New Testament Commentary. London: Hodder & Stoughton, 1930.

Marcus, Ralph, ed. *Josephus.* Vols 4–8. 10 vols. LCL. Cambridge: Harvard University Press, 1986.

Marshall, I. Howard. *The Acts of the Apostles.* TNTC. Leicester: Inter-Varsity, 1980.

Marucchi, Orazio. *Christian Epigraphy: An Elementary Treatise with a Collection of Ancient Christian Inscriptions, Mainly of Roman Origin.* 1912. Reprinted, Chicago: Ares, 1974.

Mason, Hugh J. *Greek Terms for Roman Institutions: A Lexicon and Analysis.* ASP 13. Toronto: Hakkert, 1974.

Massey, Lesly F. *Women and the New Testament: An Analysis of Scripture in Light of New Testament Era Culture.* Jefferson, NC: McFarland, 1989.

Matilla, Sharon Lea. "Jesus and the 'Middle Peasants'? Problematizing a Social-Scientific Concept." *CBQ* 72 (2010) 291–313.

———. "Revisiting Jesus' Capernaum: A Village of Only Subsistence-Level Fishers and Farmers?" In *The Galilean Economy in the Time of Jesus,* edited by David A. Fiensy and Ralph K. Hawkins. Early Christianity and Its Literature 11. Atlanta: Society of Biblical Literature, 2013.

Mayer, Anton. *Der zensierte Jesus: Soziologie des Neuen Testaments.* Olten: Walter, 1983.

Mazar, Benjamin. "Herodian Jerusalem in the Light of Excavations South and South-West of the Temple Mount." *IEJ* 28 (1978) 230–337.

———. *The Mountain of the Lord.* Garden City, NY: Doubleday, 1975.

McLaren, James S. *Power and Politics in Palestine: The Jews and the Governing of Their Land, 100 BC—AD 70.* JSOTSup 63. Sheffield: JSOT Press, 1991.

Mealand, David L. *Poverty and Expectation in the Gospels.* London: SPCK, 1980.

Meeks, Wayne A. *The First Urban Christians: The Social World of the Apostle Paul.* New Haven: Yale University Press, 1983.

Meggitt, Justin J. "The Social Status of Erastus (Rom. 16:23)." *NovT* 38 (1996) 218–23.

Meier, John P. *A Marginal Jew.* Vol. 1, *The Roots of the Problem and the Person.* ABRL. New York: Doubleday, 1991.

Meikle, Scott. "Modernism, Economics, and the Ancient Economy." In *The Ancient Economy,* edited by Walter Scheidel and Sitta von Reden, 233–50. New York: Routledge, 2002.

Mendelsohn, S. "Eleazar ben Azariah." In *Jewish Encyclopedia.* Online: http://www.jewish-encyclopedia.com/articles/5528-eleazar-b-azariah/.

———. "Eliezer ben Hyrcanus." In *Jewish Encyclopedia.* Online: http://www.jewishencyclo-pedia.com/.

Metzger, Bruce M. *A Textual Commentary on the Greek New Testament.* London: United Bible Societies Press, 1971.

Meyers, Eric M. "An Archaeological Response to a New Testament Scholar." *BASOR* 297 (1995) 17–26.

———. "Galilean Regionalism as a Factor in Historical Reconstruction." *BASOR* 221 (1976) 93–101.

———. "Jesus and His Galilean Context." In *Archaeology and the Galilee: Texts and Contexts in the Greco-Roman and Byzantine Periods,* edited by Douglas R. Edwards and C. Thomas McCollough, 57–66. South Florida Studies in the History of Judaism 143. Atlanta: Scholars, 1997.

———. "The Problems of Gendered Space in Syro-Palestinian Domestic Architecture: The Case of Roman-Period Galilee." In *Early Christian Families in Context,* edited by David L. Balch and Carolyn Osiek, 44–69. Religion, Marriage and Family. Grand Rapids: Eerdmans, 2003.

———. "Roman Sepphoris in Light of New Archaeological Evidence and Recent Research." In *The Galilee in Late Antiquity,* edited by Lee I. Levine, 321–38. New York: Jewish Theological Seminary, 1992.

Meyers, Eric M., et al. *Excavations at Ancient Meiron.* Meiron Excavation Project 3. Cambridge: American Schools of Oriental Research, 1981.

Meyers, Eric M., et al. "Sepphoris 'Ornament of all Galilee.'" *BA* 49 (1986) 4–19.

———. *Sepphoris.* Winona Lake, IN: Eisenbrauns, 1992.

———. "The Meiron Excavation Project: Archeological Survey in Galilee and Golan, 1976." *BASOR* 230 (1978) 1–24.

Michael, Otto. "οικονομος." In *TDNT* 5:149–51.

Michell, H. *The Economics of Ancient Greece.* 2nd ed. Cambridge: Heffer & Sons, 1957.

Migdal, Joel S. *Peasants, Politics, and Revolution: Pressures toward Political and Social Change in the Third World.* Princeton: Princeton University Press, 1974.

Millar, Fergus. *The Roman Near East 31 BC–AD 337.* Cambridge, MA: Harvard University Press, 1993.

Millar, Fergus, and G. Bertholme. "Salarium." In *Oxford Classical Dictionary,* edited by N. G. L. Hammond and H. H. Scullard, 945–946. Oxford: Clarendon, 1970.

Miller, S. S. "Sepphoris, the Well Remembered City." *BA* 55 (1992) 74–83.

———. "Studies in the History and Traditions of Sepphoris." PhD diss., New York University, 1980.

———. *Studies in the History and Traditions of Sepphoris.* SJLA 37. Leiden: Brill, 1984.

Moore, Barrington Jr. *Social Origins of Dictatorship and Democracy.* Boston: Beacon, 1966.

Moore, G. F. *Judaism in the First Centuries of the Christian Era.* 3 vols. Cambridge: Harvard University Press, 1954.

Morris, Ian. "Archaeology, Standards of Living and Greek Economic History." In *The Ancient Economy,* edited by J. G. Manning and Ian Morris, 91–126. Social Science History. Stanford: Stanford University Press, 2005.

———. "Foreword." In *Ancient Economy,* by M. I. Finley, ix–xxxvi. Berkeley: University of California Press, 1999.

Mossé, Claude. *The Ancient World at Work.* Translated by Janet Lloyd. Ancient Culture and Society. New York: Norton, 1969.

Moule, C. F. D. "Once More, Who Were the Hellenists?" *ExpTim* 70 (1958–59) 100–102.

Mousnier, Roland. *Peasant Uprisings in Seventeenth-Century France, Russsia, and China.* Translated by Brian Pearce. New York: Harper & Row, 1970.

Moxnes, Halvor. "The Construction of Galilee as a Place for the Historical Jesus, Part I." *BTB* 31 (2001) 26–37.

———. "The Construction of Galilee as a Place for the Historical Jesus, Part II." *BTB* 31 (2001) 64–77.

Munier, C. "Labour." In *Encyclopedia of the Early Church*, edited by Angelo Di Berardino, 1:469. 2 vols. New York: Oxford University Press, 1992.

Mussies, G. "Greek in Palestine and the Diaspora." In *The Jewish People in the First Century*, edited by S. Safrai and M. Stern, 2:1040–64. 2 vols. CRINT I/2. Assen: Van Gorcum, 1976.

Nation Master. "Economy Statistics: GDP (per capita) (most recent) by Country." Online: http://www.nationmaster.com/graph/eco_gdp_percap-economy-gdp-per-capita/.

Naquin, Susan. *Millenarian Rebellion in China: The Eight Trigrams Uprising of 1813.* Yale Historical Publications: Miscellany 108. New Haven: Yale University Press, 1976.

Naveh, J. "A New Tomb Inscription from Giv'at at Hamivtar." In *Jerusalem Revealed: Archaeology in the Holy City,* edited by Y. Yadin and E. Stern, 73–74. Jerusalem: Israel Exploration Society, 1975.

———. "The Ossuary Inscriptions from Givat ha-Mivtar." *IEJ* 20 (1970) 33–37.

Neusner, Jacob. *From Politics to Piety: The Emergence of Pharisaic Judaism.* 1973. Reprinted, Eugene, OR: Wipf & Stock, 2003.

———. *The Rabbinic Traditions about the Pharisees before 70.* 3 vols. 1971. Reprinted, Eugene, OR: Wipf & Stock, 2005.

Neyrey, Jerome H. "Luke's Social Location of Paul: Cultural Anthropology and the Status of Paul in Acts." Online: http://www.nd.edu/~jneyrey1/location.html/.

———. "Preface." In *The Social World of the New Testament*, edited by Jerome H. Neyrey and Eric C. Stewart, xxi–xxiv. Peabody, MA: Hendrickson, 2008.

Neyrey, Jerome H., and Eric C. Stewart, eds. *The Social World of the New Testament.* Peabody, MA: Hendrickson, 2008.

———. "Healing." In *The Social World of the New Testament,* edited by Jerome H. Neyrey and Eric C. Stewart, 201–2. Peabody, MA: Hendrickson, 2008.

Newhauser, Richard. *The Early History of Greed: The Sin of Avarice in Early Medieval Thought and Literature.* Cambridge Studies in Medieval Literature 41. Cambridge: Cambridge University Press, 2000.

Oakman, Douglas E. "The Archaeology of First-Century Galilee and the Social Interpretation of the Historical Jesus." In *SBLSP* (1994) 220–51.

———. "Jesus and Agrarian Palestine: The Factor of Debt." In *SBLSP* 34 (1985) 57–73. Reprinted in Oakman, *Jesus and the Peasants*, 11–32.

———. *Jesus and the Economic Questions of His Day.* Studies in the Bible and Early Christianity 8. Lewiston, NY: Mellen, 1986.

———. *Jesus and the Peasants.* Matrix: The Bible in Mediterranean Context 4. Eugene, OR: Cascade Books, 2008.

Oscher, S. "Tarfon." In *Jewish Encyclopedia.* Online: http://www.jewishencyclopedia.com/art-icles/14247-tarfon/.

Oppenheimer, A'haron. *The Am Ha-aretz: A Study in the Social History of the Jewish People in the Hellenistic-Roman Period.* ALGHJ 8. Leiden: Brill, 1977.

Overman, J. Andrew. "Jesus of Galilee and the Historical Peasant." In *Archaeology and the Galilee: Texts and Contexts in the Greco-Roman and Byzantine Periods,* edited by Douglas R. Edwards and C. Thomas McCollough, 67–73. South Florida Studies in the History of Judaism 143. Atlanta: Scholars, 1997.

———. "Who Were the First Urban Christians?" In *SBLSP* 27 (1988) 160–68.

Paige, Jeffery M. *Agrarian Revolution: Social Movements and Export Agriculture in the Underdeveloped World.* New York: Free Press, 1975.

———. "Social Theory and Peasant Revolution in Vietnam and Guatemala." *Theory and Society* 12 (1983) 699–737.

Parsons, J. B. *The Peasant Rebellions of the Late Ming Dynasty.* The Association for Asian Studies. Monographs and Papers 26. Tuscon: University of Arizona Press, 1979.

Pastor, Jack. *Land and Economy in Ancient Palestine.* London: Routledge, 1997.

Patrich, Joseph. "Warehouses and Granaries at Caesarea Maritima." In *Studies in the Archaeology and History of Caesarea Maritima: Caput Judaeae, metropolis Palaestinae,* 225–36. Ancient Judaism and Early Christianity 77. Leiden: Brill, 2011. Online: http://pluto.mscc.huji.ac.il/~patrichj/my_web_site/A_Complex_of_Warehouses-full_abstract.pdf/.

Pesch, Rudolf. *Die Apostelgeschichte.* EKKNT 5. Zürich: Benziger, 1986.

Pines. Shlomo. *An Arabic Version of the Testimonium Flavianum and Its Implications.* Publications of the Israel Academy of Sciences and Humanities. Section of Humanities. Jerusalem: Israel Academy of Sciences and Humanities, 1971.

Pitmann, H. *Cornelii Taciti Annalium Libri XIII–XVI.* Oxford: Clarendon, 1904.

Plummer, A. *The Gospel according to Luke.* Edinburgh: T. & T. Clark , 1922.

Pöhlmann, Robert von. *Geschichte der sozialen Frage und des Sozialismus in der antiken Welt.* 3rd ed. Munich: Beck, 1925.

Polanyi, Karl. *The Great Transformation.* Beacon Paperbacks 45. Boston: Beacon, 1944.

Popkin, Samuel L. *The Rational Peasant: The Political Economy of Rural Society in Vietnam.* Berkeley: University of California Press, 1979.

Powell, J. D. "On Defining Peasants and Peasant Society." *Peasant Studies Newsletter* 1 (1972) 94–99.

Price, James L. *Interpreting the New Testament.* New York: Holt, Rinehart, and Winston, 1971.

Prost, Antoine, and Gerard Vincent, eds. *A History of Private Life.* Histoire de la vie privée 5. Cambridge, MA: Belknap, 1991.

Puech, Emile. "Notes sur le manuscript de 11Q Melkisedeq." *RevQ* 12 (1987) 483–513.

Quasten, J. *Patrology.* 4 vols. Westminster, MD: Christian Classics, 1950.

Rabin, Chaim. *Qumran Studies.* Scripta Judaica 2. Oxford: Oxford University Press, 1957.

Rad, Gerhard von. *Theologie des alten Testaments.* 2 vols. Munich: Kaiser, 1961.

———. *Theology of the Old Testament.* 2 vols. Translated by D. M. G. Stalker. New York: Harper, 1962–65.

Rajak, Tessa. "Justus of Tiberias." *CQ* 23 (1973) 345–68.

Rapinchuk, Mark. "The Galilee and Jesus in Recent Research." *Currents in Biblical Research* 2 (2004) 197–222.

Rappaport, U. "John of Gischala: From Galilee to Jerusalem." *JJS* 33 (1982) 479–93.

Redfield, Robert. *Peasant Society and Culture.* Phoenix Books. Chicago: University of Chicago, 1956.

Reed, Jonathan L. *Archaeology and the Galilean Jesus: A Reexamination of the Evidence.* Harrisburg: Trinity, 2000.

―――. "Galileans, Israelite Village Communities and the Sayings Gospel Q." In *Galilee through the Centuries*, edited by Eric M. Meyers, 87–108. DJS 1. Winona Lake, IN: Eisenbrauns, 1999.

Reinhardt, Wolfgang. "The Population Size of Jerusalem and the Numerical Growth of the Jerusalem Church." In *The Book of Acts in Its Palestinian Setting*, edited by R. Bauckham, 237–65. Book of Acts in Its First Century Setting 4. Grand Rapids: Eerdmans, 1995.

Rhoads, David M. *Israel in Revolution: 6–74 CE: A Political History Based on the Writings of Josephus*. Philadelphia: Fortress, 1976.

Richardson, A. *The Biblical Doctrine of Work*. Ecumenical Biblical Studies 1. London: SCM, 1952.

Richardson, Peter. *Building Jewish in the Roman East*. Waco: Baylor University Press, 2004.

―――. "Towards a Typology of Levantine/Palestinian Houses." *JSNT* 27 (2004) 47–68

Rilinger, Rolf. "Moderne und zeitgenössische Vortellungen von der Gesellschaftsordnung der römischen Kaiserzeit." *Saeculum* 36 (1985) 299–325.

Ringe, Sharon H. *Jesus, Liberation, and the Biblical Jubilee: Images for Ethics and Christology*. OBT. Philadelphia: Fortress, 1985.

―――. "The Jubilee Proclamation in the Ministry of Jesus: A Tradition Critical Study in the Synoptic Gospels and Acts." PhD diss., Union Theological Seminary, 1981.

Rohrbaugh, Richard L. "A Peasant Reading of the Parable of the Talents/Pounds: A Text of Terror?" *BTB* 23 (1993) 32–39.

―――. "The Pre-Industrial City in Luke-Acts: Urban Social Relations." In *The Social World of Luke-Acts: Models for Interpretation*, edited by Jerome H. Neyrey, 125–49. Peabody, MA: Hendrickson, 1991.

―――. "The Social Location of the Markan Audience." *Int* 47 (1993) 380–95.

Rostovtzeff, Michael. *A Large Estate in Egypt in the Third Century B.C.* University of Wiscon-sin Studies in the Social Sciences and History 6. Madison: University of Wisconsin, 1922.

―――. *The Social and Economic History of the Hellenistic World*. 3 vols. Oxford: Clarendon, 1941.

―――. *Social and Economic History of the Roman Empire*. 2 vols. 2nd ed. Revised by P. M. Fraser. Oxford: Clarendon, 1957.

Sabean, David. "Markets, Uprisings and Leadership in Peasant Societies: Western Europe 1381–1789." *Peasant Studies* 2 (1973) 17–19.

Safrai, S. "Eleazar ben Harsom." *EncJud* 6:589.

Safrai, S, and M. Stern, eds. *Jewish People in the First Century*. 2 vols. CRINT I/1. Assen: Van Gorcum, 1974–1976.

Saldarini, Anthony J. *Pharisees, Scribes, and Sadducees in Palestinian Society: A Sociological Approach*. Wilmington, DE: Glazier, 1988.

Saller, Richard. "Framing the Debate over Growth in the Ancient Economy." In *The Ancient Economy*, edited by J. G. Manning and Ian Morris, 223–38. Stanford: Social Science History. Stanford University Press, 2005.

Sanders, E. P. *Judaism: Practice and Belief, 63 B.C.E.—66 C.E.* London: SCM, 1992.

Schalit, A. *König Herodes: Der Mann und Sein Leben*. SJ 4. Berlin: de Gruyter, 1969.

Shaw, B. D. "Bandits in the Roman Empire." *Past and Present* 102 (1984) 3–52.

Scheidel, Walter. "Real Wages in Early Economies: Evidence for Living Standards from 1800 BCE to 1300 CE." *Princeton/Stanford Working Papers in Classics* (2009). Online: http://www.princeton.edu/~pswpc/pdfs/scheidel/090904.pdf/.

———. "Stratification, Deprivation and Quality of Life." In *Poverty in the Roman World*, edited by Margaret Atkins and Robin Osborne, 40–59. Cambridge: Cambridge University Press, 2006.

Scheidel, Walter, and Sitta von Reden, eds. *The Ancient Economy*. New York: Routledge, 2002.

Schille, Gottfried. *Die Apostelgeschichte des Lukas*. THKNT 5. Berlin: Evangelische, 1983.

Schlatter, A. *Die Tage Trajans und Hadrians*. BFCT 1/3. Gütersloh: Bertelsmann, 1897.

Schneider, Gerhard. *Die Apostelgeschichte*. HTKNT 5. Freiburg: Herder, 1980.

Schulz, Siegfried. *Q—Die Spruchquelle der Evangelisten*. Zurich: Theologischer, 1972.

Schürer, Emil. *The History of the Jewish People in the Age of Jesus Christ (175 BC–AD 135)*. Translated by T. A. Burkill et al. 3 vols. in 4 parts. Edinburgh: T. & T. Clark, 1973–87.

Schwank, Benedikt. "Das Theater von Sepphoris und die Jugendjahre Jesu." *Erbe und Auftrag* 52 (1976) 199–206.

Scott, James C. *The Moral Economy of the Peasant: Rebellion and Subsistence in Southeast Asia*. New Haven: Yale University Press, 1976.

———. "Revolution in the Revolution: Peasants and Commissars." *Theory and Society* 7 (1979) 97–134.

Sevenster, J. N. *Do You Know Greek? How Much Greek Could the First Jewish Christians Have Known?* NovTSup 19. Leiden: Brill, 1968.

Shanks, Hershel. *Judaism in Stone: The Archaeology of Ancient Synagogues*. Jerusalem: Steimatzky, 1979.

Shiloh, Yigal, dir. *Excavations at the City of David*. Vol. 1, *1978–1982: Interim Report of the First Five Seasons*. 7 vols. Jerusalem: Institute of Archaeology, Hebrew University, 1984.

Sjoberg, Gideon. *The Preindustrial City: Past and Present*. Glencoe, IL: Free Press, 1960.

———. "The Pre-Industrial City." In *Peasant Society: A Reader*, edited by J. M. Potter et al., 15–24. Little, Brown Series in Anthropology. Boston: Little, Brown, 1967.

"Six Orders of the Talmud Bavli," http://www.mechon-mamre.org/b/l/l2116.htm/.

Smallwood, E. Mary. "High Priests and Politics in Roman Palestine." *JTS* 13 (1962) 14–34.

Smith, Morton. *Jesus the Magician*. San Francisco: Harper & Row, 1978.

Smith, P., and J. Zias. "Skeletal Remains from the Late Hellenistic French Hill Tomb." *IEJ* 30 (1980) 109–15.

Smith, P., et al. "The Skeletal Remains." In *Excavations at Ancient Meiron*, edited by E. M. Meyers et al., 110–20. Meiron Excavation Project 3. Cambridge: American Schools of Oriental Research, 1981.

Sperber, Daniel. "Costs of Living in Roman Palestine I." *JESHO* 8 (1965) 248–71.

———. *Roman Palestine, 200–400: Money and Prices*. Bar-Ilan Studies in Near Eastern Languages and Culture. Ramat-Gan, Israel: Bar-Ilan University, 1974.

Stagg Evelyn, and Frank Stagg. *Woman in the World of Jesus*. Philadelphia: Westminster, 1978.

Stark, Rodney. *The Rise of Christianity: A Sociologist Reconsiders History*. Princeton: Princeton University Press, 1996.

Stegemann, Ekkehard W., and Wolfgang Stegemann. *The Jesus Movement: A Social History of Its First Century.* Translated by O. C. Dean Jr. Minneapolis: Fortress, 1999.

Stern, M. "Aspects of Jewish Society: The Priesthood and Other Classes." In *The Jewish People in the First Century,* edited by S. Safrai and M. Stern, 2:561–630. 2 vols. CRINT I/2. Assen: Van Gorcum, 1976.

———. "The Province of Judea." In *The Jewish People in the First Century,* edited by S. Safrai and M. Stern, 1:308–76. 2 vols. CRINT I/1. Assen: Van Gorcum, 1974.

Strack, H. L., and P. Billerbeck. *Kommentar zum Neuen Testament aus Talmud und Midrasch.* 6 vols. Munich: Beck, 1956.

Strack, H. L., and Günter Stemberger. *Introduction to the Talmud and Midrash.* Translated by Markus Bockmuehl. Edinburgh: T. & T. Clark, 1991.

Strange, James F. "First-Century Galilee from Archaeology and from the Texts." In *Archaeology and the Galilee: Texts and Contexts in the Greco-Roman and Byzantine Periods,* edited by Douglas R. Edwards and C. Thomas McCollough, 39–48. South Florida Studies in the History of Judaism 143. Atlanta: Scholars, 1997.

———. "Sepphoris." In *ABD* 5:1090–93.

Strange, James F., and Hershel Shanks. "Has the House Where Jesus Stayed in Capernaum Been Found?" *BAR* 8/6 (1982) 26–37.

Strange, James F., et al. "Excavations at Sepphoris: The Location and Identification of Shikhin, Part I." *IEJ* 44 (1994) 216–27.

———. "Excavations at Sepphoris: The Location and Identification of Shikhin, Part II" *IEJ* 45 (1995) 171–87.

Strange, J. R. "Excavations at Shikhin." Online: http://www.samford.edu/shikhin/.

Swidler, Leondard J. *Biblical Affirmations of Woman.* Philadelphia: Westminster, 1979.

———. *Women in Judaism: The Status of Women in Formative Judaism.* Metuchen, NJ: Scarecrow, 1976.

"Talmud Yerushalmi." Online: http://www.mechon-mamre.org/b/r/ro.htm/.

Tarn, W. W. *Hellenistic Civilization.* 3rd rev. ed. Cleveland: Meridian, 1961.

Taylor, James E. "Seleucid Rule in Palestine." PhD diss., Duke University, 1979.

Taylor, Vincent. *The Gospel according to St. Mark.* 2nd ed. 1966. Reprinted, Thorn-apple Commentaries. Grand Rapids: Baker, 1981.

Theissen, Gerd. *The Social Setting of Pauline Christianity: Essays on Corinth.* Edited and translated by John H. Schütz. Philadelphia: Fortress, 1982.

———. *Sociology of Early Palestinian Christianity.* translated by John Bowden. Philadelphia: Fortress, 1978.

Thilly, Charles. *From Mobilization to Revolution.* Reading, MA: Addison-Wesley, 1978.

Thomsen, Peter. "Die lateinischen und griechischen Inschriften der Stadt Jerusalem." *ZDPV* 44 (1921) 90–168.

Toon, P. "Papal Encyclicals." In *New Dictionary of Christian Ethics & Pastoral Theology,* edited by D. J. Atkinson and David H. Field, 649–50. Downers Grove, IL: InterVarsity, 1995.

Trocmé, André. *Jésus et la Révolution Non-violente.* Geneva: Labor et Fides, 1961. [ET = *Jesus and the Nonviolent Revolution.* Translated by Michael H. Shank and Marlin E. Miller. Christian Peace Shelf. Scottdale, PA: Herald, 1973.]

Troeltsch, Ernst. *The Social Teaching of the Christian Churches.* 2 vols. Chicago: University of Chicago, 1981. (Original German ed., 1911).

Tcherikover, Victor. *Hellenistic Civilization and the Jews.* Translated by S. Applebaum. New York: Atheneum, 1975.

———. "Palestine under the Ptolemies." *Mizraim* 4 (1937) 1–82 (in Hebrew).

Tzaferis, Vassilius. "Jewish Tombs at and Near Givat ha-Mivtar, Jerusalem." *IEJ* 20 (1970) 18–32.

Udoh, Fabian E. *To Caesar What Is Caesar's: Tribute, Taxes, and Imperial Administration in the Early Roman Palestine (63 B.C.E.—70 C.E.).* BJS 343. Providence: Brown Judaic Studies, 2005.

Urbach, E. E. "Class Status and Leadership in the World of the Palestinian Sages." *Proceedings of the Israel Academy of Sciences and Humanities* 2 (1968) 38–74.

Vaux, Roland de. *Ancient Israel.* Translated by John McHugh. London: Darton, Longman & Todd, 1961.

Vermes, Geza. *Jesus the Jew: A Historian's Reading of the Gospels.* London: Collins, 1973.

Vielhauer, Philipp. *Geschichte der urchristlichen Literatur: Einl. in d. Neue Testament, d. Apokryphen u. d. Apostol. Väter.* De Gruyter Lehrbuch. Berlin: de Gruyter, 1975.

White, K. D. *Roman Farming.* Aspects of Greek and Roman Life. London: Thames & Hudson, 1970.

White, Lynn Jr. "Die Ausbreitung der Technik 500–1500." In *Europäische Wirtschaftsgeschichte: Mittelalter,* edited by C. M. Cipolla and K. Borchardt, 91–110. Stuttgart: Fischer, 1978.

———. "The Expansion of Technology 500–1500." In *The Fontana Economic History of Europe: The Middle Ages,* edited by Carlo M. Cipolle and Knut Borchardt, 143–74. London: Collins, 1993.

Wikipedia. "List of Countries by GDP (PPP) Per Capita," http://en.wikipedia.org/wiki/List_of_countries_by_GDP_(PPP)_per_capita/.

Wilkinson, John. "Ancient Jerusalem, Its Water Supply and Population." *PEQ* 106 (1974) 33–51.

———. *Jerusalem as Jesus Knew It: Archaeology as Evidence.* London: Thames & Hudson, 1978.

Williams, C. S. C. *A Commentary on the Acts of the Apostles.* BNTC. London: Adam & Charles Black, 1957.

Winter, Bruce W. "The Public Honouring of Christian Benefactors: Romans 13:3–4 and 1 Peter 2:14–15." *JSNT* 34 (1988) 87–103.

———. *Seek the Welfare of the City: Christians as Benefactors and Citizens.* Grand Rapids: Eerdmans, 1994.

Witherington, Ben III. *Ben Witherington on the Bible and Culture.* Online: http://blog.beliefnet.com/bibleandculture/.

———. *Women and the Genesis of Christianity.* Edited by Ann Witherington. Cambridge: Cambridge University Press, 1990.

———. "Women, New Testament." In *ABD* 6:957–58.

Wolf, C. Umhau. "Carpenter." In *IDB* 1:539.

Wolf, Eric R. *Peasants.* Foundations of Modern Anthropology Series. Englewood Cliffs, NJ: Prentice Hall, 1966.

———. *Peasant Wars of the Twentieth Century.* New York: Harper & Row, 1969.

Woude, A. S. van der. "Melchizedek als himmlische Erlösergestalt in den neugefundenen eschatologischen Midraschim aus Qumran Hohle XI." *OtSt* 14 (1965) 354–73.

Wuellner, Wilhelm H. *The Meaning of "Fishers of Men."* NTL. Philadelphia: Westminster, 1967.

Wunder, H. "The Mentality of Rebellious Peasants—The Samland Peasant Rebellion of 1525." In *The German Peasant War of 1525: New Viewpoints*, edited by Bob Scribner and Gerhard Benecke, 144–60. London: Allen & Unwin, 1979.

Yadin, Yigael. "The Gate of the Essenes and the Temple Scroll." In *Jerusalem Revealed: Archaelology in the Holy City*, edited by Y. Yadin and E. Stern, 90–91. Jerusalem: Israel Exploration Society, 1975.

Yoder, John Howard. *The Politics of Jesus*. Grand Rapids: Eerdmans, 1972.

Zeitlin, Solomon. "The Am Haaretz: A Study in the Social and Economic Life of the Jews Before and After the Destruction of the Second Temple." *JQR*, n.s. 23 (1932) 45–61.

Zias, Joseph. "Death and Disease in Ancient Israel." *BA* 54 (1991) 147–60.

Ziebarth, E. "Oikonomos." In *Realencylopaedie der Classischen Altertumswissenschaft*, edited by A. Pauly and G. Wissowa, XVII, 2:2118–19. Stuttgart: Metzler, 1894.

Zuckermandel, Moses Samuel. *Tosefta*. Jerusalem: Bamberger & Varhman, 1937.

SUBJECT INDEX

Made in the USA
San Bernardino, CA
25 July 2019